Battle of Paoli

Battle of Paoli

Thomas J. McGuire

Pennsylvania Society of
Sons of the Revolution
and its Color Guard

STACKPOLE
BOOKS

Published by
STACKPOLE BOOKS
5067 Ritter Road
Mechanicsburg, PA 17055
www.stackpolebooks.com

Printed in the United States of America

10 9 8 7 6 5 4 3 2 1

FIRST EDITION

Library of Congress Cataloging-in-Publication Data

McGuire, Thomas J.
    Battle of Paoli / Thomas J. McGuire.—1st ed.
      p.   cm.
    Includes bibliographical references (p.) and index.
    ISBN 0-8117-0198-0
    1. Paoli Massacre, 1777. I. Title.

E241.P2 M37   2000
973.3'33—dc21

                                          99-086679

*To all those who worked to preserve
the Paoli Battlefield,
especially Lieutenant William P. O'Neill III
and Sergeant Major Patrick J. McGuigan*

"Forti et fideli nihil difficle."

CONTENTS

FOREWORD

The Pennsylvania Society of Sons of the Revolution and its Color Guard is pleased to underwrite the publication of *Battle of Paoli*, for in so doing we further our charter purposes of public education and historic preservation in at least four distinct ways. For more than 110 years, the Society has honored Major General Anthony Wayne as the greatest of all Pennsylvania soldiers in the American Revolution. As early as 1890 the Society placed a stone marker at Valley Forge to commemorate the quarters of General Wayne during the Continental Army's long winter there in 1777–1778. Wayne was the commanding officer of the Pennsylvania Line, the hero in the capture of the British garrison at Stony Point, New York, and the defender of West Point in the aftermath of Benedict Arnold's treason. The Society's greatest example of public art and inspiration is its equestrian statue of Wayne, which it placed on the grounds of the Philadelphia Museum of Art in 1937. In more recent decades, the Society and its Color Guard has purchased and placed on exhibit at the U.S. Mint in Philadelphia the Congressional medal struck in Wayne's honor. The Society and its Color Guard has also assisted in the purchase and restoration of Waynesborough, the Wayne family homestead, and in its interpretation to the public as a historic house museum. It is then in keeping with the traditions and core mission of the Society to note that General Wayne led the American forces at the Paoli Battlefield.

The central role of General Wayne at Paoli provided ample motivation for the participation of the Society and its Color Guard in this publication, but the complementary nature of this endeavor did not end there. For more than half a century, the Society has committed its resources to the establishment and educational effectiveness of state and national historical parks in the Philadelphia area. Both Independence National Historical Park, founded in 1948, and Valley Forge National Historical Park, founded in 1976, have benefitted significantly from the educational outreach programs of the Society and its Color Guard. Now, as a result of a three-year campaign of the Paoli Battlefield Preservation Fund, the Borough of Malvern will soon take title to the 40-acre site of the Paoli Battlefield. Even so, it will be several years before the interpretation of the Paoli Battlefield is fully integrated into the regional history programs of Brandywine Battlefield State Park and the Valley Forge National Historical Park. In the interim, the publication of *Battle of Paoli* will ably meet the needs of the public and the professional museum community as an introduction and interpretive guide to the Paoli Battlefield.

For more than a quarter century, the Society and its Color Guard has sponsored both the publication of histories of the American Revolution and the broad public distribution of general and scholarly works on the subject. In 1976 the Society published Edward S. Gifford Jr.'s monograph, *The American Revolution in the Delaware Valley*, and distributed 900 copies to public, private, and historical libraries. The Society also sponsored the publication of *Standards and Colors of the American Revolution* (1982) by Edward W. Richardson and published its own *Centennial Register* (1990), which documents the history of the Society and its Color Guard and includes the service to the Society of all Officers and Managers, a guide to all monuments and memorials of the Society, and a full account of the Society's centennial year. The Society distributed both *Standards and Colors* and the *Centennial Register* to more than 350 libraries. In this activity the Society finds a third reason to celebrate, for it is the intention of the Society and its Color Guard to purchase and distribute, without charge, a substantial number of copies of *Battle of Paoli*.

Lastly, the Society and its Color Guard takes great pleasure in its association with the author, Revolutionary War–reenactor and historian Thomas J. McGuire. Tom first came to the attention of the Society in 1993, when he appeared as the guest speaker at its annual meeting. In subsequent years, the Society and its Color Guard has provided support for the publication and distribution of his 1995 volume, *The Surprise of Germantown, or the Battle of Cliveden, October 4th, 1777* and has sponsored the 1998 reenactment of the Battle of Germantown, held on the grounds of Cliveden of the National Trust for Historic Preservation, in the Germantown section of Philadelphia. In 1999 Tom was the guest of honor at the Society's annual celebration of George Washington's Birthday. Over the past decade he has become one of the leading educators of the American Revolution in the mid-Atlantic region. Throughout its history the Society has supported the educational work of historians of the American Revolution. We take great pride in the achievements of Tom McGuire.

The Society's sponsorship of *Battle of Paoli* would not have been possible without the dedicated work of several members of the Society and its Color Guard. First and foremost, two successive Captains of the Color Guard—George Ireland Wright III and Andrew Jackson Salisbury II—pledged the Color Guard to match the Society's level of support. Three members of the Board of Managers of the Society—Winchell Smith Carroll, James Whitney Marvin Jr., and Harvard Castle Wood III—worked closely with the Paoli Battlefield Preservation Fund to develop support within that organization for this project. Tom McGuire helped make the fund-raising easy by providing the Society with a copy of the final draft of the entire manuscript. Finally, Kyle R. Weaver, Editor of the Pennsylvania line at Stackpole Books, assured a successful partnership by extending every professional courtesy we asked of him in accommodating the interests of the Society and its Color Guard. On behalf of the Pennsylvania Society of Sons of the Revolution, I express my sincere gratitude to each and every one of these men.

Mark Frazier Lloyd
President
Pennsylvania Society of Sons of the Revolution
January 2000

NOTE

The Paoli Battlefield Preservation Fund was created in 1996 with the following primary objectives: To rescue the Paoli Battlefield from the developer's bulldozer and to educate America about the circumstances of the battle and its impact on the American Revolution. On November 5, 1999, the first objective was fulfilled and the battlefield was saved. The second objective is an ongoing process that will continue well into the future. This book represents a significant milestone in that process and was made possible by the commitment of the Pennsylvania Society of Sons of the Revolution and its Color Guard, the Malvern Preparatory School, and the Pennsylvania State Society Children of the American Revolution.

It is fair to say that in both of these objectives, many children from across the country became the catalysts for success: They wrote letters to their congressmen, collected contributions for the Pennies for Paoli and Footsteps to Paoli programs, and attended and testified at a congressional hearing to save the battlefield.

The successful fundraising campaign for the illustrations in this book and other educational causes conducted by the Pennsylvania State Society Children of the American Revolution, conceived and led by their state president, Elizabeth Ellen Fritsch, have capstoned the efforts of our board, the Malvern Preparatory School, and the Pennsylvania Society of Sons of the Revolution and its Color Guard to promote education and awareness of this battle for posterity. These children are a credit to their families, their schools, and their communities.

Patrick McGuigan, President Emeritus
Michael Steinberger, President
Paoli Battlefield Preservation Fund
January 2000

AUTHOR'S
ACKNOWLEDGMENTS

I gratefully acknowledge the following individuals and organizations for their part in the production of this work: the Pennsylvania Society of Sons of the Revolution and its Color Guard and its president, Mark Frazier Lloyd, for their generosity in providing a grant that made the publication of this book possible; Malvern Preparatory School and its head, James Stewart, for funding the research; the Pennsylvania State Society Children of the American Revolution, its state president Elizabeth Ellen Fritsch and senior president Mrs. James T. Sweeney for funding the maps and illustrations; and the Paoli Battlefield Preservation Fund board members for giving me constant support and encouragement.

The actual research and technical study of primary materials involved individuals and facilities on both sides of the Atlantic: in Great Britain, Sir Richard Osborn, Bt., and Sarah Saunders-Davies, Col. Graeme Hazlewood of the Royal Logistics Corps, the Public Records Office at Kew, and the National Army Museum in Chelsea; in the United States, thanks to Stacey Sweigert of the Valley Forge Historical Society, Col. J. Craig Nannos of the Pennsylvania National Guard, Don Troiani, Steve Gilbert and Herman Benninghoff, Catharine Simmons and Dr. David Wood, Richard Dietrich, Pam Shenk and Estelle Cremers of Tri-County Historians, Dave Fowler and the staff of the David Library, Ed Redmond of the Library of Congress, and the staffs of the Historical Society of Pennsylvania, Chester County Historical Society, the Huntingdon Library, and the Maryland Historical Society. Lee Boyle at the Valley Forge National Historical Park Library provided invaluable assistance in locating primary sources in the Park Collection.

Thanks to Dr. Russell Weigley and Arthur Lefkowitz for their professional support, and to Tom Fleming and David McCullough for their inspiration, guidance, and friendship. Thanks also to Sandy Lloyd and Richard Roper, for proofreading, and Kyle Weaver, of Stackpole Books, for his work, advice, and patience.

Finally, hugs and kisses to my wife Susan, for her support, encouragement, and boundless love.

RESPECTED FRIEND,

Cast thy Eyes down into Chester County.
See the numbers there engaged
in Mutual Distruction of our friends and Country Men,
by a Banditi Sent by a monster,
head'd by a villain,
guided and directed
by Rascalls and Trators to their Country.
My heart recoils at the thought
of Such numbers of fine Plantations pillaged,
laid waste and ruined.
Barns, Barracks & Mills filled with Grain and Hay
wantonly distroyed and burnt,
Dwelling houses with all their Furniture
following the same fate,
Roads deluged with Blood,
Gardens and Orchards laid waste & Cutt down,
Humankind in Horrors,
Women Weeping
for Husbands and Sons Slain,
their selves and daughters at the Mercy of Worse than brutes,
being by them denied their own bread & Sustenance,
and all this is the dire Effect
of Tyrannous Ambition . . .

Here my good friend at present,
I Cease to remind thee any further of so Unpleasing a theme
yet the friends of Zion do mourn . . .

— *Christopher Marshall,*
Lancaster, Pennsylvania
September 20, 1777

INTRODUCTION

The Philadelphia area is well known internationally for the key role it played in the American Revolution. Places such as Independence Hall and Valley Forge have become immortalized in world history and are icons to those who cherish liberty. In the shadows of these great monuments are other places integral to the full story of the Revolution. They mark lesser-known events that have become obscured by the passage of time or shrouded by myth and legend. Yet when old documents surface, they reveal the significant role these forgotten events played in the shaping of the nation.

The Great Valley of Chester County was a seat of war in mid-September 1777. The Battle of Paoli, known in popular history as the Paoli Massacre, was a small and terrible battle fought near Valley Forge. It occurred as a result of Washington's third attempt in ten days to prevent the British capture of Philadelphia. The battle's unusual circumstances left a vivid impression on the participants of both sides and served as a rallying cry for Pennsylvania's soldiers. It also marked a low point in the early military career of Anthony Wayne, Pennsylvania's most famous Revolutionary general. The criticism of his leadership at Paoli led him to demand a court of inquiry and a court-martial to clear his name for the record. Yet as the years passed, the details of what happened at Paoli were lost in myth, and its significance was eclipsed by its own legends. What actually occurred is a truly fascinating story of people engaged in the many-faceted struggle to achieve American independence.

The search for factual evidence of what happened at Paoli turned up much previously unpublished primary material, and this served as the basis for this book. The most important new information is the testimonies of fifteen officers from Wayne's court of inquiry and a manuscript map, drawn by Wayne himself, that includes data about the Paoli Camp and its surroundings. These documents are part of the Peter Force Papers in the Library of Congress. Two other documents from the inquiry, the list of evidences and the testimony of a sixteenth officer, are found in the Wayne Papers at the Historical Society of Pennsylvania, together with Wayne's defense; thus the Court of Inquiry testimony is complete. The Force Collection also holds letters from Col. Thomas Hartley and Col. Adam Hubley, two officers who wrote in splendid detail about Paoli and the events preceding it.

In reading later descriptions of this battle, it becomes clear that the better historians have relied largely on published sources of primary documents, especially those of Anthony Wayne's papers relating to Paoli. Many other writers based their versions of what occurred on colorful traditions, assumptions, or overactive imaginations, thus perpetuating tales that range from the improbable to the absurd. To my knowledge, no prior writer has used the Court of Inquiry documents.

The Battle of Paoli was the result of circumstances that went beyond the mere movements of armies and the strategies of commanders. It occurred as a result of the particular circumstances of the Continental Army's development in 1777, the divisions within Pennsylvania over the war, and the realities of the Philadelphia region at that time. It was also a result of the British Army's internal operations, their attitudes toward their opponents, and General Howe's objectives in this campaign. For a glimpse into these circumstances, the story begins with the objectives of both armies, embodied in the form of two Philadelphia parades.

CHAPTER 1

Philadelphia

Friday Morning, September 26, 1777

It was a cool, crisp morning after a night of rain, and the crimson glow of an early-autumn sunrise gradually gave way to hues of scarlet and gold against a brilliant blue sky. A light breeze from the north gently carried fresh country air into the city of Philadelphia, along with the rumble of drums approaching from the north, across the green meadows and pale amber fields along Germantown Road. Above the rhythmic throbbing of the distant drums could be heard the shrill chirp of fifes playing a vaguely familiar tune. As the sounds reached the Northern Liberties, the citizens could make out the ancient melody: "God save great George our king."[1]

Brick red coats reflected in the shimmering windows of buildings along Second Street as nearly 200 horsemen from the 16th or Queen's Own Light Dragoons trotted south across the muddy lane called Vine Street and officially entered the city proper. After a month of hard campaigning, these mounted warriors presented to civilian eyes a curious mixture of weather-beaten but picturesque pageantry: well-mended, fading crimson coats faced with washed-out dark blue lapels and cuffs laced white; sword belts pipe-clayed a dazzling white; shining black leather tack and saddlery with brasses burnished to a glow; black leather helmets surmounted by rows of chains, a fur crest, and a cloth turban painted to resemble leopard skin.[2] No one observing this procession could miss the ominous, awe-inspiring weapons drawn and carried at the shoulder—dragoon broadswords, nearly 3 feet of steel gleaming in the morning sun, capable of intimidating even the most hardened veteran.

The windows of Second Street now reflected coats of many colors as the column behind the horsemen entered the city. Above the large Palladian window of Christ Church, the cameo sculpture of King George II gazed down upon several rows of fifers and drummers in shades of yellow,

1

black, green, red, and white. Each coat was heavily decorated with lace and was faced with red, following the British Army regulation of reversed coat colors for musicians. Excepted from this rule were the musicians of royal regiments, such as the 42nd or Royal Highland Regiment, who wore red coats with dark blue facings and special royal livery lace of blue and yellow.[3] All the fifers and drummers wore tall, black bearskin caps bearing ornamental front plates of silver and black metal. The red-rimmed wooden drums, their fronts brilliantly painted in regimental colors with the king's cypher "GR" surmounted by a crown,[4] swayed rhythmically as the drummers beat the cadence, their arms raising the sticks to eye level with mechanical precision. The red-faced fifers puffed and strained, lips pursed.

Another group of horsemen came into view, quite different in appearance from the dragoons. At the head of the infantry, brilliant scarlet coats faced with dark blue velvet and a profusion of glittering gold lace proclaimed the arrival of the Right Honourable Lieutenant General Charles Earl Cornwallis, together with Brigadier General Sir William Erskine, and a host of aides and staff officers.[5] Lord Cornwallis embodied those qualities that nobility and generalship required: an ancient and aristocratic family, a soldierly reputation, and a dignified bearing that commanded awe and respect. His presence announced that law and order had returned to Philadelphia—"to the great relief of the inhabitants who have too long suffered the yoke of arbitrary Power; and who testified their approbation of the arrival of the troops by the loudest acclamations of joy," wrote seventeen-year-old Loyalist Robert Morton.[6]

Less conspicuous by their appearance, but certainly not by reputation, were a number of familiar Philadelphia faces accompanying Lord Cornwallis. These included the Allen brothers, William, John, and Andrew, sons of the prominent Philadelphia merchant and politician Judge William Allen, who himself had gone to England. Andrew Allen was a former delegate to the Second Continental Congress. William, Jr., served in the Continental Army before independence was declared. As lieutenant colonel of the 2nd Pennsylvania Battalion, he fought in Canada alongside Col. Anthony Wayne of the 4th Battalion at the disastrous Battle of the Three Rivers in early 1776. This was Wayne's first battle; he wrote to Benjamin Franklin, "I believe it will be Universally allowed that Col. Allen & myself have saved the Army in Canada."[7] Defense of American rights was one issue, but a war for independence was treasonous in William Allen's view. He resigned from the army July 24, 1776, and later raised a regiment of Pennsylvania Loyalists.[8]

The most prominent Loyalist in the group was Joseph Galloway, a wealthy Philadelphian whose career in law and politics was extraordinary.[9] Born of Quaker parents in Maryland, Joseph married Grace Growden at Christ Church in 1753. He served as Speaker of the Pennsylvania Assembly for fourteen years before the war; his closest personal friend and political ally was Benjamin Franklin. At the First Continental Congress in 1774, Galloway worked to avert conflict with Britain by proposing a moderate "Plan of Union," but the radicals, led by Sam Adams, managed to have the plan stricken from the record. Not long afterward, Franklin returned to Philadelphia from England, having become an ardent rebel. He failed to persuade Galloway to support independence, and their close friendship soon faded. Galloway refused to attend the Second Continental Congress and retired to his Bucks County estate, Trevose, rather than remain in the city, especially as anonymous threats against him and his family mounted. In late November 1776, as Washington's disintegrating army retreated across New Jersey and Congress prepared to abandon Philadelphia, Joseph Galloway fled for his life and put himself under the protection of Sir William Howe's army. A Philadelphia newspaper vilified him with a satirical verse:

> Galloway has fled and joined the venal Howe
> To prove his baseness, see him cringe and bow.
> A traitor to his country and its laws.
> A friend to tyrants and their cursed cause.
> Unhappy wretch! Thy interest must be sold,
> For continental, not for polished gold;
> To sink the money, thou thyself cried down,
> And stabbed thy country, to support the Crown.
> Go to and fro, like Lucifer on earth,
> And curse the being that first gave thee birth . . .[10]

Now, almost a year later, having served as the chief guide and spymaster for General Howe during the past month of campaigning through southeastern Pennsylvania, Joseph Galloway returned to the Seat of Congress with a triumphant Royal Army. Describing Lord Cornwallis's entry into the city, Galloway wrote, "No Roman General ever received from the citizens of Rome greater acclamations than the noble General did on this occasion from the loyal citizens of Philadelphia."[11]

At High Street, or Market Street, following the generals, rank upon rank of British grenadiers filled Second Street as far as the eye could see. Tall soldiers, these grenadiers were made to appear taller by their black bearskin caps. Although the uniforms and faces were weathered by the campaign, they were magnificent in their soldierly bearing. The gleaming black and silver plates on their caps bore the king's crest and a scroll with the motto *Nec Aspera Terrent*—"hardship does not deter us"—borne out by their performance in the previous weeks. Company by company they passed, each distinguished by the color of their coat facings and the design on their buttons.[12] The pale buff facings of the 40th Regiment's Company, commanded by Capt. John Graves Simcoe, were seen among the units in the 1st Grenadier Battalion. Close behind the 40th came the 55th's grenadiers with dark green facings. One ten-year-old Philadelphia boy, identified simply as J. C., never forgot the scene:

> Their tranquil look and dignified appearance have left an impression on my mind, that the British grenadiers were inimitable . . . I went up to the front rank of the grenadiers when they had entered Second street, when several of them addressed me thus,— "How do you do, young one—how are you, my boy"—in a brotherly tone, that seems still to vibrate on my ear; then reached out their hands, and severally caught mine, and shook it, not with the exulting shake of conquerers, as I thought, but with a sympathizing one for the vanquished.[13]

Loyalist Sarah Logan Fisher noticed that the soldiers "looked very Clean & healthy & a remarkable solidity was on their countenances, no wanton levity, or indecent mirth but a gravity well becoming the occasion, seemed on all their faces."[14] And so they went, row after row, muskets at the shoulder, gleaming bayonets by the hundreds, south on Second Street past the Old Court House at Market Street.

As the column reached Chestnut Street, it turned right and headed west, passing Christopher Marshall's apothecary shop, which had supplied the Pennsylvania Battalions with much-needed medical kits. It continued past Third Street and Carpenter's Hall, where the First Congress met in 1774, and on beyond Fourth.[15] Up the street, fifteen-year-old Debby Norris watched the parade from her house near Fourth & Chestnut. "We were upstairs, and saw them pass to the State house; they looked well, clean, and well-fed. . . . It was a solemn and impressive day—but I saw no exultation in the enemy."[16] Ahead on the left past Fifth Street soared the bell tower of the Pennsylvania State House, the very symbol of the rebellion. Here in the summer of 1776, the Declaration of Independence was debated, adopted, and signed. Now, on Friday, September 26, 1777, a month and a day after landing near Head of Elk, Maryland, His Majesty's forces were in possession of their prize: the seat of Revolution.

On the previous Friday, the street scene had been quite different. Congress, along with thousands of citizens, had abruptly fled the city in the middle of the night after receiving news that the British Army was about to cross the Schuylkill River. Concerning that episode, Robert Morton wrote in disgust, "Thus we have seen the men from whom we have received, and from whom we still expect protection, leave us to fall into the hands of (by their accounts) a barbarous, cruel, and unrelenting enemy."[17]

Six Royal Artillery 12-pounders, together with four Royal howitzers and some light cannon, rumbled past the State House on Chestnut Street. Escorting the guns were Royal Artillerymen, resplendent in dark blue coats faced with red, the buttonholes laced yellow, the crossbelts and leather accoutrements a dazzling white.[18] Sunlight glinted from the polished bronze cannon barrels, their embossed Royal cyphers and crowns proclaiming to the world the might of the British Empire. Stout, gray-painted oak carriages reinforced with black ironwork creaked under the weight of the gun barrels as they lumbered along, pulled by sturdy draft horses.

The two battalions of British grenadiers, a red column of over 1,000 troops, and the guns of the Royal Artillery were followed by a dark blue column with a more ominous air. Shining brass drums, each with a rampant lion embossed on the front and rimmed with red and white diagonal stripes, announced the arrival of two Hessian grenadier battalions. Nearly 800 strong, these German soldiers of the Von Linsing and Von Lengerke Battalions wore blue coats with facings of various colors and tall polished brass or tin "mitre-caps" with embossed decorations and colored pompoms. Unlike the clean-shaven British, the Hessian grenadiers all wore blackened mustaches waxed into sharp points, which added to their fierce appearance.[19] Their blank, expressionless faces were quite a contrast to those of the British grenadiers. As ten-year-old J. C. later recalled:

Their looks to me were terrific—their brass caps—their mustaches—their countenances, by nature morose, and their music, that

sounded better English than they themselves could speak—plunder—plunder—plunder—gave a desponding, heart-breaking effect,
as I thought, to all; to me it was dreadful beyond expression.[20]

Following behind the Hessians came officers' aides, Royal Engineers,
and Quartermasters, while "Baggage Wagons, Hessian Women & Horses
Cows Goats & Asses brought up the rear, they encamped on the Commons."[21] All told, about 3,000 personnel took possession of Philadelphia;
"thus was this large City surrendered to the English without the least opposition whatsoever."[22] The main part of the army, commanded by Sir William
Howe, K.B. (the general and commander in chief), and numbering over
10,000, remained in camp at Germantown, 5 miles to the north. There
they would stay until a line of fortifications could be built across the northern approaches to the city. Another 2,000 British and Hessian troops occupied Wilmington, Delaware, along with many of the sick and wounded
from the campaign.[23]

With all the various uniforms passing through town this day, there was
one curious element: To add a festive air to the occasion, the dragoons, the
British and Hessian grenadiers, the fifers and drummers, and the artillerymen all had "tied greenery and bands to their hats and on the horses
pulling the cannon."[24] The sprigs of green were a remarkable echo of
another parade that had passed by the State House about a month before, a
parade whose participants had hoped to prevent *this* parade, carrying with
its bits of greenery the hopes of victory in the fields of Chester County.

CHAPTER 2

Philadelphia

Sunday Morning, August 24, 1777

Early on Sunday morning, August 24, 1777, coats of many colors reflected in the windows of Chestnut Street as leather-helmeted dragoons led Washington's army through Philadelphia. Green sprigs in the hats of the troops passing the State House not only lent an air of festivity to the march, but also provided an element of uniformity. It was just about the only uniformity present. Some of the dragoons in the column wore red coats with blue facings; others were clad in white jackets with sky blue lapels; still others had on uniforms of brown faced with green. Many of the horsemen wore linen hunting shirts and a mixed bag of clothing and accoutrements ranging from like new to sorely distressed.[1]

The force that marched through Philadelphia that day was called the Grand Army, or the main Continental Army, but it was only part of a wide-ranging force stationed over hundreds of miles. The backgrounds of its members were as varied as their uniforms. Adventuresome Frenchmen, fearless Poles, and Germans from all over central Europe marched side-by-side with Americans from a wide range of origins—Virginians of English descent, New Yorkers with Dutch names, Scots-Irish Pennsylvanians who spoke with the brogue and burr of Northern Ireland, steady New Englanders, and hot-tempered Scots from the Carolinas. Sprinkled among troops from New England and the Middle States were free Africans, some shouldering muskets despite Congressional disapproval. Most of the blacks present were relegated to noncombatant status as teamsters, musicians, or laborers. As was the custom of the day, numerous officers, including the commander in chief, had servants called waiters, some of whom were Africans, both slave and free. Most of the officers' waiters were indentured servants, hired civilians, or soldiers drawn from the ranks.[2]

The air in town was thick and humid. August in Philadelphia is rarely pleasant, and the summer houses of wealthy residents dotting the areas north and west of the city attested that those who could afford to escape the heat, dust, and stench of summer in the city did so. "A Thunder Gust, very sharp and violent, attended with plentifull Rain" had drenched Philadelphia the previous evening, and an early-morning shower "which will spoil our Show, and wett the Army" guaranteed that the day's march in 80-degree weather would be dust-free in the morning but exhausting by afternoon.[3] With luck, by that time the army would have passed through the city, crossed the Schuylkill River on the floating bridge, and set up camp at Darby, thus avoiding marching during the hottest part of the day.

The skies cleared just in time for the march. Thousands of Philadelphians of all backgrounds and loyalties watched the Continental Army as it passed through that morning. George Washington informed John Hancock, the president of Congress:

> I think to march it thro' the City, but without halting. I am induced to do this, from the opinion of Several of my Officers and many Friends in Philadelphia, that it may have some influence on the minds of the disaffected there and those who are Dupes to their artifices and opinions. The March will be down Front and up Chesnut Street, and, I presume about Seven O'Clock.[4]

The loyalties and opinions of 40,000 Philadelphians were nearly as diverse as the army's appearance. Watching the march from the "Coffee House Corner" at Front Street and Market Street was Capt. Alexander Graydon, who noted that "The sight was highly interesting to persons of all descriptions; and among the many who, perhaps, equally disclaimed the epithet of Whig or Tory [i.e., claimed neutrality], Mr. [Chief Justice Benjamin] Chew, from an upper window in the house of Mr. Turner, appeared a very anxious spectator."[5]

Chief Justice Chew was arrested a few days after the march on suspicion of Toryism and was held prisoner with Pennsylvania proprietor John Penn, grandson of William Penn. In a city founded on toleration, extremism flourished in this crisis. Those who remained loyal or neutral often found themselves the target of extremists. Family members, neighbors, or friends sometimes became bitter, unforgiving enemies. Benjamin Franklin, the most well-known Philadelphian of the age, had broken permanently with his son William, the now-imprisoned royal governor of New Jersey. Franklin's trusted friend and long-time political crony, Joseph Galloway, was at that very moment preparing to guide Howe to Philadephia. The Quakers were largely suspected of Loyalism, along with the Anglican and Methodist clergy, who were torn between loyalty to the king and revolutionary fervor.[6]

"Gen. Washington has none but Southern Troops with him," wrote John Adams. "The New England Troops and N. York Troops are every Man of them at Peeks Kill [New York] and with Gates. The Massachusetts Regiments are all with Gates."[7] (At that time, New Englanders referred to anyone from south of Connecticut as southern; New Englanders were often referred to as eastern.) In the ranks of the army were hundreds of Pennsylvania troops, some with families in the crowd. Maj. Gen. Benjamin Lincoln's Division of two Pennsylvania brigades was led by Brig. Gen. Anthony Wayne, a thirty-two-year-old native of Chester County, whose in-laws, the Penrose family, were Philadelphians. Anthony's marriage to Mary "Polly" Penrose took place in Christ Church on Second Street in 1766.[8] Numerous others in the Pennsylvania Line, from officers to privates, had connections in the city. The temptation to visit or even stop and chat was strong; if allowed, it would cause a breakdown of order and mobility. In an army still learning the rudiments of organization and operation, basic discipline was essential but often lacking.

The orders of march were strict and detailed. Every officer, without exception, was to keep his post while passing through the city, and under no circumstance was he to leave it. Any soldier who dared quit the ranks during the march was to be given thirty-nine lashes at the first halting place afterward; the officers were to pay special attention to this, both in their own units and others. They were also to keep the crowds from pressing on the troops. Washington paid special attention to the army's baggage train and some of the timeless problems associated with armies on the march:

> Men who are able to bear arms (except the necessary guards) [are to] march in the ranks; for it is so great a reflection upon all order and discipline to see such a number of strollers (for they cannot be called guards) with the waggons, that it is really shocking . . . wag-

gons, baggage, and spare horses, are to file off to the right, avoid the
City entirely, and move on to the bridge at the middle ferry. . . .
Not a woman belonging to the army is to be seen with the troops
on their march thro' the city.[9]

Nearly all of the women, many with young children, following the
Continental Army were wives or relatives of soldiers. Often driven to follow the army by commitment or sheer necessity, their appearance was
bedraggled, pathetic, and unmilitary. An army unable to properly clothe its
soldiers had little, if any, clothing to spare for camp followers, a term used
to describe all nonmilitary personnel. Armies also attract some disreputable
characters, both male and female, as do cities; the Continental Army and
Philadelphia were no exception. The General Orders given at Darby on
August 24 stated: "The Commander in Chief possitively forbids the straggling of soldiers . . . and likewise to prevent an inundation of bad women
from Philadelphia; and for both purposes, a guard is to be placed on the
road between the camp and the city, with particular orders to stop and
properly deal with both."[10]

The army's appearance made an impression on John Adams, who wrote
to his wife, Abigail:

> Four Regiments of Light Horse . . . Four Grand Divisions of the
> Army—and the Artillery. . . . They marched Twelve deep, and yet
> took up above two Hours in passing by. . . . We have now an
> Army, well appointed between Us and Mr. Howe. . . .
> I find [the army] to be extreamly well armed, pretty well
> clothed, and tolerably disciplined. . . . Much remains yet to be
> done. Our soldiers have not yet, quite the Air of Soldiers. They
> dont step exactly in Time. They dont hold up their Heads, quite
> erect, nor turn out their Toes, so exactly as they ought. They dont
> all of them cock their Hats—and such as do, dont all wear them
> the same Way.[11]

The General Orders instructed the fifers and drummers that "a tune
for the quick step [be] played, but with such moderation, that the men
may step to it with ease; and without *dancing* along, or totally disregarding
the music, as too often has been the case."[12] Rhode Island congressman
Henry Marchant noted, "From the State House We had a fair View of

Them as They passed in Their several Divisions . . . passing with a lively smart Step."[13]

The nine regiments of the 1st and 2nd Pennsylvania Brigades illustrated some of the problems of uniformity in the army. Each state was responsible for providing clothing for its troops, and Gen. Anthony Wayne firmly believed that proper uniforms were essential to the pride, discipline, and morale of soldiers. He wrote to the Pennsylvania Board of War on June 3, 1777:

> I now send Major Miller for Arms & Clothing for the first Penn'a Regiment Commanded by Col. Chambers—they never Rec'd any Uniform except hunting Shirts which are worn out—and Altho a body of fine men—yet from being in rags and badly armed—they are viewed with Contempt by the Other Troops, and begin to Despise themselves—Discontent ever produces Desertion. . . . I am Confident that you have the Honor of your State at Heart—and that you will use every means in your Power to expedite the Arming & Clothing of our People as Soldiers in Order to support it.[14]

But in spite of Wayne's repeated and emphatic requests, supplies of basic clothing, let alone proper uniforms, remained a nagging problem for months.

The best information about the clothing of Pennsylvania soldiers in 1777 can be found in newspaper descriptions of deserters. Fringed linen hunting shirts were the most common outer garment; some of them were dyed yellow, brown, black, and even purple. Regimental uniform coats were described as being brown, blue, black, or green, with facings of red, scarlet, white, buff, green, or brown. Other coats were described as "light colored, snuff colored, dark serge, dark drab, brown broadcloth, and blue sagathy," along with jackets of gray, blue, red, white, brown, or green. Buckskin breeches were common, with woolen trousers, checked trousers, striped trousers, linen drawers, and overalls of white or blue mentioned. Stockings appeared in blue yarn, white worsted, white yarn, white milled, white wool, or blue wool. Headgear included round hats bound (edged), felt hats, wool hats, "fashionable" wool hats, fur hats, beaver hats, slouched hats, cocked hats, and light infantry caps.[15] Captain Graydon noted that the army, "though indifferently dressed, held well burnished arms, and carried them like soldiers."[16]

As they marched southward to meet the king's army of 18,000 well-equipped professionals, this American army of 8,000 regulars, soon to be reinforced by 3,000 more Continentals and hundreds of local militia, was beset by problems that would have daunted most good leaders. Rebuilding and reorganization after the exhausting 1776 campaign left many officers bitter and disgusted. Problems of supplying food, clothing, ammunition, and equipment were perpetual, and the inability of Congress and state governments to provide consistent and appropriate support to the army caused increasing frustration at all levels. To this dismal picture, add political chicanery, incompetence, favoritism, and an influx of "foreign experts" to court favor from overseas, particularly from France. In August 1777, despite the optimism of John Adams and others, the odds were stacked against American independence.

CHAPTER 3

Camp on the Lancaster Road

Sunday, September 14, to
Monday, September 15, 1777

From the tavern door, as far as Mary Miller could see, the Lancaster Road was filled with traffic, the likes of which had rarely been seen: wagons, cannons, horses, and cattle by the hundreds, and soldiers by the thousands. A widow, Mary had run this tavern herself since the death of her husband, Joseph, five years earlier. The Sign of the Buck stood on the line between Philadelphia County and Chester County in the far-northern corner of Haverford Township, virtually surrounded by Lower Merion Township.[1] This was not obvious without looking at a map, however, for nothing in the character of the farmland or woods nearby indicated any sudden changes in political boundaries between the counties and townships.

Changes in another type of political boundary were, on the other hand, readily visible to anyone attempting to return home from church or the Friends' meetings in Merion or Radnor. Here, on this sunny, pleasant Sunday morning, September 14, 1777, the Continental Army was on the move. As clouds began to gather in the afternoon, General Washington arrived at "the Buck" with the headquarters staff on the first leg of the army's march to regain the offensive against General Howe in Chester County. And here on the Lancaster, or Conestoga, Road, as the skies grew overcast, the Continental Army of over 10,000 troops was preparing to set up camp, stretching from milestone 14 near Radnor Meeting House back beyond milestone 8 near Merion Meeting.[2] The road was virtually impassable because of the congestion.

Three Sundays earlier, this army had marched proudly through Philadelphia. Two Sundays ago, they were preparing defensive positions near Wilmington, Delaware. The previous Sunday, they were about to move to Red Clay Creek in Delaware to entrench and prepare for battle. Early last week, they withdrew from Delaware and took up positions along Brandywine

Creek in Chester County, Pennsylvania. And three days ago, on a hot and muggy Thursday, September 11, they fought in the largest and longest battle of the war to date, the Battle of Brandywine.

Brandywine became a subject of controversy among military experts from the moment it ended. As a study of strategy, generalship, and lost opportunities, it was one of the more remarkable battles of the war. Lt. Col. Adam Hubley, commander of the 10th Pennsylvania Regiment, writing from "Camp Lancaster Road, near Sorrel Horse" (Radnor Township) at 6 P.M. on September 14, commented to his brother John about the outcome of the battle: "Never was Men more surpriz'd, men from private to his Excellency[,] than we were, after Carrying every thing before us, from early in the morning untill ab[out] 3 'OClock in the Afternoon, & then after that time every thing Carry'd against us & we [were] Obldg'd to Leave the field."[3]

The Continentals were outmaneuvered and defeated, but not discouraged; portions of the army had fought extremely well and gave the British no easy victory. Hubley continued:

Our men Nothwithstanding we were obldg'd to Leave the feild are in the highest spirits & eager to have at them again. Nothing but misconduct lost us the feild, the men behav'd like Vetrans, and Fought with the Greatest brevary . . . its evident the Enemy were sorely put to it, on that day when the[y] did not think proper to Come on and are at this time at the Same Place and Oblidge'd to have out heavy Pickets between us & them.[4]

The halt by the British after the battle has remained a mystery ever since. General Grant and General Cornwallis were sent toward Chester on September 12 and 13 in a halfhearted pursuit, while the bulk of the British Army remained encamped around Dilworth and Chadds Ford. Two thousand troops, mostly Hessians and Scottish Highlanders, were sent to occupy Wilmington, Delaware, and establish hospitals for the great number of wounded from the battle. Speculation about the halt abounded; rumor in the American camp had it that the Royal Army was hobbled by high casualties and unable to proceed.

In 1779, General Howe testified before the House of Commons that he had halted because the army was tired from its long flank march during the battle. This feeble explanation drew bitter criticism from Joseph Galloway,

PENNSYLVANIA

N

**THE SEAT OF WAR
SEPTEMBER 1777**
With key locations relevant to
the Battle of Paoli

Reading

Schuylkill River   Parkers Ford

Jones Tavern

Pennibecker's Mills

Trappe

Reading Furnace

French Creek
Powder Mill

Valley Forge

Yellow Springs   White

Swedes Ford   Germantown

Leverings

Lancaster

Red Lion   Horse   Tredyffrin   Merion   Ford
Meeting

Downingtown   Boot

McClellan's Tavern

Paoli   Buck   Falls of Schuylkill

Turks Head

Middle

Cochrane's Tavern

Aston   Darby Ferry   **Philadelphia**

New
London

Chads Ford   **Chester**

Oxford

Susquehanna River

Wilmington

NEW JERSEY

Nottingham

Christiana

Head
of
Elk

*Chesapeake
Bay*

Johnson's Ferry

MARYLAND   DELAWARE

*Delaware River
and Bay*

Map by Thomas J. McGuire

who, having lost everything in Pennsylvania for his loyalty, wrote a series of scathing attacks on Howe's conduct. These attacks, published in pamphlet form in England, all but directly accused Howe of treason for allowing the rebel army to withdraw and regroup after Brandywine.[5] Washington took full advantage of Howe's lethargy and pulled his army back behind the Schuylkill River to "the Falls" (East Falls) near Germantown on September 12. With no immediate British pursuit threatening the city, the Continental forces were permitted the next day to rest and refit—clean their weapons, receive new ammunition, and put themselves in order as best they could.

About 9 A.M. on September 14, Washington seized the initiative and went on the offensive by marching his army from the Falls to Levering's Ford (present-day Manayunk), crossing the Schuylkill and moving up the Lancaster Road back into Chester County. Col. Timothy Pickering, the adjutant general of the Continental Army, described the river crossing:

The army . . . marched up a few miles & recrossed Schuylkill at
Leverings ford, the water being nearly up to the waist.—We lost
here much time, by reason of mens stripping off their stockings &
shoes & some of them their breeches. It was a pleasant day, & had
the men marched directly over by platoons without stripping, no
harm could have ensued, their cloaths would have dried by night
on their march, & the bottom would not have hurt their feet. The
officers too discovered a delicacy quite unbecoming soldiers; quitting their platoons, & some getting horses of their acquaintences
to ride over, and others getting over in a canoe. They would have
better done their duty had they kept to their platoons & led in
their men.[6]

Sgt. John Hawkins of Hazen's Regiment related his experience in his
diary entry for September 14: "Passed Sweede's [Levering's] Ford, up to
our Middle in Water, proceeded on—passed till we came to Merion
Meeting House, when we turned into the Lancaster Road and kept on till
we came near the Eleventh Mile Stone were we halted in the Woods and
rested this Night."[7]

Milestone 11 was located about 100 yards east of the Buck Tavern and
nearly 12 miles from where Sergeant Hawkins began his march that day at
the Falls of the Schuylkill.

The army had brought some of its tents along, but sleeping accommo-
dations were tight, as Washington had wanted the baggage train lightened
so as not to hinder the army's movements. Orders issued the previous day
directed:

The following proportion of Tents is allowed the Army upon its
next March, Vizt
    1 Soldiers Tent for the Field Officers [colonels, lieutenant
       colonels, majors] of each Regt
    1 D[itto] for every 4 Commission'd Officers [captains, lieu-
       tenants, ensigns]
    1 D[itto] for 8 Sergts, Drummers and Fifers
    1 D[itto] for 8 Privates
. . . one Wagon for every 50 Tents and no more. No Woman
under any pretence whatsoever to go with the Army, but to follow
the Baggage. The Soldiers are to Carry their Camp Kettles.[8]

According to the British Army regulations of the period, "The tents of private men are 6½ feet square and 5 feet high, and hold 5 soldiers each." This soldiers' tent pattern was generally followed by the Continental Army.[9]

Before leaving the camp at the Falls on the morning of the 14th, Washington issued orders to Pennsylvania Militia general John Armstrong to take the floating bridge at Middle Ferry and detach it to the Philadelphia side. He also directed that any boats at Schuylkill River ferries were to be drawn up on the left bank of the river. Washington further instructed Armstrong to fortify the upper fords of the Schuylkill in order to oppose a British crossing[10] and sent a group of French volunteers headed by Col. Louis Lebegue Du Portail, chief engineer of the Continental Army, to build the fortifications. They began laying out earthworks to emplace several heavy iron cannons (12- or 18-pounders) at Swedes Ford (present-day Norristown). Washington cautioned Armstrong and the engineers:

> As it is not expected that these Works will have occasion to stand a long defence, they should be such as can with the least labour and in the shortest time be completed, only that part of them which is opposed to cannon, need be of any considerable thickness and the whole of them should be rather calculated for dispatch than any unnecessary Decorations or regularity which Engineer's are frequently too fond of.[11]

September 15 dawned cloudy and raw. The army was to strike tents and march "as soon as it is well light."[12] At dawn, the commander in chief, with some of his officers, rode down the Lancaster Road toward the rear of the army near Merion Meeting, pausing for breakfast at the home of Philip Syng Jr., at milestone 10 and a mile east of the Buck. The seventy-four-year-old master silversmith from Philadelphia had bought the old Prince of Wales Tavern, made it a private residence, and was living there in retirement. Washington's "Daily Expences" records note, "To Cash paid at Mr. Syngs for fowls & Breakfast £3.10" and contains a receipt "for Hay & Oats used by General Washington & Company £4.10."[13]

A mile or so west of the Buck stood the Sorrel Horse Tavern, surrounded by Anthony Wayne's two Pennsylvania brigades. Wayne himself was farther ahead, at the 14th milestone near Radnor Meeting House and just beyond the Sign of John Wilkes, or Old Plough, Tavern.[14] As always, Anthony Wayne was willing to pick a fight with the British—if only some

of the other generals would push the issue. He wrote to Gen. Thomas
Mifflin that morning:

> The Enemy sore from the Other days Action [Brandywine] lay in
> a Supine State—part at Dilworths, part at Chads's ford, & the
> Remainder Advance at Concord.
>
> We Intend to push for the White Horse this Evening in Order to
> gain their left flank the soonest Possible. Query[:] may they not steal
> a March and pass the fords in the Vicinity of the falls [of Schuylkill]
> unless we immediately March down and Give them Battle[?] come
> then and push the Matter and take your fate with [me].[15]

The "White Horse" to which Wayne referred was the White Horse
Tavern in East Whiteland Township, about 13 miles west of the Sorrel Horse.

As the army moved on, the Sorrel Horse Tavern, kept by Jacob Waggoner, hosted the commander in chief. The expense records for General
Washington indicate a payment of £9.4 to "Mr. Waggoners bill at the
Sorrel horse" on September 15. The bill itself lists charges for "10 breakfasts, Servants breakfasts, 18 dinners, Servants dinners, 2 bottles of wine,
Toddy, Spirits, and 1 quart Rum for Servants." Dinner was in the early
afternoon, and by that time, most of the Continental Army was well on
the march toward the White Horse.[16]

Earlier that day, before the troops marched, the 1st Pennsylvania
Brigade's commander, Col. Thomas Hartley, wrote to William Atlee and
Paul Zantzinger in Lancaster, about 60 miles west of Philadelphia. Using a
drumhead as a writing table, Hartley reported:

> We are favoured with yours [letters] by Express—The hurry of the
> army prevents me from writing so full as I could wish. . . . We are
> happy in your having established these Expresses & shall not fail to
> give you every Intelligence in our Power—
>
> To Morrow may be of great Consequence to America—we
> shall not wait for the Enemy again—we are just moving—our
> Troops are numerous and in high Spirits.
>
> We hope soon to finish the Campaign with Success. All your
> Friends behaved well in the action [Brandywine] and the Survivors
> are ready for Business again. My Regiment suffered the most.[17]

The Express was a system of riders established on September 12 by Atlee and Zantzinger and opened by subscription "to enable them to hire one or more Persons to ride between Lancaster & General Washington's Army with & for intelligence." The city of Lancaster was in a panic, fearing that Howe's army would arrive any day. Rumors flew, especially during the Battle of Brandywine on the 11th. About sixty-five anxious city business-men paid amounts ranging from "7/6" (7 shillings, 6 pence) to "£1.10" (1 pound, 10 shillings) for the express service. Two riders, Stephen Sutton and John Snyder, were paid at a rate of 10 shillings per one-way trip, or £1 for a round-trip. Snyder appears to have made the first ride from Lancaster to the army on September 14.[18]

Lt. Col. Adam Hubley had even less of a writing surface than Colonel Hartley's "desk." Hubley remarked to his brother John on the 14th, "Youl Excuse bad writeing as this has been done in an open feild, without any other place but my knee to write on." His camp furniture had not improved by the next morning, when he wrote to Atlee and Zantzinger:

> I was Yesterday, most agreeably, surpriz'd with your letter, to Colo. Hartley & me. And with a great deal of satisfac[tion] observ'd, the Gentlemen of Lancaster, have establish'd Riders, to bring & carry Intiligence, to & from the Army. . . . I am at this time, oblig'd to Write in an open field, and also oblig'd to substitude my knees for a Table. . . .
>
> The Men all in fine Spirits and panting to have at the Enemy again, Confident in their Abilities, in giving them a total defeat. . . . Had it not been for a certain unlucky Eastern General [John Sulli-van] . . . the day would have been our own. . . .
>
> I understand the Inhabi[tants] of your Town are exceedingly dispirited, and making preparations for a flight.—for God Sake.—stop such proceedings. . . . You may depend on my earliest Intili-gence to you, should their be a necessity for flying. . . .
>
> Why dont you send your Militia—for Heavens sake, follow the brave example of the Militia to the Northward, they have fought most resolutely, and conquer'd most manly, can you forbear to emulate their noble Spirit[?] Have you not the least ambition, to share with them the Applause of not only your Country, but of the whole world[?][19]

"The Militia to the Northward" refers to New England militia who had defeated part of Gen. John "Gentleman Johnny" Burgoyne's forces at the Battle of Bennington, Vermont, in mid-August. Word of this victory raised hopes in Philadelphia, and from the end of August into early September, there was a great deal of enthusiasm about calling out the militia of Pennsylvania, Delaware, Maryland, and Virginia. Congressmen wrote glowing letters concerning the citizen-soldiers who were allegedly flocking in to defend the capital city. John Adams described "a noble army of continental troops, and a large body of militia, which is constantly and rapidly increasing." Eliphalet Dyer of Connecticut reported, "The Militia of this Country are daily reinforcing Genll Washington" and wrote of "Militia who flock in to him on this occasion," with the result that it "is supposed our Army now Consists of near Twenty thousand men." South Carolina's Henry Laurens referred to a force of "upwards of 12,000 Continentals & an innumerable hive of Militia" awaiting Howe, who, Laurens asserted, "would not have attempted his present seeming plan if he had not been amused by that fop Burgoyne with hopes of being joined."[20]

Gen. William Smallwood of Maryland, on a newly assigned command from General Washington, would beg to differ with Lieutenant Colonel Hubley and the honorable members of Congress concerning the value of militia.

CHAPTER 4

Cecil County, Maryland, and Chester County, Pennsylvania

Saturday, August 30, to Monday, September 15, 1777

The chaos was predictable but still unbelievable, as a host of hundreds of enemy warships carrying thousands of troops sailed into the heart of the nation with impunity.

What Gen. William Smallwood and Col. Mordecai Gist of the Maryland Continental Line faced in their home state was not panic caused by bands of marauding Hessian grenadiers bent on plunder or rape, not terror caused by ruthless British dragoons hanging helpless civilians from trees, but chaos caused by poorly trained, undisciplined, leaderless militia called out by their state government for the crisis, only to discover that basic organization was practically nonexistent. How was it possible for the Continental Congress to issue a call for state militias to repel an invasion without providing arms, food, clothing, ammunition, proper officers, or even a basic system of organization? The answer lay in the confused jurisdiction between Congress and the states over responsibility for defense. Congress had authority over the Continental Army and called on the states for militia support in this emergency. The legislatures of the middle states, except for Maryland, responded by placing their militias temporarily under Continental jurisdiction. The Maryland militia's arming, training, and discipline were entirely a state matter. Issuing orders on paper was easy; the problems often lay in carrying them out. Anthony Wayne referred to this very issue in September 1777 when he wrote, "We must fight. . . . We can neither starve, sink, or Destroy them on Paper; Otherwise they would long since have been totally Annihilated."[1] Smallwood and Gist immediately discovered why *they* were needed—not just to lead the Maryland militia, but to organize them first. And that would be a formidable, frustrating, thankless task, as both officers knew before they even arrived.

Washington first wrote to Smallwood on August 23, the day before the Continental Army marched through Philadelphia, from "Camp, 3 Miles from Philadelphia [East Falls]." He passed on the joyful news that Congress was ordering the Maryland militia into action:

> On the march to day I was honoured with a Letter from Congress transmitting Sundry Resolutions for calling out reinforcements of Militia, to repel the threatned invasion by the Enemy. . . . Such as respect the Militia of Maryland . . . you will find enclosed. . . . I request . . . you will communicate the Contents to Colonel Gist and that you and he repair to Maryland without loss of time. . . . I need not urge the necessity of expedition upon this interesting occasion and flatter myself nothing in either of your powers, will be omitted to answer the views of Congress in this instance.[2]

For unknown reasons, Washington did not receive a reply or even an acknowledgment from either Smallwood or Gist. A week later, on August 30, he again wrote Smallwood from Wilmington:

> In consequence of the directions of Congress, I wrote you on the 23d . . . requesting you and Colo. Gist to repair immediately to Maryland, to arrange, march and conduct the militia of that State, which Congress has called for, Twelve Hundred and Fifty of which were to assemble at Baltimore and Hartford Towns, and Seven hundred and fifty more at George Town on the Eastern Shore. . . . As you and Colo. Gist have not arrived yet, at my Head Quarters I presume my Letter never came to hand. . . .
> . . . The Militia are in much confusion for want of Officers to arrange and bring them on. . . . I request that you will communicate this Letter to Colo. Gist, and that you and he set out upon this command . . . calling upon me on your way down. Without some Leaders are appointed, to form and command them, It is more probable, a great part will disband; or if they should not, will be in such disorder that they will be of no Service.[3]

Some of the militia units, such as Col. William Richardson's 5th Maryland Battalion, were formed and awaiting instructions. Many of the other units had no officers, and the state government had provided no authorization for officers' commissions. Not surprisingly, militiamen finding no one in charge and no food or supplies available sometimes decided to go home, especially as harvest time was close at hand.

Disorganization was not the only cause of chaos. The British presence had awakened Loyalist activity and the "wrath of the Almighty" in the Chesapeake area. Maryland congressman William Paca fingered some "culprits from pulpits" on the Eastern Shore near Chestertown. He wrote Gov. Thomas Johnson on September 6:

> I herewith send you a most incorrigible fellow, the Rev. John Patterson: he has been endeavouring to throw every Obstacle in the way of calling forth our militia. . . . He is the most provoking exasperating mortal that ever existed. . . . I hope he will be taken good care of and well guarded.
>
> I am sorry to inform you of an Insurrection of Tories on the Borders of Queen Ann's & Caroline Counties headed by some scoundrel Methodist Preachers. . . . Three have since been apprehended. The Captain & Chief Methodist Preacher are among the Captives. Col. Richardson remains in Caroline County to supress those that are there assembled.
>
> Col. Gist is at Camp & has the Command. . . . Our militia are daily assembling and our force grows formidable; but I am told the Cecil County militia & Talbot & the Counties lower down are collecting in great disorder from want of Commissions. I wrote you in my last the necessity of providing Commissions. . . .
>
> We have nothing from Washington's army. Pray send commissions & write me the Intelligence.[4]

The situation was exasperating. Militia units were gathering in several widely separated spots. Supplies trickled in. Gist's force on the Eastern Shore received a few tents, and "with the sails of Ships which necessity urged us to take, I hope we shall make out a tolerable covering for our men."[5] Smallwood, several miles up the Susquehanna, urged the governor to send him two artillery pieces, but positively insisted, "Make no doubt of their being dispatched with the number of Officers & men required as also a sufficient Stock of Ammunition."[6]

As supplies trickled in, men trickled out. Smallwood wrote the governor on September 8, "I should be obliged if you wou'd enclose me the Regulations for Governing the Militia and let me have the Deserting Poltroons apprehended." He informed Johnson that Colonel Cowan's regiment, "being badly armed," was stationed on the shore of the Chesapeake opposite the British fleet to prevent "the Negroes and Stock being Swept away." He also warned that the "lower ferry" on the Susquehanna was open at the moment but was in sight of the British fleet and "they have it in their Power in one hours Time to prevent it" if troops attempted to cross there. The harried Smallwood abruptly ended his note, "Excuse haste and Interruption for I find Trouble multiplying on me."[7]

Washington wrote to Smallwood on September 9: "[I] hope by this Time, that you have arrived at Nottingham [Maryland]. . . . You will move on with all possible expedition with all the force you have or can get."[8] Actually, Smallwood was miles away from Nottingham; he was still south of the Susquehanna at "Mr. Delham's near Swan Creek." On September 11, the day of the Battle of Brandywine, Smallwood was at Johnson's Ferry on the Susquehanna, about a mile below Rock Run, Maryland. He again wrote Governor Johnson, detailing his situation and explaining why he had not been able to move farther:

> I have wrote Gist, Richardson, & Rumsey, to form a junction with me tomorrow at the cross Roads eight miles above Nottingham [near Oxford, Pennsylvania]. I have now once more to entreat most earnestly that you woud send forward the field Pieces with their proper Officers & Men with fixed Ammunition, Musket Cartridge . . . carefully made up, and not with wet or damaged powder . . . and about 87 stand of Arms for Colo. B. Johnson's Regt., who are good men, & ought to be Armed, rather than many who come from below with much Reluctance, Regulations for governing the Militia (which I before wrote for). . . . We have not Cartridges for this Body of Militia for half an hours Action.[9]

This was a force that was supposed to harass the rear of the British Army. Together with the Maryland, Delaware, and Pennsylvania militias,

Washington's army should have been augmented by thousands of able-bodied men. Instead, Colonel Gist, who proceeded to Christiana, Delaware, to rendezvous with Gen. Caesar Rodney and the Delaware militia, found an even more absurd situation than Smallwood's. According to Maryland congressman Samuel Chase:

> General Rodney and Mr. John Dickenson war [were] at Xteen [Christeen, or Christiana] with Colo. Gist. Mr. Buchanan [of the Army Commissary Department] informs that Genl. Rodney had with him 150 of the Delaware State [militia] before he arrived at Xteen, but that so many of them deserted that Genl. Rodney discharged the remaining few. . . . Genl. Rodney had wrote to you on Fryday last [September 12], giving an account of his and Colo. Gists Situation. . . . [He] fears it has fallen into the Enemies Hand. if Mr. Howe is acquainted with the Circumstances of Colo. Gist, he may be in Danger.[10]

The Pennsylvania militia's sad state of affairs was almost as ludicrous. The collective situation regarding the militias of all three states was summed up by Col. Timothy Pickering, Washington's adjutant general and a Massachusetts man. He wrote his brother in late September:

> Here [in Pennsylvania] we are, in fact, in an enemy's country. I am told upwards of sixty-five thousand men are enrolled in the militia of Pennsylvania; yet we have not two thousand in the field, and those are of little worth and constantly deserting. After the action on the 11th [Brandywine], and the enemy took possession of Wilmington, almost all the militia of Delaware State also ran home. Some Maryland militia may join us tomorrow, perhaps a thousand men. Many that marched from home have deserted. . . .
>
> I had heard at home so much contempt and ridicule thrown by the southern gentlemen on the New England militia, that I expected something better here; but no militia can be more contemptible than those of Pennsylvania and Delaware; none can be spoken of more contemptuously than they are by their own countrymen. And how astonishing is it, that not a man is roused to action when the enemy is in the heart of the country. . . . How

amazing, that Howe should march from the head of Elk to the
Schuylkill, a space of sixty miles, without opposition from the people of the country, except a small band of militia just round Elk!
Such events would not have happened in New England. I rejoice
that I can call *that* my country. I think myself honored by it. . . .

Congressman James Lovell, also of Massachusetts, wrote, "I dare not
be more minute as to the causes than only to tell you that the Philadelphians themselves say 'it would not be so in New England, every stone wall
would rattle about their ears.'"[11]

Washington wrote to Smallwood on the afternoon of September 14
from the Buck Tavern in Haverford Township, Pennsylvania. The commander in chief expressed sympathy for the Maryland general's plight and
told Smallwood that he was "sorry to find the Force you have is so small,
and that too, so illy provided with Arms and Ammunition." He directed
Smallwood to press on with whatever force he had and "either annoy and
harass the Enemy on their Flank or Rear, or proceed to join [the main
Army]."[12]

On September 15, Gen. William Smallwood sent Washington a very
frank and descriptive letter from "Oxford Meeting House 7 Miles above
Nottingham" appraising the whole situation. He included a detailed
return of the troops collected under his command. He had five Maryland
militia regiments: Marbury's, Murdock's, Dorsey's, Say's, and Johnson's.
The force was composed of 106 officers and staff, 14 drummers and fifers,
83 sergeants and corporals, and 1,210 privates. Of these, only 866 had
"good guns." Smallwood wrote the commander in chief:

Your Excy. may depend I will do all in my Power to comply with
our Instructions . . . to annoy and harass the Enemys Rear, but the
Condition of my Troops, their Number, the state of their arms,
Discipline and Military Stores, I am Apprehensive will not enable
me to render that essential Service. . . . As you seem to expect . . .
they may detach a Body of Infantry with their light Horse to Attack and
disperse the Militia. . . .

Your Excelly. is too well acquainted with Militia to place much
Dependence in them when opposed to regular and veteran Troops,
without Regular Forces to support them. . . . It will not be in my Power

to bring these Troops for these three Days to come on the Enemy's Rear. . . . Your Excy. will excuse the freedom I have taken in offering my sentiments. . . . Your Orders in the Interim shall be most exactly complied with.[13]

As this letter sped its way along the dirt roads of southern Chester County, Washington's army arrived in the Great Valley of northern Chester County and encamped between the White Horse and Warren Taverns, just as the threatening gray skies opened with a prelude of what was to come.

CHAPTER 5

The Battle of the Clouds

Monday, September 15, to
Tuesday, September 16, 1777

The Great Valley became the "seat of war" on September 15, 1777, as Washington's army converged on Randall Malin's house. Located at the fork of the Lancaster Road and the Swedes Ford Road in East Whiteland Township, Malin's became Washington's headquarters. Those troops that may have crossed the Schuylkill at Swedes Ford[1] would have had a 10-mile march to Malin's; the bulk of the Continental Army marched westward on the Lancaster Road from Lower Merion, Haverford, and Radnor Townships, a 10- to 15-mile march. Nor was that the end, as many troops advanced beyond Malin's and encamped along the Lancaster Road near the White Horse Tavern. The White Horse, kept by John Kerlin, was among the earliest taverns established in Pennsylvania.[2] It was located at the junction of six key roads just 2 miles west of Malin's house.

From a military perspective at that moment, this six-points crossroads was one of the most crucial intersections in northern Chester County. Mill Town, or Downing's Town (present-day Downingtown), an important food and supply depot, lay 7 miles to the west on the Lancaster Road, and Lancaster was only 33 miles beyond that. Philadelphia was 26 miles east, and Swedes Ford, the best ford on the Schuylkill,[3] was 12 miles northeast by way of the fork at Malin's. Heading southeast from the tavern up the South Valley Hill was the Road to Goshen, Edgemont, and Chester. Another road immediately to the southwest led to Boot Tavern, Turk's Head Tavern, and ultimately to Wilmington. These last two roads passed through or near the British Army camps 15 to 20 miles away, which made them strategically important for blocking any British advance. Northwest from the White Horse went a road to Yellow Springs and the iron region of French Creek; this road made a tortuous climb up the steep North Valley Hill. The ironworks of Warwick, Hopewell, and Reading Furnaces, which manufactured cannon, artillery ammunition, and iron implements for the Continental Army, could be reached via this route. Finally, a road to the northeast, called the Road to Moorehall, led to Judge William Moore's mansion, Moore Hall, on Pickering Creek near the Schuylkill above another ironworks, the Valley Forge. From Moore Hall, other routes led to several Schuylkill River fords, the French Creek iron region, and Reading, the Continental Army's main supply depot. Control of these roads was imperative to protect Washington's vital sources of supply.

Just before leaving the Buck Tavern on the 15th, Washington wrote John Hancock in Philadelphia, "We are moving up this [Lancaster] Road to get in between the Enemy and the Swedes Ford and to prevent them from turning our right flank, which they seem to have a violent inclination to effect, by all their Movements."[4] Protecting his army's flanks was not the only factor the American commander in chief had to consider. By placing his army on the Lancaster Road between the Warren and White Horse Taverns,[5] with forces as far back as the Paoli Tavern, Washington hoped to block British access to the interior areas so important to the American war effort. The next move was up to Howe.

That same morning, Sir William Howe was still at Dilworth with the bulk of his army. Gen. James Grant had been sent 5 miles east to Concord Meeting on September 12 with the 1st and 2nd British Brigades. Howe sent Hessian troops and the Scottish 71st Regiment to occupy Wilmington on September 13. These troops arrived in town so suddenly that the Scots captured Delaware president John McKinley. That same day, Lord Cornwallis went with the 1st and 2nd British Grenadier Battalions and the two British light infantry battalions to Concord, where they joined Grant's force; together they moved on to the heights of Ash Town (present-day Aston) near Chester and established camp.

On September 14, the sick and wounded from Howe's army were sent to a general hospital established at Wilmington. A Hessian member of General Howe's staff, Captain Friedrich von Münchhausen, recorded his observations of events at headquarters. He wrote on the 15th:

Some stupid people are dwelling on the fact that our General does not quickly follow Washington with his whole force. Of course this would be a good thing to do if it were possible, but it is definitely not, because the General first has to send away the sick and wounded on the wagons, which carry our provisions and baggage.

It is not possible to procure enough wagons here to do both at the same time, and neither of the two could be left behind.[6]

Captain von Münchhausen further reported that General Howe rode out of camp near Dilworth at 11 A.M. on September 15 and went down to Cornwallis's camp at Aston, no doubt to confer with the lieutenant general and decide the next movement.

The British Ash Town Camp was the scene of a dramatic episode that day. Two British soldiers were hanged in front of the encampment for "mauroding," or plundering local civilians. In August, General Howe had expressly forbidden his army to plunder, under penalty of death. Until September 15, the order had been largely ignored; now it was finally being enforced, as the Orderly Book of the 64th Regiment's light infantry captain Thomas Armstrong noted in the entry for Ash Town Camp on that date:

Willim Mirret, Grenadier, 1st Battalion Grenadiers, & Willm. Harrison, 1st Battn. Light Infantry, are this day to be executed at 11 o Clock in front of the grenadiers Encampment for plundering in Disobedience of Genl. orders.

. . . It is with the greatest Concern that his Excellency The Commander in Chief is Reduced to the Disagriable Necesety . . . but the Shoking & Crule Robries that have been commited on the Enisant Inhabetants of this country who have already suffered much from the Rebels for their Loyalty Renders it absulutely Necessary—

. . . It is likeways a Justase to the good Solder, who in a land of plenty must be Deprived of Every Comfort by the out Regious Depredations of a fue Desprat Villians.[7]

Capt.-Lt. John Peebles of the 42nd or Royal Highland Regiment's Grenadier Company, commented on this episode: "A Light Infantry Man of the 5th [Regiment] & a Grr. [Grenadier] of the 28th [Regiment] were Executed to day at 11 OClock . . . for Mauroding, the 1st Examples made, tho' often threatened, & many deserved it."[8]

Howe was not the only general confronted with problems caused by plundering; Washington also had to threaten capital punishment for the same offense during the campaign. In the month of September alone, Washington addressed the issue four times in the General Orders, with few results.

Information about Washington's movements arrived at British head-quarters during the afternoon. Capt. John Montrésor of the Royal Engineers noted, "At 4 o'clock P. M. [we] learnt that the rebel army which had crossed the Schuylkill at Philadelphia had repassed it to this side of Levering's Ford and were pursuing the road to Lancaster."[9] As a result of this intelligence, Howe finally decided to put his forces in motion. Cornwallis's troops at Aston were ordered to march at 8 P.M. toward the Lancaster Road, but it was midnight before they actually moved. Howe would move the force from Dilworth at 5 A.M. the next day. The two columns were to rendezvous at Goshen Meeting House and then proceed toward the White Horse Tavern to confront the rebel forces.

Sgt. Thomas Sullivan of the British 49th Regiment described the march of Cornwallis's column: "It was 12 o'clock at night when we marched . . . [with] tedious movement and frequent halting on account of the Night being very dark."[10] Lieutenant Peebles noted, "We turn'd off at the Sign of the 7 Stars [tavern] into the Lancaster road [sic], & march'd about 2 Miles over very rough road & halted till day light, ye 16th, when we moved on for 9 or 10 Miles & made a halt."[11] The unpaved roads became a muddy quagmire, churned by the movement of horses, livestock, baggage wagons, artillery pieces, and the tramp of thousands of feet. The skies turned ugly late in the day on the 15th; intermittent showers and wind from the northeast and southeast were harbingers of a gale about to descend on the Delaware Valley. Rain and wind continued off and on throughout the night and into the morning of the 16th.

Washington was informed of the British advance about 9 A.M. on September 16. He decided to move the Continental Army up the South Valley Hill and arrange it facing south on high ground between the Chester Road (present-day Route 352) to the east and the Road to Uwchlan (now Ship Road) to the west. Command of the advance forces was entrusted to Anthony Wayne, who was sent to feel out the British advance and slow it down, while the main army moved into position.

Wayne's force was made up of Pennsylvania militia regiments and Continental regulars of the 1st and 2nd Pennsylvania Brigades. The troops on the left moved up the hill from the White Horse and placed themselves on a rise of ground along the Chester Road (near today's Greenhill Road) about 1 1/2 miles north of Goshen Meeting House, with skirmishers deployed toward the meetinghouse. This would block Cornwallis's march on this road and cover the left flank of Washington's main battle line, which was supposed to form up about half a mile back. On Washington's right, the rest of Wayne's command advanced up the road to the southwest (now fragments of Phoenixville Pike) toward the Boot Tavern (at present-day Boot Road and Phoenixville Pike) and took up positions on the heights just north of the tavern. In this location, they would encounter General Knyphausen's column advancing from Dilworth by way of the Turk's Head Tavern (in present-day West Chester). Behind these advance parties, as the morning turned into afternoon, the bulk of Washington's force slowly lumbered up the South Valley Hill under turbulent lead-colored skies.

Skirmishing began in the midafternoon on Washington's right, just north of the Boot Tavern. Howe's Hessian aide, Captain von Münchhausen, described the action:

> About two o'clock in the afternoon, in the region called The-Boot-Sign, our vanguard, consisting of the Hessian jägers . . . encountered about 1500 rebels, being the vanguard of Washington's army. . . . The Hessian grenadiers and Hessian Leib Regiment were put in line on a height. But the rebels retreated, and there was only some skirmishing with the jägers, who were in the van of our column. Colonel [Count Karl] von Donop, who had advanced a little too impetuously with a company of jägers and 40 mounted jägers, was almost surrounded and only narrowly escaped capture.[12]

Hessian Jägers (literally "hunters," also spelled yeagers, yeackears, or Yagers) were green-uniformed riflemen equipped with short rifles and hunting swords. A special force of light troops, they were sharpshooters who were well trained in ranger or partisan tactics. One of the Jäger officers, Capt. Johann Ewald, recounted this part of the battle:

> The advance guard had hardly arrived at the Boot Tavern when they learned that an enemy corps of two to three thousand men had appeared on the left flank of the [British] army.
> After receiving this information, Colonel Donop immediately took the advanced guard of the jägers under Captain Wreden and the mounted jägers under Captain Lorey to reconnoiter the enemy. . . . The colonel pursued them too far, through which mistake an enemy party passed between him and the army and cut off his retreat. . . . Captain Lorey decided to break through with

the horsemen . . . notwithstanding that the enemy had posted himself very favorably behind walls and fences and kept up a sustained rifle fire. This was successful and the colonel got off with his skin.—

Ewald observed that the colonel's actions were extraordinary: "That is not a trade for one to follow who has no knowledge of it.—We all laughed secretly over this partisan trick."[13] Von Donop's valor was noted the next day in the General Orders, as was his rescue by the Jägers. It was a reckless valor born of humiliation; still smarting over the Hessian defeat at Trenton, the count was determined to recover the honor of his countrymen. His determination cost him his life several weeks later at the Battle of Fort Mercer.

The American advance guard on the Chester Road, composed mostly of Pennsylvania militia, promptly collapsed under the assault of Cornwallis's advance guard, the 1st Battalion of British Light Infantry. Lt. Henry Stirke of the British 10th Regiment described the action north of Goshen Meeting House:

> About 3 O'Clock, the first Battn of Light Infantry, attack'd a body of 500 rebels, under the Command of Genl Waine, posted behind a fence, on a hill, about half a mile from Goshen meeting House[.] on our advancing very briskly [they] gave us one fire and run away; leaving 10 men kill'd and Wounded on the field. . . . [Of] Ours, only one man wounded.[14]

Col. Timothy Pickering, the adjutant general of the Continental Army, corroborated Stirke's account: "An advanced party of ye enemy attacked our picquet just posted (about 300 strong) who shamefully fled at the first fire."[15]

As the skirmishing began, first on Washington's right and then on his left, the main part of his army was still not in place. Pickering further described the situation:

> General Washington ordered me to the right wing, to aid in forming the order of battle. On my return to the centre I found the line not formed. Seeing the commander-in-chief with a number of officers about him, as in consultation, I pressed my horse up

The White Horse Tavern, circa 1886. Photo by Julius Sachse [?] The appearance of the White Horse Tavern has changed little since 1777 when it was an important landmark for both British and American forces. AUTHOR'S COLLECTION

to learn the object. It was a question of whether we should receive the British on the ground then occupied by our troops, or retire beyond a valley in their rear.[16]

The position was poorly chosen. Only the two roads to the White Horse left room for the army to withdraw back into the Great Valley. Considering how long it took the army to take up positions, a decision had to be made quickly. Pickering told Washington:

Sir, the advancing of the British is manifest by the reports of the musketry. The order of battle is not completed. If we are to fight the enemy on this ground, the troops ought to be immediately arranged. If we are to take the high grounds on the other side of the valley, we ought to march immediately, or the enemy may fall upon us in the midst of our movement. "Let us move," was the general's answer.[17]

Back down the South Valley Hill went the Continental Army, taking up new positions 2 miles away on a "gradual prevailing height" in the valley north of the White Horse Tavern. As the withdrawal began, so did the violent rain. The Hessian Jägers continued their skirmish with Wayne's troops near Boot Tavern. Captain Ewald wrote:

> I believe that it was about five o'clock in the afternoon, an extraordinary thunderstorm occurred, combined with the heaviest downpour in this world. The army halted. On the left was a thick wood, from which our flank patrols had been dislodged by the enemy.
>
> General Knyphausen, who arrived at my company on horseback, ordered me to attack the people in the wood. . . . I had to cross open ground for several hundred paces . . . exposed to enemy fire, which did not seem to be very heavy, since most of the rifles did not fire owing to the heavy rain. . . . I ordered the hunting swords to be drawn. I reached the wood at top speed and came to close quarters with the enemy, who during the furious attack forgot that he had bayonets and quit the field, whereby the jägers captured four officers and some thirty men. The entire loss of the Jäger Corps in this fight consisted of five killed, seven wounded, and three missing.[18]

Maj. Karl Baurmeister, another Hessian officer, wrote of the same events:

> The rebels . . . were posted on high ground covered with a cornfield and orchards. The jägers, ducking behind the fences around the fields and woods, had an opportunity to demonstrate to the enemy their superior marksmanship. . . . The enemy, who soon retired to a dense forest, left behind many killed and wounded. I wish I could give a description of the downpour which began during the engagement and continued until the next morning. It came down so hard that in a few moments we were drenched and sank in mud up to our calves.[19]

The storm was a classic "nor'easter," part of a hurricane or tropical storm that pounded the Mid-Atlantic region that day. Under such conditions, it was nearly impossible to keep either firearms or gunpowder dry for firing. Mobility and visibility, critical for commanders when deciding on battlefield strategy, were also severely restricted for both armies, as was horseback communication. Because of the deluge, the Royal Army simply stopped in its tracks and hastily established camp.

Thus ended the Battle of the Clouds, an engagement that in dry conditions would probably have become a major battle on the scale of Brandywine. In reality, it amounted to little more than two widely separated skirmishes that petered out in the rain. But according to Captain Ewald, the rain was not the only reason for the halt:

> The army encamped in the vicinity of Boot Tavern in a quadrangle formation. This terrible rain caused the roads to become so bottomless that not one wagon, much less a gun, could get through. . . .
>
> I firmly believe that we still could have caught up with the greater part of the enemy army, at least the baggage . . . if it had been the will of General Howe. But the three-day delay on the battlefield [Brandywine] convinced me that we certainly would have halted even if no rain had fallen, because we surely knew that we were hard on Washington's heels.[20]

Howe's soldiers had no tents; they had been left behind to lighten the baggage train, so the troops crowded into barns and farm sheds or scrambled to build "wigwams" out of brush, fence rails, and tree limbs. Dry firewood no doubt was at a premium. The high-ranking officers took up the best lodgings they could find in the local farmhouses and taverns. Howe's aide, Captain von Münchhausen, wrote, "Our headquarters was established in a miserable small house, called The-Boot-Sign, which has given this region its name."[21]

Washington's army re-formed for action at the new position in the Great Valley, even as the drenching downpour rendered the muskets inoperable. Worse still, the Continental Army's cartridge boxes were so poorly constructed that practically all of the ammunition was ruined; the army's firepower was gone. Maj. Samuel Shaw of Massachusetts wrote:

> [The] rain coming on very fast, the General filed off, choosing to avoid an action in which the discipline of the enemy in the use of their bayonets (the only weapon that could then be of any service,

and which we were by no means generally supplied with) would give them too great a superiority.[22]

As darkness approached, the troops were ordered to march northward to Yellow Springs, 6 miles away over the steep North Valley Hill, to distance themselves from the British. A very young Continental artilleryman, thirteen-year-old Jacob Nagle, years later described the army's withdrawal and march:

The rain continuing so constant that small runs of water ware overflowed by the rain, that the foot soldiers could scarcely get a cross without swimming in several different places. We came to a regular decented hill [the North Valley Hill], the ground being so soft that they had to onhich the horses from one piece of artilery and hitch them to another till they got them all up[.] The nights was so dark you could not tell the man next to you. I being a horseback, I kept close behind one of the ammunition waggons but driping wet and shivering with cold.

All this time Morgans riffelmen ware on the wings, next to the enemy, against the Hissions [Jägers], as they could use their rifels, having bearskins over their locks, and every now and then you would give a crack at each other. We could always tell when a Hession fired, from our rifels, cracking so much lowder than our rifels.[23]

Everyone was soaked to the skin. Washington's aide, Lt. Col. John Laurens, son of Congressman Henry Laurens from South Carolina, later wrote his father, "My old [green aide's] sash [was] rather disfigur'd by the heavy Rain which half drown'd us on our march to the Yellow Springs, (and which by the bye spoilt me a waistcoat and breeches of white Cloth and my uniform Coat, clouding them with the dye wash'd out of my hat)."[24]

Night fell amid relentless sheets of rain as the Continental Army inched forward, slogging over steep hills and raging streams through a quagmire of Chester County mud. For over eight exhausting hours they marched, the soldiers pushing and pulling the horses and wagons, the artillery pieces, and each other, on bottomless roads to the Yellow Springs, a place known for rest and healthful waters.

CHAPTER 6

Northern Chester County, Pennsylvania

Wednesday, September 17, to Thursday, September 18, 1777

Upon examining the State of our Ammunition, I find it so generally hurt by the Rain, that we are not in Condition to make a stand against the Enemy," wrote Washington from Yellow Springs on the morning of September 17. "I have therefore thought best to move up towards Warwick Furnace, in order to obtain a Supply."[1] The "equinoxial gale" that began during the late afternoon of the 16th continued unabated until the early afternoon of the 17th. The effects of this deluge were felt for several days. Robert Morton of Philadelphia, attempting to travel to Reading that day, recorded in his journal:

> In the morning we crossed Skippack [Creek] though very rapid, and proceeded on to Perkioming [Creek], where we found it dangerous to pass owing to the rapidity of the stream. . . . We thought it most advisable to proceed to Pawling's Ferry upon Schuylkill, which having raised above 8 feet perpendicularly, and great numbers of trees and other rubbish coming down so fast, the Boatman would not go over.[2]

Washington's adjutant general Timothy Pickering wrote, "The brooks were swolen with the heavy rain, & Pickering's Creek up to the horses bellies, so that the passage of ye artillery and waggons was difficult. The foot [soldiers] passed over in a single file on a log laid across as a bridge for foot passengers."[3]

Col. Thomas Hartley of the Pennsylvania Line notified his friends in Lancaster that day, "We had Yesterday one of the hardest Marches known by any Soldiers in our army—neither Floods Storms Myres Nor any Thing else, prevented us from [effecting?] the Point."[4]

The condition of the roads and the flooding of French Creek dictated the army's route. The raging waters were impassable except at French Creek bridge on the Reading Road (present-day Route 23). To get to Warwick Furnace, Washington's army had to slog the 6 or so miles from Yellow Springs to the Reading Road and make a left-hand turn to cross the swollen torrent. The men then continued their tortuous march, with frequent halts and endless delays, to the Ridge Road and moved another 13 miles through hilly country to Warwick Furnace. Washington left General Greene's Division at Yellow Springs to cover the army's march and "Gen'l Wayne's between this and Warwick until the baggage can be got off."[5]

At Trappe, a few miles away over the Schuylkill, the sixty-nine-year-old Reverend Dr. Henry Muhlenberg, the senior Lutheran Church minister in Pennsylvania, observed that day:

Since yesterday, and through the night, it has stormed and rained, and it still continues to rain. The poor men of both armies are in a bad way, for they must be out in the cold wind and rain, without tent or roof, and thinly clothed. This can cause grave illness, especially in this time of the equinox.[6]

Pastor Muhlenberg's observations rang true. The British Army, waiting out the storm in Goshen and the Whitelands, was having its own problems due to the weather. The chief of the Royal Engineers, Capt. John Montrésor, noted on September 17 that the "rain and wind continued at N. E. but not so incessant. . . . Our troops suffered much from the weather." The following day he added, "Near 1/2 of my artificers, labourers, and waggoners as well as the Engineers are fallen sick with the prevailing distemper of the Fever and Ague."[7]

As the storm abated on the 17th, marching orders were issued at 3 P.M. from Howe's headquarters at the Boot Tavern. His Majesty's forces were without their tents, so the men had encamped in farm buildings or hastily constructed "wigwams" in the fields and woods along the roads, while the higher-ranking officers were quartered in farmhouses and taverns. The orders were to decamp and rendezvous at the White Horse Tavern on the Lancaster Road in the Great Valley.[8] The British Army encampments stretched along the roads from Goshen Meeting House northward to the crest of the South

Valley Hill and westward to the Road to Pottsgrove, a distance of more than 5 miles.[9] No sooner had the main part of the army in the area around Boot Tavern begun their march toward the White Horse than a halt was called. Capt. Friedrich von Münchhausen of Howe's staff explained:

> Everybody was already on the move when the heavy artillery, which was somewhat ahead, took the wrong road, a mistake of one of our guides. It took until nine o'clock in the evening before the artillery, over ravined and bad roads, was brought back to the main force. This unhappy mistake made us halt.[10]

Nearly twelve hours after the marching orders were given, von Münchhausen reported: "At half past two in the morning [of the 18th] the General left with all the troops for White Horse, where we arrived a little after dawn and met Lord Cornwallis. Here we halted until 10 o'clock [A.M.]."[11] Cornwallis's troops, encamped along the Chester Road from Goshen Meeting House to the Road to the White Horse, had moved down the South Valley Hill and arrived at the White Horse Tavern after midnight. The distance each of these columns moved in the dark was about 3 miles (from different directions), yet the movement was painfully slow and exhausting. "The roads were extremely bad, partly because of the heavy rains and partly because Washington, with the large part of his army, artillery, and all his baggage, had passed this way last night."[12]

Word of the British movement reached Washington in the early-morning hours of September 18. By this time, the bulk of the Continental Army had arrived at Warwick Furnace and continued on another 2 miles to nearby Reading Furnace. Washington commented, "The Army here is so much fatigued that it is impossible I should move them this Afternoon."[13] Nevertheless, it was at this very moment that Washington began to formulate yet another plan to foil Howe's advances through the region. This plan would use select Continental troops and militia units to outflank and harass the British, buying time for the main army to rest and then move to block Howe's crossing of the Schuylkill.

A force of Continental Light Infantry, commanded by Gen. William Maxwell of New Jersey, together with Pennsylvania militia under Gen. James Potter, was "near Potts's Forge" on the 17th; they were ordered by Washington to stay there "until that part of the baggage and Stores at the

Valley can be got away."[14] It is difficult to positively identify just which Potts's Forge they were near, as there were several ironworks in the region associated with the Potts family, but the following letter to Washington from Col. Clement Biddle of the Commissary Department, writing from Valley Forge at 9 P.M. on September 16, strongly points to the Mount Joy Forge, more commonly known as the Valley Forge, which was co-owned by David Potts:

> I removed the Baggage to Howell's Tavern 4½ Miles from the Warren Tavern & there waited for orders . . . to send the Provisions & Rum for the different Divisions to the Yellow Springs & having sent back on the road which lead there, found that Genl. Potters Baggage coming that road would interfere with the Rum & Provisions. . . . Colo Mifflin who came with orders from your Excellency . . . ordered the Baggage as well as the Provisions & Rum by this rout to the Bull Tavern.[15]

Maxwell's force numbered about 1,500, but the men ran the gamut from combat-hardened Continental light infantrymen chosen from many regiments to raw, untrained Pennsylvania militiamen called out for the crisis.[16] Some of the militia had seen action during the previous year, but collectively they were undependable. Militiamen were sometimes useful in secondary roles, such as guarding military depots, but their lack of experience, poor discipline, and short term of service (often sixty days) caused them at times to be more of a liability than an asset. Nevertheless, the realities of the situation meant that Washington did not have the luxury of choice; numbers were important in this campaign, even if badgering the state of Pennsylvania to supply its quota of militia in 1777 was a near-hopeless task. In addition, enlistments for the understrength regular Pennsylvania Line regiments were disappointingly low; the overall poor showing of recruits in Pennsylvania was downright embarrassing, especially for Anthony Wayne.

Wayne's Continentals were near Yellow Springs at "Camp three miles from the Red Lion"[17] on the 18th when Washington formulated his new strategy for stopping Howe's advance toward Philadelphia. Since the roads were deep in mud and the Schuylkill River was running high, British movements would be slowed for a few days. It might be possible to harass the Royal Army by sending Maxwell's and Wayne's forces to the flanks and

Reading Furnace Mansion, 1999. Photo by Andrew Cordray. From this house on September 18, Washington directed Anthony Wayne to move his division behind the British Army to watch their movements and cut off their baggage if possible, thus setting events in motion that resulted in the Battle of Paoli. AUTHOR'S COLLECTION

rear—the weak spots of any army—to hover, strike, and run, perhaps inflicting enough damage on British outposts and patrols to worry them into pursuit and exhaustion. Militia could be useful simply by their numbers. Their presence might confuse British intelligence gathering in two ways: by giving the impression of larger Continental forces or, if identified as militia, by catching the British off guard by concealing American regulars.

From Reading Furnace in northern Chester County, Washington wrote to Wayne on the morning of September 18:

> As I have receiv'd Information that the Enemy have turn'd down
> that Road from the White Horse which leads to Swedes Ford on

Schuylkill I have to desire that you will Halt your Troops wherever this meets you if coming this way and set them to Cleaning their Arms[,] drawing Ammunition & Cooking Provision.

I must call your utmost Exertion in fitting yourselves in the best manner you can for following & Harassing their Rear—Genl Maxwell will have a Similiar Order & will Assist you with the Corps under his command.

. . . I shall expect by return of the light Horse Man to Know where you are & when it will be in power to Comply with this order.[18]

As the circumstances changed daily, so did Washington's specific plans. From Yellow Springs on the 17th, Washington had sent General Smallwood the following instructions in response to his difficulties with the Maryland militia at Oxford:

As it may be dangerous for the Troops under your command to act alone, and the service may be more advanced by drawing Our Whole Force together, I earnestly request, that you will form a junction with the Main Army as soon as you possibly can. . . . I cannot mark out any particular Rout[e] for you, as that will depend upon the situation of the Enemy, of which you will obtain the best information in your power, that you may be secure in your Line of March. There is one Futhay, about Two Miles this side of Cockran's [Tavern], who is said to be a Trusty person and acquainted with the Country. I woud once more urge the necessity of the utmost expedition.[19]

Fortunately for Washington, Smallwood was still delayed by the problems of dealing with the militia, together with "the shameful neglect in the Commissarys Department [which] throws many Obstacles in my way and retards my March."[20] Now the idea was taking shape to use the Maryland militia, which was somewhere near Cochran's Tavern in West Fallowfield Township, in conjunction with Wayne's troops. Combining this body of 2,000 militiamen with Anthony Wayne's 1,500 Continentals could create a formidable threat to the rear of the British Army. From the "Camp three Miles from the Red Lion," at 1 P.M. on September 18, Colonel Hartley wrote his friends in Lancaster:

The Enemy . . . are kind enough to say the Rebels behaved well [at Brandywine]—we will let them know upon a proper Occasion that the American Bravery is equal to that of Britain.—

Forward on your [Lancaster] Militia. the Enemy are advancing towards Philada. We have I think gained their left Flank. the Communication between us and Lancaster is open—Smallwood can join us—the Day is approaching when, if we are successful, American Liberty will stand fair to be established; if the contrary a long war will be intailed upon us.[21]

Thomas Hartley concluded this portion of his letter with an optimistic, "God bless our operations; & put an End to all our Trouble."

CHAPTER 7

Near the Yellow Springs

Thursday, September 18, 1777

The problems faced by American forces in September 1777 were not limited to fighting the British, marching through rain, and constant shortages of supplies. The internal politics of organizations in general and of the American states specifically were just as real threats to the Continental Army's survival. The reorganization of the army in early 1777 left many officers bitter and disgusted, especially concerning the appointments of officers chosen for political reasons rather than for merit or seniority. In May, John Adams wrote: "I am wearied to Death with the Wrangles between military officers, high and low. They Quarrel like Cats and Dogs. They worry one another like Mastiffs. Scrambling for Rank and Pay."[1] James Lovell, another congressman from Massachusetts, commented in July, "There is as much pulling and hauling, about rank and pay, as if we had been accustomed to a military establishment here 150 years."[2]

Combined with these factors was the general nature of the people involved. Pulled together from a wide spectrum of backgrounds and beliefs, they were often proud, self-reliant, fractious, and provincial. To secure ultimate victory, Americans had to learn to cooperate with each other in spite of their differences. Though many were familiar with hunting or outdoor living, they were impatient with military life and discipline. The war had dragged on for more than two years already, with the end always in sight but just out of reach.

Maintaining a regular army in the field was a major challenge. In the New York Campaign of 1776, the Continental Army disintegrated due to a catastrophic cycle of expired enlistments and military defeats. Between the two victories at Trenton and Princeton, Washington had to personally beg the few remaining troops to stay beyond their terms of enlistment simply to keep a force in the field. At the commander in chief's insistence, the army of 1777 was composed of men signed up for long-term enlistments (three years or "during the war") who would become a professional force. In spite of the overwhelming evidence from the 1776 campaign that demonstrated the need for this, Congress was divided over the issue. Some Congressmen believed that no freedom-loving American would submit to the "tyranny" of soldiering for more than a few months; others feared a long-term standing army as a threat to free government; still others worried about an American military too reliant on foreign professionals in positions of command.

Despite the admirable efforts and remarkable success in rebuilding the Continental forces during the spring and summer of 1777, the ranks of the army were far from filled, especially in the Pennsylvania Line. By September, a number of Pennsylvania's generals had been reassigned or relieved of command. Colonels were called upon to temporarily command brigades, leaving their regiments to be commanded by lieutenant colonels or majors. The issues of seniority, promotion, job security, and pay were paramount, especially to those who had been serving for more than a year. To all of this, add battle casualties, sickness, jealousy, personality clashes, bickering, and politicking.

The troops under Anthony Wayne's command were the 1st and 2nd Pennsylvania Brigades of the Continental Line. Together these two brigades formed Maj. Gen. Benjamin Lincoln's Division. Wayne, a thirty-two-year-old native Pennsylvanian with no formal military training prior to the war but with no shortage of zeal and spunk, was commissioned brigadier general in February 1777, along with Philip De Haas. Wayne was given command of the 1st Pennsylvania Brigade, and De Haas was assigned to the 2nd Brigade. For unknown reasons, De Haas never took command of his brigade and soon resigned. General Lincoln was sent to upstate New York with the Northern Army under Gen. Horatio Gates in 1777, so command of his division devolved to Wayne. The rest of the Pennsylvania Line's command structure was a managerial nightmare. Some officers were doing extra duty, while others became supernumerary and left the army in disgust as regiments were reorganized. The unsettled state of affairs caused much tension among the officers, and the generals were at the forefront of the issues.[3]

Officers of the same rank derived their seniority in relation to each other based on date of commission. This process was complicated in the

Continental forces by the arrival of European officers, mostly from France, whose reputed expertise, titles, or political connections often gained them high ranks, much to the frustration of American officers. British- and Irish-born officers, many of whom had gained experience in the king's service, also abounded in the Continental Army and in the Pennsylvania Line. Forty-four-year-old Col. Richard Humpton, commander of the 2nd Brigade, was Wayne's second in command. A British Army veteran and twelve years Wayne's senior, Humpton was a native of Yorkshire, England, coincidentally the birthplace of Wayne's grandfather Capt. Anthony Wayne, who had served in King William III's army. The "York connection" in Wayne's command was remarkable: By coincidence, the third in command, twenty-nine-year-old Col, Thomas Hartley of the 1st Brigade, was a prominent resident of York, Pennsylvania.[4]

The two Pennsylvania brigades, each commanded by a colonel acting as a brigadier general, totaled nine infantry regiments. At full strength, the musketmen alone should have numbered over 6,000, but the surviving compiled records—payrolls, muster sheets, and brigade returns—along with descriptions from eyewitnesses, paint a different picture. Several contemporary accounts number Wayne's command at 1,500; other sources give the number as 2,000. The records indicate 1,767 musketmen (NCOs and privates) and 319 officers, staff, and musicians, for a total of 2,086 infantry personnel.[5] The 1st Pennsylvania Brigade, commanded by Col. Thomas Hartley, was made up of the following five regiments (the numbers include all personnel):

1st Pennsylvania Regiment (Col. James Chambers), 230
2nd Pennsylvania Regiment (Maj. William Williams), 187
7th Pennsylvania Regiment (Lt. Col. David Grier), 325
10th Pennsylvania Regiment (Lt. Col. Adam Hubley), 170
Hartley's "Additional" Regiment (Lt. Col. Morgan Connor), 265
Total personnel: 1,177

The 2nd Pennsylvania Brigade, under Col. Richard Humpton, was made up of four regiments:

4th Pennsylvania Regiment (Lt. Col. William Butler), 237
5th Pennsylvania Regiment (Col. Francis Johnston), 245

8th Pennsylvania Regiment (Col. Daniel Brodhead), 225
11th Pennsylvania Regiment (Maj. Francis Mentges), 202
Total personnel: 909

Attached to Wayne's force was Capt. Thomas Randall's Independent Company of Artillery, with four light cannon and thirty-seven personnel. Randall was from Massachusetts, but it is unclear whether his artillerymen were from Massachusetts or New Jersey. There were also three troops of light dragoons from two regiments: Bland's, raised in Virginia, and Sheldon's, from Connecticut. Numbering upward of sixty horsemen, their functions were to scout, patrol roads, and carry messages to and from the main army. Finally, Wayne's baggage train included an estimated total of twenty to twenty-five wagons from the Quartermaster Department transporting ammunition and certain camp equipment, along with Commissary Department wagons loaded with food and other equipment, all driven by civilian teamsters. The grand total of personnel under Wayne's command was about 2,200.[6] To keep the baggage train to a minimum, the tents were left behind. In clear weather, the soldiers would sleep in the open; in rainy conditions, they would build shelters called "booths" (same as the British "wigwams") out of brush and other available materials.

On September 18, Colonel Hartley wrote from "near Red Lion" at 2 P.M.:

The Enemy are in full March to Philada we shall March after them in a few Minutes. We have them in such a Situation that I think & if we defeat them, then will none of them get of[f.] almost all my Baggage . . . has fell into the Enemys Hands—I have no Breeches—send me a Pair of the best Buckskin ones by the express [rider]—a few Minutes earlier Notice would have given us the Enemys Baggage.[7]

Clothing problems plagued Wayne's force; many of the officers, including Hartley, lost their baggage after Brandywine and were left with only the clothes on their backs. The wear and tear of marching, along with the sun, sweat, dust, and rain, caused unchanged clothing to wear out quickly.[8] The following inventory provides an interesting glimpse into one officer's personal baggage:

Memorandum of Cloathing Lost at Brandywine By Capt. Wm. Alexander of the 7th Pennsylvania Regt. Commanded by Col. Wm. Irvin[e]

1 Uniform Coat blue & Red	1 Pair superfine black broadcloth
1 thick flannel Coat	Breeches
1 Coarderoy Vest	1 Pair Coarderoy .... Ditto
1 Nankeen Ditto	1 Pair fine Drilling .... D[itt]o.
1 thick flannel Ditt[o]	4 Pair Cotton Stockings
1 fine Swanskin	3 Pair thread Ditto
1 Jacket Pattern Not made up	3 Pair Worsted Ditto
	1 Pair Silk .... Ditto

1 bed sheet	6 Ruffld. Shirts
1 Table Cloath	2 Plain Ditto
2 Pair Shoes	4 White Stocks [worn at the
1 Case Razors & box	neck]
1 Pair Silver knee buckles	2 Black Ditto
	3/4 yd. Cambrick [fine linen]
	3 Pocket Handkerchiefs
	1 Black Barsalona silk Handker-chief
	1 Beaver hatt Laced. and Gold band

I do Certify Upon Honour that I Lost the Above mentioned Articles with some Others Which I Cannot Recollect at Present[9]

The enlisted men were in much worse shape. Uniforms were reduced to faded tatters by the constant wear from marching and countermarching. Sometimes shoes were sucked off in the calf-deep mud and filth created by the armies' passage. Occasionally some soldiers threw away blankets or extra clothing to lighten their loads on the march or in the haste of retreat.

Nonetheless, many of Wayne's men were veterans of months of army life and a few battles; some were going into their second or third year of campaigning and had established a reputation as stubborn, fairly well-disciplined veteran infantry. Wayne was proud of his troops and ceaselessly

wrote to all authorities for more shoes, proper uniforms, muskets, bayonets, and equipment.

The British Army, experiencing the same weather and road conditions
but without the organizational, supply, or discipline problems of the rebels,
moved from the White Horse Tavern eastward along the Lancaster Road
during the late-morning hours of September 18. Capt. John Montrésor of
the Royal Engineers noted:

> Several shot fired during the course of this day and some prisoners
> taken from the rebels. Some deserters and a Light Horse. The
> Army passed over the rebels late encampment where they had a
> most favourable position[,] being a prevailing gradual height in the
> valley. . . . We found the Inhabitants in general at their Homes.
> Several small hills in getting to this Encampment, which made the
> rear long and Baggage late.[10]

The last remnants of the tropical storm were clearing out on the morning of the 18th. The previous night, a cold, stormy wind with a little rain
continued into the morning hours but gradually diminished; by the afternoon of the 18th, conditions near Philadelphia were recorded at "3 PM . . .
68° . . . Cloudy & Sunsh[ine] at Interv[als]."[11] The roads throughout the
area remained a mess, especially those in the vicinity of the armies.

The townships of East and West Whiteland, called by the early Welsh
settlers Duffryn Mawr ("Great Valley"), and the Welsh township of Tredyffrin ("Valley Town") were witnessing a sight not soon to be forgotten: the
arrival of 15,000 troops of His Britannic Majesty. Rain soaked and mud
spattered as the men were, the British Army's appearance was nontheless an
awesome sight to the staid assortment of Quaker, Anglican, and Baptist farm
folk, most of them descendants of Welsh settlers. Sprinkled among the
Welsh were pockets of Scots-Irish Presbyterians and some German and
Swiss "Mennonists and Omish." This area was a microcosm of Pennsylvania
itself. Having sampled a taste of war by the Continental Army's encampment
three days before, these communities would now experience the presence of
thousands of British, Hessian, and Loyalist troops for the next few days.

Reaching the fork at Randall Malin's house, Howe's army divided into
two columns. Gen. Wilhelm von Knyphausen's column, the bulk of the
army, led the march and moved to the left onto the Swedes Ford Road.
Captain Montrésor wrote:

The whole army moved on towards Philadelphia, until we arrived at Randel Malins, being 2½ miles further. There we struck off (the roads forking) the road to the Swedes Ford to Treduffrin, one mile beyond Howell's Tavern, being 4½ to that Tavern and encamped one mile further, making 5½ miles more, in all this day [from Boot Tavern], Eleven miles.[12]

The 10,000 troops that marched on Swedes Ford Road through the Great Valley were led by the green-uniformed Hessian Jägers, both on foot and mounted. Blue-uniformed Hessian grenadiers and the Hessian musket battalions followed. The thousands of British redcoats included the Guards Battalions, the 16th or Queen's Own Light Dragoons, the 4th Brigade, the 3rd Brigade, and the 2nd Light Infantry Battalion. The blue-coated Royal Artillerymen, struggling to move dozens of fieldpieces through the muck, also accompanied this part of the Royal Army, along with hundreds of supply wagons and herds of livestock.

This seemingly endless column trudged through the mire eastward from the fork at Malin's, past the road leading to the Anglican Church of St. Peter-in-the-Great Valley. The church's Loyalist pastor, the sixty-nine-year-old Reverend William Currie, was also pastor of St. James's Church near Trappe and St. David's Church in Radnor, where Anthony Wayne was one of his parishoners. The split within the congregations was so hostile that Currie had ceased preaching entirely in May 1776.[13] Ahead was the Great Valley Presbyterian Church, whose congregation, by contrast, was solidly rebel. A Hessian officer later wrote, "Call this war, dearest friend, by whatsoever name you may, only call it not an American Rebellion, it is nothing more or less than an Irish-Scotch Presbyterian Rebellion."[14] About a mile beyond the Presbyterian church was David Howell's Tavern, known before the war as the Sign of George III. As the army arrived in Tredyffrin, Maj. Gen. Charles Grey took up quarters in this tavern, while Sir William Howe established headquarters at the house of Samuel Jones.[15] Other houses in the neighborhood were also occupied by officers. A few hundred yards east of Howe's headquarters stood the Great Valley Baptist Church, whose firebrand pastor, the Reverend David Jones, was chaplain of Wayne's 1st Pennsylvania Brigade.

On the Lancaster Road, Lord Cornwallis's Division slogged eastward from the fork at Malin's past the Admiral Warren Tavern,[16] named for British naval hero Sir Peter Warren, his portrait gazing down from the tav-

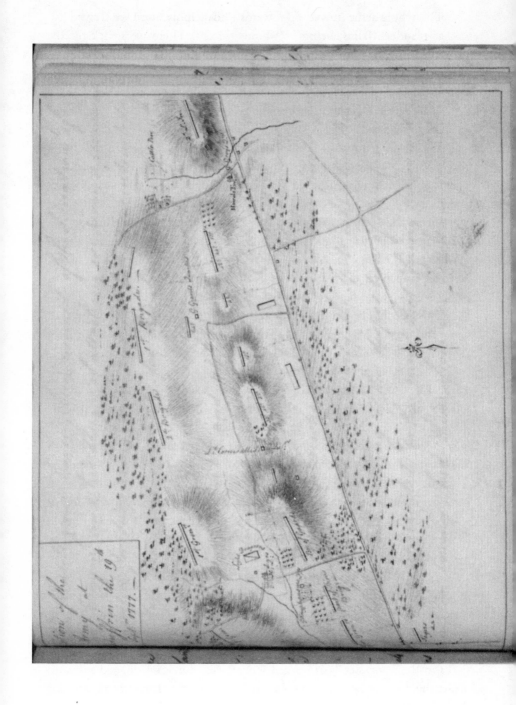

ern sign at his countrymen's progress. Later tradition maintained that the proprietor, Peter Mather, was known for his Loyalist views.[17] Up the South Valley Hill through the Warren Pass[18] marched the 1st Light Infantry Battalion, the 1st and 2nd British Grenadier Battalions, and the eight regiments of the 1st and 2nd Brigades, nearly 5,000 British troops in all.

About 2 miles east of the Warren Tavern, in a dell atop the South Valley Hill, stood the General Paoli Tavern. Named for Gen. Pasquale Paoli, Corsican hero and champion of liberty, this tavern was reputed as a gathering place for local Whigs, including a feisty young country squire named Anthony Wayne, whose home, Waynesborough, stood just over a mile away.[19]

Cornwallis's troops passed the General Paoli and continued 2 miles farther east to the Blue Ball Tavern. The British took up positions on the north side of the Lancaster or Conestoga Road for nearly 2 miles beyond the Blue Ball on bluffs overlooking the Great Valley and the main British camp below. For the second time in two days, the roads were filled with soldiers, officers, wagons, cattle, and horses all day and into the night. Sgt. Thomas Sullivan of the 49th Regiment, part of the 1st Brigade, remarked, "It was 12 o'clock at night before our Brigade that covered the rear, reached their Ground."[20]

The British high command was already aware of rebel movements in the vicinity, through reconnaissance patrols, deserters, and captured Continental dragoons carrying dispatches. Even before Wayne's force moved behind him, Howe knew that something was in the wind. At the Tredyffrin headquarters, Howe's Hessian aide, Capt. Friedrich von Münchhausen, wrote on September 18:

> We are told that several thousand men are still stationed in front of us behind the Schuylkill in the region of Swedes Ford, which is supposedly eight miles from here. Washington is said to be awaiting support from Maryland, Virginia, etc., after which, as the rebels say, he will hem us in completely at the Schuylkill.

Opposite page: *"Position of the Army at Truduffrin the 19th Septr. 1777," manuscript map by Capt. John André. Note that the orientation of the map has N at the bottom. In addition to other superb details, this map clearly shows General Grey's Quarters at Howel's Tavern at the west side, or rear of the camp, near the 2nd Light Infantry Battalion.* HUNTINGDON LIBRARY

Regarding the neighborhood, von Münchhausen observed: "We marched through the Great Valley to Tredyffrin. They call this region Great Valley because there are chains of high hills covered with woods on both sides
of the valley. The Valley Creek, part of which flows through our camp, has
the best water I have tasted here in America."[21]

Across the Great Valley, the delightful waters of Valley Creek enter the
gorge between Mount Joy and Mount Misery and flow down to the
Schuylkill River near some mills and an ironworks called The Valley Forge.

CHAPTER 8

Valley Forge and Philadelphia

Thursday, September 18, to
Friday, September 19, 1777

There was much activity on Valley Creek not 3 miles downstream from Howe's Tredyffrin headquarters, where a handful of American personnel feverishly worked to remove a veritable mountain of army supplies stored at Valley Forge. Later famous for the winter encampment of 1777–78, Valley Forge was the name of an ironworks established in 1742. Known also as Valley Creek Forge or Mount Joy Forge, the ironworks converted pig iron into bar iron, which was then used to make items such as tools, hardware, and horseshoes. The forge was one of several iron-producing enterprises connected to the Potts family of Pottsgrove, an early Pennsylvania iron dynasty.

At the time of the Revolution, the forge was owned by ironmaster William Dewees, Jr., son of the Philadelphia County sheriff, in partnership with David Potts, son of ironmaster John Potts of Pottsgrove. David's brother Isaac was a businessman who owned a sawmill and a gristmill a few yards downstream from the forge, near where the Valley Creek empties into the Schuylkill.[1] These enterprises became the nucleus of a small community nestled at the foot of Mount Joy and Mount Misery, where the Nutt Road met the "Great Road" (present-day Gulph Road) at Valley Creek. A few yards from the mills, Isaac owned a small, elegant house built a few years before the Revolution.[2]

In early 1777, Congress established a Continental magazine, or military depot, at Valley Forge. Although he was a colonel in the Pennsylvania militia, William Dewees was reluctant to allow military supplies to be stored there, fearing that the forge would become a target for Loyalist sabotage or British attack during an invasion. The magazine was established despite his protests, so the ironmaster requested that a sergeants' guard of militia be stationed at the forge for security. Both the Continental Commissary Department and the Quartermaster General stored supplies there during the summer of 1777. Most of the stores were flour and grain— upward of 4,000 barrels (1 barrel of flour equals 196 pounds)—along with large quantities of iron goods for the army.[3] As Howe's army moved into the region, the American military made hasty efforts to remove supplies from the Philadelphia area into the upcountry of northern Chester, Philadelphia, and Berks Counties.

On the stormy night of the Battle of the Clouds, with British forces only 10 miles away, Colonel Dewees quickly compiled an inventory of supplies stored at the magazine:

Estimate of Stores at Valley Creek forge
Tuesday Evening 1/4 after 8 O'Clock 16: Sep: 1777
Qur: Mr: Genls. [Quarter Master Generals] Stores & Forage
   3000 bushels Wheat part ground
   20,000 Tomahawks or rather more
   5:000 Sets horse Shoes
   3: or 400: axes helved [having handles] & ground
   A great quantity of Spades}
      Shovels & Pick Axes}
   4 or 3 Tonns Barr Iron—
   20 or 30 Cask Nails
   6 or 700 Camp Kettles—
   A Number of other Articles of less Value not included in the
      above—

Commissary's Stores
   2000 Barrels Flour
   1,000 D[itto] Bread which with some of the Flour is to go off
   to the Army at the Yellow Springs in the Morning with Five
   Waggons—Both are orderd the Waggons to hawl them to the
   landing as early as possible & Colo. Biddle has directed them to
   the East Side of Schuylkill.[4]

Only one small problem remained: Who was going to move all of this material? No one seemed to know. The haste of the situation, the confusion of jurisdiction among military departments, the call-up of workers for Pennsylvania militia duty—all played a part in the supplies not being moved in a timely manner. Now, with the teeming rain, the roads flooded, the Schuylkill rising, and Washington withdrawing to Yellow Springs, the chances of removing so many supplies to a safe location diminished by the hour.

From Valley Forge at 9 P.M., Col. Clement Biddle, the Continental Army's Forage Master General, sent a message to Washington along with Dewees's inventory:

> I have stopd at this place (sending a Good Guide & Conductor with the Waggons to the Bull Tavern where I shall soon overtake them) to examine the state of the Stores at this place & I inclose to your Excellency an Estimate hastily taken from the Gentleman in Charge which he says may be incorrect—I have desired him to procure Boats & Teams to hawl them to the landing (not 400 yards from the Stores) & and as he complains that his hands have all been taken from him who did this Business I have taken the Liberty to assure him that any persons employd in that Service should be exempted from Militia Duty while engaged therein.[5]

The next morning, Washington wrote to Gen. William Maxwell, who was somewhere near Valley Forge with light infantry and militia, "I would have you remain where you are until that part of the baggage and Stores at the Valley can be got away, which I wish to be effected as expeditiously as possible."[6]

Between the mired roads, the raging Schuylkill, and the general chaos of the invasion, little seems to have happened regarding the stores at Valley Forge until the afternoon of September 18, when Washington's aide, Col. Alexander Hamilton, accompanied by Capt. Henry "Light Horse Harry" Lee and a party of eight dragoons, arrived to assist Colonel Dewees in removing the supplies. That same afternoon, Howe's army arrived at Tredyffrin, only 4 miles away by foot. Lee wrote:

> Contiguous to the enemy's route lay some mills stored with flour. . . . Their destruction was deemed necessary by the commander-in-chief; and his aid-de-camp, Lieutenant-Colonel Hamilton, attended by Captain Lee, with a small party of his troop of horse, were dispatched in front of the enemy, with the order of execution. The mill, or mills, stood on the bank of the Schuylkill. Approaching,

you descend a long hill [present-day Gulph Road] leading to a bridge over the mill-race. On the summit of this hill two vedettes [mounted sentries] were posted; and soon after the party reached the mills, Lieutenant-Colonel Hamilton took possession of a flat-bottomed boat.[7]

A local girl, eighteen-year-old Sarah Stephens, observed the activity and recounted the scene often in later years. She was returning from Philadelphia with her aunt and was unable to cross the Schuylkill at Swedes Ford due to the high water. They proceeded upriver to Pawling's Ferry, nearly opposite to Valley Forge, "from which place they were then removing the stores on temporary rafts, constructed for the purpose, as expeditiously as possible." The two women were ferried over on a return trip by one of the rafts. Sarah saw "Col. Dewees hurrying to cross the river . . . and Col. Lee, who was stationed here to guard the stores, in company with Col. Hamilton, busily engaged in moving them away."

As Sarah and her aunt continued on their way up the Gulph Road toward home,

at the junction of the Gulf and Baptist roads, hearing a noise in the woods on their right, [Sarah] looking in that direction, saw coming toward them a body of British cavalry, moving in the most perfect order, their horses being so trained that they made but little noise in their march. In their front, in company with an officer, rode a guide or pilot, whom she knew, but who shall in this description be nameless [possibly William S. Moore]; one who, if report be true, was often engaged in similiar expeditions during the war. They passed on without noticing or molesting them, except that an officer left his station, rode up to them, and inquired of them whether they had been at Valley Forge and seen Colonel Dewees? and whether they were removing the military stores? Receiving from her an affirmative answer, he took his leave and resumed his station in the company, who proceeded on to the river.[8]

Back at British headquarters, Capt. Friedrich von Münchhausen noted: "In the evening Colonel Harcourt (16th Dragoons) left with two squadrons of dragoons, three companies of light infantry, and 200 dismounted dragoons. His destination is Valley Forge, four miles from here [by foot]. . . .

He plans to seize a deserted magazine there."[9] As the British cautiously approached the crest of the ridge overlooking the creek and river, they discovered that the magazine was not quite deserted. Captain Lee wrote:

> Hamilton took possession of a flat-bottomed boat for the purpose of transporting himself and his comrades across the river, should the sudden approach of the enemy render such a retreat necessary. In a little time . . . the fire of the vedettes announced the enemy's appearance. The dragoons were ordered instantly to embark. Of the small party four with the lieutenant-colonel jumped into the boat, the van of the enemy's horse in full view, pressing down the hill in pursuit of the two vedettes. Captain Lee, with the remaining two, took the decision to regain the bridge, rather than detain the boat.
>
> Hamilton was committed to the flood, struggling against a violent current, increased by the recent rains; while Lee put his safety on the speed and soundness of his horse. . . . The two vedettes preceded Lee as he reached the bridge; and himself with the two dragoons safely passed it, although the enemy's front section emptied their carbines and pistols at the distance of ten or twelve paces.

Lee and his horsemen escaped westward on the Nutt Road; the British quickly gave up pursuit. As for Hamilton, Lee could hear "volleys of carbines discharged upon the boat, which were returned by guns singly and occasionally."[10] Hamilton's horse, also in the boat, was hit in the middle of the river. In the return of gunfire, "the Commanding Officer of the Light Infantry [Maj. Peter Craig, 57th Regiment] had his horse shot."[11]

Thus ended the "Battle of Valley Forge," though just a skirmish, the largest military engagement that ever actually took place there. The British won; their spoils included, according to Captain Montrésor, "3800 Barrels of Flour, Soap and Candles, 25 Barrels of Horse Shoes, several thousand tomahawks and kettles, and Intrenching Tools and 20 Hogsheads of Resin."[12] They also now occupied this critical area, with roads leading to Reading, the French Creek iron region, Lancaster, and several Schuylkill River fords.

Hamilton made it safely across the Schuylkill; two others with him were not so fortunate. He immediately scribbled a hasty note to president of Congress John Hancock, warning:

If Congress have not yet left Philadelphia, they ought to do it immediately without fail, for the enemy have the means of throwing a party this night into the city. I just now crossed the valleyford, in doing which a party of the enemy came down & fired upon us in the boat by which means I lost my horse. One man was killed and another wounded.

A little later, being marginally more composed, Hamilton again wrote Hancock at 9 P.M.:

I did myself the honor to write you a hasty line this Evening giving it as my opinion that the city was no longer a place of safety for you. I write you again lest that should not get to hand.

The enemy are on the road to Sweedes ford, the main body about four miles from it. They sent a party this evening to Davesers ferry, which fired upon me and some others in crossing it, killed one man, wounded another, and disabled my horse. They came on so suddenly that one boat was left adrift on the other side, which will of course fall into their hands and by the help of that they will get possession of another, which was abandonned by those who had the direction of it and left afloat, in spite of every thing that I could do to the contrary.

These two boats will convey 50 men across at a time so that in a few hours they may throw over a large party, perhaps sufficient to overmatch the militia who may be between them and the city. This renders the situation of Congress extremely precarious if they are not on their guard. . . .

The most cogent reasons oblige me to join the army this night or I should have waited upon you myself. I am in hopes our army will be up with the enemy before they pass Schuylkill. If they are, something serious will issue.[13]

Hancock was the recipient of much news that night, none of it good. At 10 P.M., before Hamilton's notes arrived, he was visited by "a certain Joseph Burns of Chester County," one of Anthony Wayne's scouts. After receiving Washington's orders to move forward on the rear of the British Army, Wayne sent Burns to reconnoiter the British camp. Burns, "being unable to get back again, was under a Necessity of making the best of his

Way to this City." He told Hancock that the British were "within seven or eight Miles of the Swede's Ford" and that some Pennsylvania light horse had captured two British soldiers "within Eighteen Miles of this City on the Lancaster Road," which was near the front of the Tredyffrin Camp. Hancock wrote Washington, "I thought it best to lay this Intelligence before you, and to transmit it immediately by Express."[14]

Hamilton's urgent warning arrived in Philadelphia about midnight. Within the first hours of Friday, September 19, the City of Brotherly Love was transformed into pandemonium. The official record in the *Journals of the Continental Congress* states that "the president received a letter from Colonel Hamilton, one of General Washington's aids, which intimated the necessity of Congress removing immediately from Philadelphia; Whereupon, the members left the city."[15] Such are the bare bones of government records; personal accounts reveal a much more interesting picture. John Adams wrote Abigail:

> the Congress were alarmed in their beds by a letter from Mr. Hamilton, one of General Washington's [military] family, that the enemy was in possession of the fords over the Schuylkill, and of the boats, so they had it in their power to be in Philadelphia before morning. The papers of Congress . . . had, before this, been sent to Bristol. The president and all the other gentlemen had gone that road, so I followed.[16]

The news traveled quickly; exaggerated rumors and panic spread even faster. The resulting scene spread smug satisfaction among Loyalists, disillusionment among Patriots, and disgust among the sensible. Seventeen-year-old Robert Morton, whose stepfather, James Pemberton, and uncles Israel and John Pemberton were under arrest without charge by order of Congress, wrote:

> This morning, about 1 o'clock, an Express arrived to Congress, giving an acco. of the British Army having got to the Swedes Ford on the other side of the Schuylkill, which so much alarmed the Gent'n of the Congress, the military officers and other Friends to the general cause of American Freedom and Independence, that they decamped with the utmost precipitation, and in the greatest confusion, insomuch that one of the Delegates, by name Fulsom

[Nathan Folsom, New Hampshire], was obliged in a very *Fulsom* manner to ride off without a saddle.[17]

Hamilton's report of the possibility of a British crossing of the Schuylkill was quickly exaggerated into an actual crossing and Howe's imminent arrival in the capital. Sarah Logan Fisher, whose husband was also in custody and en route to exile, vividly captured the chaos of the moment:

> The City was alarmed about two oClock [A.M.], with a great knocking at peoples Doors & desiring them to get up, that the English had crossed the Swedes ford at 11 oClock & would presently be in the City. had I not had my Spirits too much depressed with the absence of my dear Companion, the scene would really have diverted me, Waggons rattling, Horses Galoping, Women running, Children Crying, Delagates flying, & all together the greatest consternation, fright & terror that can be imagined, some of our Neighbours took their flight before Day, & I believe all the Congress mov'd off before 5 oClock, but behold when Morning came . . . the English had only made their appearance opposite the Swedes ford & some of our People whose fears had magnified it into a reality that they had crossed brought the alarm to Town, & terrour & dismay spread itself amongst them, thus the guilty fly when none pursue.[18]

Not twelve hours earlier, Congressman Henry Laurens of South Carolina had written to a friend: "Fright sometimes works Lunacy. This does not imply that Congress is frightened or Lunatic but there may be some Men between this & Schuylkill who may be much one & a little of the other." Now Laurens described his reaction to the alarm:

> About 4 oClock next Morning I was knocked up by Sir Patrick Houston who informed me that advice had been received of General Howes crossing Schuylkill at 11 oClock & that part of his Army would be in the City before Sunrise. I could feel no impression. I judged differently from the City people. . . . I considered the difficulty of crossing a ford with an Army of 6 or 7 Thousand men, Cannon, Horses, Waggons, Catle &ca . . . & detaching a respectable force to a distance of 22 Miles. . . . I however would

not fly, I stayed Breakfast & did not proceed till 8 oClock. . . . My bravery however was the effect of assurance for could I have believed the current report, I should have fled as fast as any Man, no Man can possibly have a greater reluctance to an intimacy with Sir William Howe than my Self.[19]

Mrs. Elizabeth Drinker, whose husband, Henry, was also among the Philadelphians exiled to Virginia for refusing to swear allegiance, noted the rumors and reactions:

> Jenny awoke us this Morning about 7 o'clock, with the news that the English were near; we find that most of our Neighbors and almost all the Town have been up since one in the Morning[.] The account is that the British Army cross'd the Sweeds-Foard last night, and are now on their way heather; Congress, Counsil [state government] &c are flown, Boats, Carriages, and foot Padds going off all Night; town in great Confusion.[20]

Common Sense author Thomas Paine painted the scene for Benjamin Franklin: "The confusion, as you may suppose, was very great. It was a beautiful, still, moonlight morning, and the streets as full of men, women and children as on a market day."[21]

The main roads out of the city to the north—the Old York Road and the Frankford-Bristol Road—were choked with refugees. Congressman Laurens observed:

> The Scene was equally droll & melancholy. Thousands of all sorts in all Appearances past by in such haste that very few could be prevailed on to answer to the Simple question what News? . . . I proceeded to Bristol, the little Town was covered by fugitives . . . the Road choaked by Carriages, Horses & Waggons. The Same was disgustingly Specked by Regimental Coats & Cockades, Volunteer blades I suppose who had blustered in that habit of the mighty feats they would perform if the English should dare to come to Philadelpa. Upon these I looked with deep contempt.[22]

News of Congress's hasty departure reached the British camp at Tredyffrin within a few hours. Capt. John Montrésor recorded in his journal on

September 19, "This morning between 2 & 3 the Rebel congress precipi-
tately abandoned Philadelphia, owing to a false alarm."[23] No doubt His
Majesty's officers had a good chuckle when the reports arrived, accompanied by the usual exaggerations and stories that such events also precipitate.

A few miles west of the Tredyffrin Camp that night, gray shadows from
a ghostly river of troops poured steadily down the North Valley Hill, as
Anthony Wayne's two brigades made their way through the Great Valley. A
full harvest moon illuminated the valley, revealing blankets of mist in the
rills and dells of the valley floor. Glimmers of moonlight pierced the rising
vapors and caused the muskets of the soldiers to glisten as they moved
through the valley in a column, the sounds of their movement muffled by
the thick, damp air. Onto the Lancaster Road they trudged in silence, past
the darkened windows of the Admiral Warren and up through the gloomy
Warren Pass, where Cornwallis's men had marched but a few hours earlier.
The rutted clay mire made footing uncertain; the tree-shrouded slopes of
the South Valley Hill cast deep shadows, making the ascent slow and difficult. Reaching the crest of the hill, the weary column halted near the
moonwashed walls of the General Paoli, there to await the next move.

CHAPTER 9

The Great Valley, Chester County

Friday, September 19, 1777

Anthony Wayne was within hailing distance of his birthplace and home, Waynesborough, in the predawn hours of September 19. His force of about 2,200, including infantry, artillery, dragoons, and supply wagons, had moved through the Great Valley during the night and arrived at the Sign of General Paoli on the Lancaster Road, only 2 miles southwest of the rear of the British camp at Tredyffrin.[1] From Reading Furnace the previous day, Washington had ordered Wayne to advance from Yellow Springs to get behind Howe. Evidently some of the messages did not reach Wayne in a timely manner or at all, for an exasperated Washington wrote him personally at 6 P.M. with explicit instructions:

> I have this Inst[ant] rec[eived] yours of 1/2 after 3 Oclock—having wrote twice to you already to move forward upon the Enemy, I have but little to add.—Genl. Maxwell and Potter are order'd to do the same (being at Potts' Forge)—I could wish you and those Genl. would act in conjunction, to make your advances more formidable. . . . I shall follow as speedily as possible with jaded men. . . .
> —give me the earliest Information of every thing Interesting & of your moves that I may know how to govern mine by them— the cutting of the Enemy's Baggage would be a great matter—*but take care of Ambuscades.*

As more information about British movements arrived at Reading Furnace, Washington directed his aide John Fitzgerald to add a postscript to Wayne's marching orders:

Since Sealing the within [letter] his Excellency Orders me to mention to you that as the Enemy will probably find some opposition at Swedes ford, they will Endeavor to make a push at some of the Fords lower down on Schuylkill—he therefore wishes you to keep a constant Guard towards their Right that you may be able either to give Information or Oppose them *if the Party should not be an overmatch for you*[.] He is fully satisfied you will do every thing in your power to Harass & Distress them on their March, *without suffering yourself to be reduc'd to any disagreeable Situation.*[2]

The British Tredyffrin Camp was established according to the troops' line of march on two nearly parallel roads, the Swedes Ford Road and the Lancaster/Conestoga Road. The *front* of the march was headed northeast toward Swedes Ford (Norristown); therefore, their *right flank* was to the east, southeast, and south along the Lancaster/Conestoga Road toward Easttown Township. The "Fords lower down on Schuylkill" included Matson's Ford (Conshohocken), Levering's Ford (Manayunk), and several others, all of which were accessible via the Lancaster/Conestoga Road and its many crossroads. The British *left flank* was to the north and northwest of Tredyffrin in the region of the North Valley Hills and Valley Forge; there were also several river fords in that direction. The *rear* of Howe's force was to the west and southwest toward the Paoli and White Horse Taverns. By moving to the Paoli Tavern, Wayne placed his force southwest of the Tredyffrin Camp in the *right rear* of the British Army.

Following the commander in chief's explicit instructions to keep him informed of "every thing Interesting & of your moves that I may know how to govern mine by them," Wayne wrote enthusiastically to Washington at 7:30 that morning:

On the Enemies Beating the Revillee I ordered the Troops under Arms and began our March for their left flank—But when we Arrived within half a Mile of their Encampment found they had not Stired, but lay too Compact to admit of an Attack with Prudence—Indeed their Supineness Answers every Purpose of giving you time to get up—if they Attempt to move I shall Attack them, at all Events—

this Moment Capt. [Llewellyn] Jones of Blands Dragoons brought in four Prisoners—three of them belong to the Queens Rangers & One Artillery man, they don't seem to know much about the Movements of the Enemy nor the loss they sustained at Brandywine but have heard it was very great—

There never was, nor never will be a finer Opportunity of giving the Enemy a fatal Blow than the Present—, for Gods sake push on as fast as Possible.[3]

The reveille in the British camp sounded sometime between 1 and 2 A.M. Capt. Johann Ewald of the Hessian Jägers noted: "On the 19th, at two o'clock in the morning, the army received orders to march. . . . [Later] the army received counterorders." Wayne was close enough to hear the Royal Army's fifers, drummers, pipers, and trumpeters "beat reveille."[4]

A brilliant harvest moon shone on this "beautiful, still, moonlight morning"; the temperature dropped into the upper 50s during the night.[5] Movement in the night was much easier by moonlight, although exhaustion from constant marching combined with the soaking rains and cooler temperatures was taking a toll on the armies. Capt. John Montrésor of the Royal Engineers wrote:

19th. Wind N. W., very fine weather, which comes very seasonably to refresh the troops and dry the roads which are very sloughy about this place. The halting this day very necessary for the men and particularly for our horses. . . . As many men have lately fallen sick, empty waggons are ordered to each of the Corps. . . . Heavy dews.[6]

Wayne, ever impatient for action, wrote Washington a second message at 10:45 that morning:

The Enemy are very quiet, washing & Cooking—they will Probably Attempt to move towards Evening—I expect Genl. Maxwell on their left flank every Moment and as I lay on their Right, we only want you in their Rear—to Complete Mr Hows buisness—I believe he knows nothing of my Situation—as I have taken every precaution to Prevent any intelligence getting to him—at the same time keeping a Watchful Eye on his front Flanks & Rear.

I have not heard from you since last Night.[7]

Wayne's last remark may be the first indication that the statement "he knows nothing of my situation" was erroneous. While Wayne may have indeed "taken every precaution to Prevent any intelligence getting to him," Captain Montrésor noted in his diary that same day, "A Dragoon deserter came in. . . . Couriers constantly going towards and returning from the Enemy's Camp."[8] Some of these couriers did not reach their destinations; at least one dispatch sent from Washington to Wayne on the 19th passed into Howe's hands that day and revealed American plans to the British high command:

> By the advice of the general officers, I have determined, that the army, under my immediate command, cross the Schuylkill at Parker's ford, and endeavour to get down in time to oppose the enemy in front, whilst the corps under your command, in conjunction with gen. Smallwood and col. Gist, act to the greatest advantage in the rear.[9]

The ramifications of this new situation were enormous. Washington's decision to march to Parker's Ford was a daring gamble that left Wayne in a dangerously exposed position, precluding any notion of Washington arriving behind Howe's army with Continental troops. Instead, the army began a 16-mile march northeast from Reading Furnace to Parker's Ford, where the troops faced a river crossing in chest-high water, and another 20-mile march southeast to the region of Swedes Ford. This motion completely outflanked Howe's army. It also put Wayne entirely on his own to "act to the greatest advantage in the rear" as soon as Smallwood and Gist joined him—with militia. Though Wayne had never been one to shrink from a risky challenge, he was now virtually unsupported and within less than 3 miles of a professional force seven times larger than his own. Further, since Washington's instructions stated that the army's motions would be governed by his moves, Wayne was certain that the main army would soon arrive in the Great Valley to pin Howe against the flooded Schuylkill, with Wayne on the right and Maxwell on the left. The interception of this dispatch deprived Wayne of the knowledge that the main army was actually moving *away* from him and over the Schuylkill. For the British high command, it laid Washington's plans before them and confirmed Wayne's presence somewhere behind their army.

The first indication to Wayne that his position at the Paoli Tavern might be known to the British occurred shortly after he wrote his second note to Washington. Col. Daniel Brodhead of the 8th Pennsylvania Regiment recalled, "[We] lay on our arms untill about 10 o'Clock when the Genl. informed us the Enemy were Advancing & Ordered us to Retire, which we did to a piece of high Ground about 1-1½ Miles to our Rear."[10] Col. Adam Hubley and Col. Thomas Hartley also noted this movement. Hartley related, "General Wayne on the 19th of Sepr in the Afternoon changed the position of his Troops on understanding the Enemy intended to attack us, and took Post on some high Ground above the Warren Tavern on the Lancaster Road."[11] Allowing for the slight discrepancies in time, Wayne withdrew from the Paoli during the midday hours and moved westward back up the Lancaster Road toward the Warren Tavern.

About a mile and a half west of the Paoli, the Pennsylvania brigades descended toward the Warren Pass in the South Valley Hill. Just before the pass was the upper portion of the Long Ford Road, a steep, narrow road that ran up the hill to the left. The Continentals swung to the left and marched up this road through dense woods that covered the slopes of the South Valley Hill in Willistown Township. Just over the crest of the hill, about half a mile from the Lancaster Road, the woods gave way to open meadows and farm fields surrounded by stands of trees and fences. Here the soldiers filed off to the right through a narrow strip of woods and halted in the fields of Ezekiel Bowen and Cromwell Pearce.

The British Tredyffrin Camp, which Wayne described as very quiet at 10:45 A.M., was buzzing with movement by noon. Howe's Hessian aide, Capt. Friedrich von Münchhausen, explained:

> At noon news arrived that our detachment at Valley Forge was being attacked. Two English regiments were sent off at once; they arrived there in an incredibly short time, whereupon the enemy retreated. In the afternoon the English grenadiers and the 1st battalion of light infantry left for Valley Forge, and the detachment under Colonel Harcourt, as well as the two English regiments sent there today, came back here.[12]

Most likely the troops spotted by the British near Valley Forge were part of Maxwell's and Potter's force, which was in the vicinity. Rebel forces were in clear view across the Schuylkill from the Gulph Road at the ridge of Mount Joy. Grenadier Lt. John Peebles of the 42nd Royal Highland Regiment observed:

The Light Infantry & Grenadrs. march'd in the Afternoon about 3
OClock to the Hill above the Valley forge which is near the
Sckuylkill at the Mouth of Valley Creek, Major Craig with some
Compys. of Light Infy. having taken possession before. . . . Some
Scouting partys of the Rebels seen hovering about, they Lit fires
t'other side of the River.—a fine Prospect from this Hill.[13]

There may also have been some rebel skirmishers west of Valley Creek.
Whether any actual shooting took place or if it was simply that the appearance of large numbers of rebel troops in the neighborhood was sufficient to
call for reinforcements is unclear. What is clear is that General Howe sent
Lord Cornwallis with more than 1,500 of his best troops, the two battalions
of British grenadiers and the 1st Light Infantry Battalion, to hold the position at Valley Forge. In addition, some Hessian light troops went along for
reconnaissance, as Capt. Johann Ewald of the Hessian Jägers noted:

> Since the enemy threatened to cross the Schuylkill . . . to destroy
> the magazine at Valley Forge . . . Lord Cornwallis went at once to
> Valley Forge with the 2d [1st] Battalion of Light Infantry and the
> English grenadiers to cover the magazine. Today Quartermaster
> General Erskine took twenty mounted and twenty foot jägers
> under Captain Lorey to reconnoiter the hilly area on the left [west]
> of the Valley Creek, but found it was not occupied by the enemy.[14]

Captain Montrésor wrote, "At 2 this afternoon Lord Cornwallis's column marched and encamped within 2 miles of French Creek at the Bull's
Head and Mouth [Bull Tavern, Charlestown Township], all upon the
neighboring Height."[15] Officers took up quarters in some of the nearby
houses. One grenadier officer, Capt. John Graves Simcoe of the 40th Regiment, later wrote that "he had been . . . quartered in the house that was
[later] Washington's head quarters, and had made himself minutely master
of the ground about it."[16] This house was Isaac Potts's small mansion near
the mouth of Valley Creek. Most likely other British officers shared the
elegant premises with Simcoe.

It was probably the alarm in the main British camp concerning rebel
forces near Valley Forge and the call to arms of the grenadiers and 1st
Light Infantry Battalion encamped on the heights of Tredyffrin just north

of the Lancaster Road that caused Wayne to pull back from the Paoli. As no British force appears to have actually headed toward Wayne's position during the early afternoon on September 19, the intrepid Pennsylvania general may still have believed that his presence was unknown at the Tredyffrin headquarters. In reality, Sir William Howe was well aware of rebel activity all around his army. Reconnaissance patrols, captured couriers, rebel deserters, and loyalists in the vicinity all were sources of information, as were dispatches signed by George Washington.

CHAPTER 10

The Great Valley and the Schuylkill River, Chester County

Friday Evening, September 19, to Saturday, September 20, 1777

The local Loyalists were persons who believed that George III was their lawful king and that war for independence was treasonous. Loyalists, or Tories, came in all genders, races, and creeds, as did rebels, or Whigs. They viewed this "unnatural rebellion" as the work of New England radicals and their local adherents. Joseph Galloway was their main contact at British headquarters, along with the Allen brothers, William, John, and Andrew. Congressman James Lovell wrote, "Consider that Galloway, the Allens &c are conducting the enemy thro the most torified tracts assisted by Sherrifs of counties who know all the paths accurately."[1] Nathaniel Vernon, sheriff of Chester County (1774–76), continued his law-enforcement service to the king in 1777 by guiding Howe's army through the region with his son, Nathaniel Jr. Ironically, another son, Job, was a lieutenant in the 5th Pennsylvania Regiment—in Wayne's force.[2]

After the war, many Loyalist refugees filed compensation claims with the British government for services and lost property. In these claims are found the names of some Chester Countians who served General Howe in the Philadelphia Campaign:

- Jacob James, of Goshen Township, keeper of the Turk's Head Tavern, ". . . manifesting his loyalty . . . joined the British Army the 12th Sepr. 1777 the day after the battle of Brandy Wine . . . was from this time constantly employed as a guide to the British Army & in procuring . . . intelligence for the Commander in Chief [who] employed him to find guides [and] twice acted as a guide himself . . . was well qualified to offer from his knowledge of the Country. What were the Importance or Officacy of them he submits to Sr. Wm Howe—Earl Cornwallis & Col: Balfour.

- Curtis Lewis, a blacksmith from East Caln Township, property owner in West Bradford, "on the arrival of the British Army at the head of Elk immediately joined them where from his Knowledge of the Country he . . . [acted] as a Guide at the Battle of Brandywine and also through the Country to . . . Philadelphia . . . [he] joined the British at Kennett Square."

- William S. Moore of Moore Hall (grandson of County Judge William Moore) of Charlestown Township, "at great personal risque . . . went out of the Lines with a Party of Dragoons to secure Guides and get intelligence."

- George Peters, "a Miller . . . native of Pennsylvania . . . a Negro Man, came into the King's Army in America on its approach to the Schuylkill River in Sept. 1777 . . . was serviceable in pointing out the Fords in that River—was afterwards employed in different capacities—such as Waggoner, Labourer, &ca. attending the Army."

- Richard Swanwick, landowner in West Caln and Charlestown Townships. "The day after the Battle of Brandywine, Joseph Galloway Esqr. came to [him] in the name of Sir Wm. Howe who requested [his] services in pointing out the Roads and obtaining Intelligence of the force and Situations of the American Army."[3]

These were individuals whose names are part of the record. Others are lost to history, as are the names of many who actively supported independence by risking their lives to deliver intelligence to the Continental Army. Most of the people in the area chose to ignore the war until it arrived in their cornfields and meadows, their barns and houses, and occupied their places of worship.

Behind Howe's army, Wayne's troops encamped 1 mile south of the Warren Tavern on farmland surrounded by woods. The wooded heights of the South Valley Hill provided a screen beyond which Wayne established his camp on the reverse slope. Wayne later stated:

To you . . . who know and are Acquainted with the Nature and Manner in which Encampments are and Ought to be Chosen in

the face of an Enemy—I need say no more than, that the Ground
we lay on was the Strongest and best suited for our Purpose, that
could be found for many Miles . . . the Disposition was Perfect for
Defence.[4]

Colonel Thomas Hartley described the camp layout as follows:

[It was] on some high Ground above the Warren Tavern on the
Lancaster Road. the Right of his Division towards Philada. In Part
of the Front was a small wood and a Corn Field—on the Right a
small wood and some open Fields—there were Roads passing the
Flanks. . . . Genl. Wayne being acquainted with the Country
chose the Ground himself.[5]

On the left of the camp were at least two well-fenced fields all the way
to the Road from the Admiral Warren to Chester (present-day Sugartown
Road). The distance from this road on the left flank back to the upper
Long Ford Road (now Longford Avenue and Channing Avenue) on the
right flank was about 4,400 feet, or 8/10 mile. Behind the camp on the
south side was a thick wood, beyond which was a farm recently owned by
Levi Bowen but now owned by Daniel Cornog. The farms of Ezekiel
Bowen (probably a relative of Levi) and Cromwell Pearce were the chosen
site for the camp. Both farmers were "friends of Independence." Pearce
was a major in the Chester County militia. On the Pearce property, a
house located "a Small Distance in the [left] Rear of the Incampment"
with access to the Sugartown Road served as Wayne's headquarters.[6]
Ezekiel Bowen's log farmhouse stood to the right rear of the camp, on the
slope of a notch in the hills. It is not certain whether any officers used this
house or whether the Bowen family or others were living there. The
notch contained numerous springs, which flowed southward to Crum
Creek, and the bottom of the notch area was marshy and wet. Thus
Wayne's force had plenty of access to water, an important consideration
when choosing a campsite.

Other considerations were made by the Continentals. Anthony Wayne
was a stickler for military order and a strict disciplinarian. He was also a
farmer who knew the difficulties of maintaining a farm under normal
conditions. His men were not permitted to destroy farmland, buildings, or
fences at random, especially the farms of active Patriots like the Pearces.

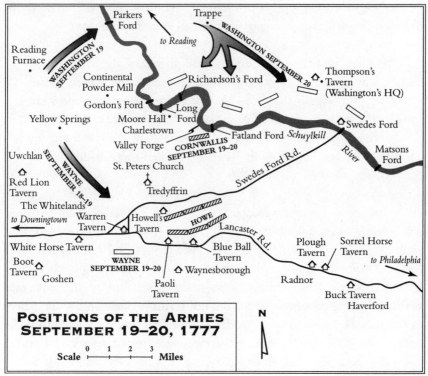

Parkers Ford

Trappe

to Reading

WASHINGTON SEPTEMBER 20

Reading Furnace

WASHINGTON SEPTEMBER 19

Continental Powder Mill

Richardson's Ford

Thompson's Tavern (Washington's HQ)

Gordon's Ford

Long Ford

Yellow Springs

Moore Hall

Charlestown

Swedes Ford

Valley Forge

CORNWALLIS SEPTEMBER 19–20

Fatland Ford *Schuylkill*

Uwchlan

WAYNE SEPTEMBER 18–19

St. Peters Church

Swedes Ford Rd.

River

Matsons Ford

Red Lion Tavern

Tredyffrin

The Whitelands

to Downingtown

Warren Tavern

Howell's Tavern

HOWE

Lancaster Rd.

White Horse Tavern

Blue Ball Tavern

Plough Tavern

Sorrel Horse Tavern

to Philadelphia

Boot Tavern

WAYNE SEPTEMBER 19–20

Waynesborough

Goshen

Paoli Tavern

Radnor

Buck Tavern

Haverford

POSITIONS OF THE ARMIES SEPTEMBER 19–20, 1777

N

Scale 0 1 2 3 Miles

Map by Thomas J. McGuire

Already, in General Orders issued at Wilmington on September 4, Washington had admonished his army about random destruction and plundering of civilians:

> Nothwithstanding all the cautions, the earnest requests, and the positive orders of the Commander in Chief, to prevent *our own army* from plundering *our own friends and fellow citizens,* yet to his astonishment and grief, fresh complaints are made to him. . . . We complain of the cruelty and barbarity of our enemies; but does it equal ours? They sometimes spare the property of their *friends:* But some amongst us, beyond expression barbarous, rob even *them!* Why did we assemble in arms? Was it not, in one capital point, to protect the property of our countrymen? . . . If officers in the least connive at such practices, the licentiousness of some soldiers will soon be without bounds.

On September 10 at "Burmingham," the day before the Battle of Brandywine, Washington again blasted both men and officers:

The General hears the frequent complaints of the farmers, on account of the destruction of their fences &c by which means their fields of grain and grass are exposed to devastation and ruin. He wishes that officers of every rank . . . [would not allow] such practices to prevail in a country, abounding with wood, and by men with hatchets in their hands . . . when there is no kind of necessity for them .[7]

Some damage was unavoidable—a force of 2,200 camping on farmland will trample crops and cause some disruption—but wanton destruction of property, often committed by undisciplined troops, did not happen here. Fences, so time-consuming to split and set, were removed only where necessary. Unlike the British troops, who were permitted to use the fence rails in the region for firewood, Wayne did not let his soldiers remove the fences adjacent to the camp. When, "in the Evening [we] were Ordered to make Fires & take Rest," the surrounding woodlands provided firewood.[8] Besides, this was a temporary camp, for Wayne was waiting here only until Small-wood joined him. Earlier that day, Smallwood had been at James McClellan's Tavern (Parkesburg), about 25 miles west of Wayne's position, and was at that very moment marching toward Downingtown.

The troops were in camp just a few hours when "we received Orders to March to the Rear about two Miles which we did."[9] This was actually a movement out the left flank of camp onto Sugartown Road. According to Wayne's second in command, Col. Richard Humpton, "the Fences were put down for the wagons & ye rear of the Division but the Front march'd in the road."[10] The troops moved onto Sugartown Road and marched northward to a crossroads. There they turned left onto a new road (opened in 1774) that ran along the township lines of Willistown and the Whitelands. This road, now called King Road, was described by Wayne as "a Road leading on the Summit of the Hill towards the White Horse [Tavern],"[11] 4 miles distant. The Continentals moved southwest on this road about 2 miles to the Road to White Horse and Goshen Meeting (present-day Route 352) and halted.

Although he later referred to it, Anthony Wayne never offered any explanation for this sudden movement, nor has any firm explanation for it come to light from his officers. What makes this so curious is that a possible explanation is found in the journal of General Howe's Hessian aide Captain von Münchhausen, who wrote on the 19th:

> In the evening it was reported that General Wayne had been detached by General Washington with 800 men to make the region behind us insecure. Consequently, the 2nd battalion of light infantry and the English riflemen were dispatched to break camp quietly and attempt to surprise these gentlemen. They found General Wayne two and a half miles behind us, and they had almost surrounded him when fate intervened. Two drunken Englishmen fired at a picket, which touched off an alarm, and permitted their escape, though in great confusion. At two o'clock in the morning the light infantry returned, without having attained its objective.[12]

Further proof of this first British attempt to attack Wayne's force came from later evidence of Col. Thomas Hartley and Col. Morgan Connor, who said they had received information the following day that the British would have attacked Wayne's camp the night before, "but he had changed his ground."[13] Col. Daniel Brodhead of the 8th Pennsylvania Regiment noted that "about 7 or 8 o'Clock in the Evening the Genl. desired me to follow the Troops & order them back to the Same Ground, which I did & returned with them, Nothing material happened During the Night."[14] If Wayne or anyone else in the American camp was aware of the approach of the British light infantry that evening, they made no mention of it.

Why, then, did this movement take place? Was it the result of intelligence received? Was it just another false alarm, as the earlier movement away from the Paoli Tavern seems to have been? Was the maneuver simply an evacuation drill in case of attack? If it was, which is highly unlikely, the coincidence of timing—the evacuation of a camp about to be attacked—is truly astonishing. If not, it was the second time that day that Wayne moved his troops to avoid a possible British attack.

Late in the afternoon and into the evening, a small force of British dragoons made an excursion into the countryside south of the Tredyffrin Camp. The Royal Army badly needed horses; many of their mounts had died on the voyage to the Head of Elk, and though earlier foraging had helped make up for the deficiency, the strenuous march on mired roads after the Battle of the Clouds took a serious toll on the animals. Captain Montrésor remarked on September 19, "The halting this day very necessary for the men and particularly for our horses." To remedy the problem, "Lt. Col. Harcourt with a party of dragoons and Light Infantry made an Excursion on the Philadelphia road and brought in 150 horses which were much wanted, got from New Town square 6 miles from hence."[15] This force headed down the Lancaster/Conestoga Road into Radnor Township, where they purchased or seized horses for the army. Some Radnor residents later submitting claims for "Damages Sustained by the Brittish Army under the Command of Coll. Hariot [Harcourt] the 19th day of Sept. 1777" included the following:

> John Jones, "3 Horses taken by the Light Horse, £60"
> Lewis Lewis, "4 Horses valued @ £60"
> Mordecai Morgan, "3 Horses"
> George White, "3 horses Value £50"
> Aquila Evans, "1 Young Mare 3 years old £20"
> Adam Siler, "4 Horses £60, Rec'd of British paymaster £30"
> Paul Sherading, "1 Horse £18, Cash Rec'd £8.15s"
> Fredk. Beetle, "3 horses £42.10, 2 Cotton & 2 hatters pr Chains & Crupper Back & Belly Band £22, Chains & a Great Coat Saddle & Bridle £3.5s"

Harcourt and his troopers continued out as far as Marple Township, where some "Light Horse belived to be Commanded by Col. Harcourt on the 19th day of September 1777 took two Creators [creatures] worth Thirty six pounds" from William Burns. They swung back toward camp through Newtown Square, where Samuel Caley reported that they took "2 Horses to the Value of £50, By Cash Rec'd of the payment £19.31." On the last leg of their sweep, Easttown residents Robert Stephens, Casper White, and Peter Ubles each reported losing a horse; Michael Bingers reported losing three mares.[16] A few other families put in smaller claims; many others chose not to do so.

The war touched the personal lives of the local people in many different ways. On the Newtown Road about a mile west of Radnor Meeting lived an elderly couple, eighty-four-year-old David Cornog and his seventy-eight-year-old wife, Catherine, who that evening lost "1 Mare valued @ £18." Catherine died in 1779 and David a few months later in 1780, before a claim could be made, so their son and executor, Daniel Cornog, submitted the claim. At the time of Harcourt's raid, Daniel lived in Willistown Township, miles away from his parents' house, but not out of the seat of war. Far from it—Daniel had recently purchased the farm of his neighbor Levi Bowen, which was adjacent to Ezekiel Bowen's, the site of Wayne's camp. Several hundred yards north of Cornog's house, Wayne established a picket post to protect the right flank of his camp. The war touched more than home and family. Daniel's church was the Great Valley Baptist Church, now part of the British camp and a target of desecration and plundering. Daniel's pastor, the Reverend David Jones, was just up the road in Wayne's camp serving as chaplain of the 1st Pennsylvania Brigade. Friday, September 19, was a truly unsettling day in the lives of the Cornog family.[17]

The morning of Saturday, September 20, dawned fair, with temperatures in the high 50s. Washington's army had crossed the Schuylkill the previous evening at Parker's Ford, with the river still high from the storm of the 16th and 17th. Pastor Henry Muhlenberg at Trappe noted the condition of the soldiers as thousands of them trudged past his front door: "The American troops then marched through the Schulkiel, four miles from us. . . . They had to wade through the river up to their chests. . . . The passage of the troops lasted through the night. . . . To get wet up to one's chest and then to march in the cold, foggy night . . . is hard for the poor men."[18]

An American officer, Capt. Enoch Anderson of the Delaware Regiment, described his unit's method of crossing the flood-swollen Schuylkill:

The late rains had raised the waters. We entered the river in platoons,—the river was about two hundred yards wide. I now gave orders to link arm in arm,—to keep close and in a compact form, and to go slow,—keeping their ranks. We moved on,—we found the river breast deep,—it was now night as we gained the western shore [left bank] all wet, but in safety.[19]

The Continentals rested for a few hours along the eastern banks of the Perkiomen Creek and resumed their march during the midday hours. By afternoon, Washington's main army, about 7,000 troops, was moving into position along the left bank of the Schuylkill River from Long Ford and Richardson's Ford (present-day Oaks), past the mouth of the Perkiomen Creek (Audubon) across the river from Valley Forge and all the way down to Swedes Ford (Norristown). The American line was nearly 8 miles from flank to flank. With Maxwell's force nearby and Pennsylvania militia units at Swedes Ford, Washington now had over 10,000 soldiers in place to block Howe's advance across the Schuylkill.

Washington's brilliant, if exhausting, strategic maneuver was noted at British headquarters. This new threat to the British Army caused General Howe to send 1,000 more of his best troops, the two battalions of Guards, over to Valley Forge to reinforce the grenadiers and light infantry. Another small skirmish erupted there. Captain Montrésor reported on the 20th:

> Weather extremely fine. At 2 this morning the guards moved off and posted themselves with the Light Infantry at the Valley Forge. Waggons employed in carrying off from the magazine there, the rebel stores. This morning 5 rebel centries fired on the Guards who took the whole. They slightly wounded 1 of our officers.[20]

In his journal, Captain von Münchhausen wrote at length about Washington's movement and its strategic significance. His comments in his entry for September 20 reveal the in-depth knowledge that the British high command possessed of rebel moves and intentions:

> Early in the morning the Guards marched to Valley Forge. Washington, having achieved his aim by his forced marches . . . has now gained our left flank. He has uncontested access to supplies as well as a route of retreat to the lower provinces. He himself is positioned behind the Schuylkill with a strong force in the region where, opposite him, Valley Creek empties into the Schuylkill, his line extending a little beyond Swedes ford. He has sent all his baggage, etc. to Reading.
>
> It is said that he intends to prevent our crossing of the Schuylkill, which is wider and deeper than the Brandywine. In order to achieve this more effectively, he has detached 4,000 men to this side of the Schuylkill, 2,000 of whom are on our left flank [Maxwell] and 2,000 are close behind us, under the command of General Wayne. Both corps have orders to attack us if we march again, and, particularly, if we try to cross the Schuylkill River.[21]

General Howe found himself in a dangerous situation. Washington, whose army had been defeated at Brandywine and had narrowly escaped defeat at the Battle of the Clouds, had once again seized the initiative and was on the offensive—all within the same week. Not only that, but Howe was now outflanked and surrounded by smaller forces. An anonymous American "Gentleman in the Army" commented: "We shall be able to be totally round them. . . . Howe has brought himself into a fine Predicament, A few days will convince the World, unless Providence turns against us."[22] But Providence did turn; the British high command reacted and planned to break out of the "fine Predicament."

CHAPTER 11

Near the Warren and Paoli Taverns on the Lancaster Road

Saturday Evening, September 20, 1777

Little direct information has come to light regarding the details of the planning of Howe's response to Washington's "encirclement," as secrecy was an important facet of the British Army's operations. What is known is pieced together from a number of sources and from the operations themselves. The British intelligence network was excellent; the information gathered was timely and accurate. Howe's aide, Capt. Friedrich von Münchhausen, recorded in his journal some of the intelligence received on September 20:

> In the evening the General received reliable information that General Wayne, who is said to be highly regarded by Washington because of his personal bravery, is only three miles behind us. We are informed that his 2,000 men are not militia but the best troops Washington has in his entire force. We are further informed that Wayne intends to attack our rear guard and our baggage, as soon as we are in march again.[1]

This intelligence was gathered from many sources, including British patrols. Lt. Martin Hunter, an officer in the 2nd Battalion of Light Infantry, described one such patrol: "three Companies of our battalion were sent out under the command of Major [Turner] Straubenzie [17th Regiment] to get all the information they could of the situation of General Wayne's encampment. They returned about four o'clock in the evening."[2] Just what specific information they brought back is not known.

Wayne's camp appears to have been quiet on the morning of the 20th. In the early afternoon, Wayne left camp with his commanding officers, Col. Richard Humpton, Col. Thomas Hartley, and Brig. Maj. Michael Ryan, on a reconnaissance mission, "to examine some Roads and Ground to the Right or rather in the Rear of our then Encampment as a Passage by which he said he belived he should shortly afterwards move the troops—we viewed the Ground with him." Colonel Humpton recalled that the group went "on the road to the right of the Division ('upper' Long Ford Road) & returned the road near Genl. Waine's Quarters (Sugartown Road)."[3]

At the same time, Wayne was awaiting the arrival of Gen. William Smallwood and Col. Mordecai Gist, along with 2,100 Maryland militiamen and three iron cannons. This force had arrived the previous evening at Downingtown, 11 miles to the west. According to Colonel Hartley, "I understood from Genl. Wayne during the Day of the 20th of Sepr. that he certainly expected Genl. Smallwood would join him—almost every Minute. . . . Two Persons had been sent to Genl. Smallwood to show him the Way[;] the last was Col. Chambers" of the 1st Pennsylvania Regiment. Wayne himself confirmed, "I had sent Col. Chambers As a Guide to Genl. Smallwood to Conduct him into my Rear—he was expected to Arrive every hour from 2 in the Afternoon."[4]

The skies began to cloud up late in the day. Col. Daniel Brodhead stated that at 4 P.M., the division received orders to prepare for a march. "Accordingly the Division formed but the weather being Cloudy and threatening Rain we were Ordered to build Booths to secure our Arms & Ammunition & go to Rest."[5] This was the first indication of shelters being constructed in the camp. The men would have cut saplings, tree branches, and cornstalks to build "booths." After the disastrous loss of ammunition in the rain at the Battle of the Clouds only four days earlier, Wayne's precaution to protect the arms and ammunition was certainly appropriate.

Once the orders to build booths were issued and carried out, Colonel Hartley observed, "Genl. Wayne rode out afterwards with some Gentlemen—as I understood towards Genl. Smallwood or to reconnoitre—I remained at our Quarters."[6] It was at this time that Hartley wrote a revealing letter to his friends William Atlee and Paul Zantzinger in Lancaster. This letter, written at 6 P.M. and sent by express rider, was perhaps the last letter written from the camp that night, and it contains some startling information:

The Hour of Decision is not yet come but believe it near at Hand[;] perhaps to Morrow will do something[.] this Division is now in the Post of Danger—I hope we may acquit ourselves with Honour and fidelity to our Country—the Mayn [main] of our army has crossed the Skookyl—*I understand General Howe means to have us attacked to Morrow Mornng—perhaps he may do it—he will find Frost*—thoo he may have Success—*this Manuovere of ours to get in their Rear—has surprized our Enemy's not a little*—& especially as we have had the Impurtence [impertinence] to lie within long Cannon Shot of them—for two Days—General Smallwood will join Us to Night—I fear I shall have no Leasure to write till this Man [rider] goes of[f] as we must make immediate Dispositions. Do send me some Paper & Sealing Wax—D[itt]'o Mr Zantzinger send me the Leather Breeches[;] a Pair which will fit you will do for me—I am naked and ragged. . . .[7]

The implications of this letter are significant and raise some serious questions. It indicates that Hartley, the third in command, possessed information of a possible British attack to be made the next morning. Further, the statement that the presence of Wayne's force "has surprized our Enemy's not a little" strongly points to some knowledge of reaction in the British camp. By writing this letter, Hartley obviously was not keeping this information to himself. The question is whether Wayne was aware of it. The answer is yes, for intelligence gathering was personally directed by Wayne, not Hartley.

The acting commanding officer of Hartley's Additional Continental Regiment, Lt. Col. Morgan Connor later testified: "I Suped in Company with Genl. Wayne, Colo. Hartley & Col. Brodhead, there was also a Mr. Bartholomew of Chester County in Company Who Sayed he believed the Enemy wou'd attack us that night,—the reasons he gave for Such an opinion I do not recollect."[8] Mr. Bartholomew was a thirty-year-old Chester County militia officer, Lt. Col. John Bartholomew of East Whiteland Township, whose home was in the Great Valley just down the hill from Wayne's camp. He was a major in the militia in 1775 and saw severe action in the New York Campaign of 1776 as part of the "Flying Camp." His twenty-three-year-old brother Benjamin was a member of the Provincial Assembly for Chester County, served on the Chester County Committee of Safety chaired by Anthony Wayne in 1775, and was presently a captain in the 5th Pennsylvania Regiment, Wayne's former unit. Ben was wounded in the leg

at Brandywine; whether he was convalescing or back with the regiment in
the Paoli Camp is uncertain.[9] Based on Hartley's letter and Connor's testimony, it would appear that supper occurred between 4 P.M., the time when
the orders to build booths were issued, and 6 P.M., the time Hartley wrote
his letter and after Wayne had left camp the second time to reconnoiter. The
tone of Hartley's letter indicates that he was convinced of the validity of
John Bartholomew's warning. The Bartholomews were both personally well
known to Wayne as active and committed local Patriots with some military
experience, and thus John's warning was certainly credible.

A second warning was brought by another local person known to the
commander. Between 8 and 10 P.M., a Mr. Jones, an "old Gentleman" who
lived near the encampment, came to Wayne's headquarters. Wayne was still
out of the camp, as was his brigade major, Michael Ryan. Col. Thomas
Hartley recalled:

> In the Evening Mr. Bartholamew came up, and spoke of the vicin-
> ity of the Enemy and their Numbers—an Old Man of the Name
> of Jones also visited us. he said he came to see Genl. Wayne to tell

*The Paoli Tavern, circa 1886. Photo by Julius Sachse. The original General Paoli
Tavern is the small stone rear section in the middle of the photo. The main
building, shown here, was constructed in the 1790s. Fire destroyed the tavern in
1892.* AUTHOR'S COLLECTION

him he had been down at the Paoli [Tavern] where he had seen a
servant or some other Person who had been in with the enemy,
where the Soldiers had told him, that they would attack Genl.
Wayne's Party that Night. that they would have done it the Night
before had he not changed his Ground. Mr. Jones was for returning home but I persuaded him to stay till the general came to his
Quarters—Genl. Wayne came to his Quarters a little after Dark
according to my Recollection. When he received the foregoing
Information from Messrs. Bartholamew and Jones—Mr. Bartholamew insinuated that our Situation was a little Dangerous.[10]

Wayne had a decision to make: whether to move his force immediately or risk staying put so that General Smallwood could find him. Smallwood's force was supposed to arrive any minute. Yet indications were
strong of British knowledge of his presence and of a possible imminent
attack. Wayne later partially explained his decision to stay:

I had the fullest and Clearest Advice that the Enemy would March
that Morning at 2 OClock for the River Schuylkill. In Consequence of that Advice I had Reconnoitered a Road leading Immediately along the Right flank of the Enemy and that in Company
with Coll. Humpton and Hartley and had the men laying on their
arms to Move as soon as Gen. Smallwood should arrive.[11]

Another puzzling question is whether Wayne informed his second and
third in command of what was transpiring. Hartley simply stated that they
examined some roads with Wayne "as a Passage by which he said he
belived he should shortly afterwards move the Troops." Humpton's statement is more startling. When later asked by Wayne if he knew why they
had reconnoitered the road, Humpton responded, "[I suppose] it was in
order to change ye Ground of the Division." When Wayne asked, "Do
you know whether General Smallwood with his Brigade was to join me
that day[?]," Humpton replied, "No, he never heard of it, but understood
he was to be at the [White] Horse."[12]

Another question put to Humpton, "Did [you] hear on the evening of
the 20th any information of the enemy's intention to attack[?]," prompted
a response that revealed a perplexing and disturbing issue about the chain
of command: "[I] never did." Further, Humpton testified that it was only

on the morning of September 24, *four days later,* that Lt. Col. Benjamin Temple of Bland's Dragoons "inform'd Me that Genl. Wayne had notice of the Enemies Intention, which I scarcely could believe as I never before then had heard any thing of the Matter."[13]

Somewhere along the line there was a terrible communication gap between Anthony Wayne and Richard Humpton. Col. Thomas Hartley, Col. Daniel Brodhead, and Col. Morgan Connor all were present when John Bartholomew relayed his intelligence. Colonel Hartley, Colonel Brodhead, and Col. Benjamin Temple were present when Mr. Jones spoke to Wayne about his information. For unknown reasons, Humpton was left out. Humpton's plain statement that "the Genl. had received intelligence some hours before the Attack that the Enemy intended it, as Second in Command I think the Genl. ought to have acquainted Me with it,"[14] indicates a breakdown at the top in the chain of command. At such a critical moment, on such an important mission, communication needed to be clear and constant; anything less could result in dire consequences.

CHAPTER 12

On the Lancaster and Swedes Ford Roads

Saturday Night, September 20, 1777

Colonel Humpton was not the only officer to experience communication difficulties that night. An incident regarding the placing of the extra pickets in response to Mr. Jones's warning further points to communication problems in the command structure between Wayne and some of his subordinate officers. This episode involved Brig. Maj. William Nichols of Colonel Hartley's 1st Pennsylvania Brigade. His duty on the evening of September 20 was to inspect the camp pickets and report their status to the commander. Hartley noted, "Pickets ware placed on the several Roads— and I sent Major Nicholl to forward them on to their several Posts—Major Nicholl acted as Brigade Major to me at that Time—& was very industrous and assiduous that Night."[1]

Each picket post was made up of one subaltern officer (lieutenant or ensign), one sergeant, one corporal, and sixteen privates. The job of the pickets was to examine anyone going near the camp and to give fair warning of the enemy's approach. They were also charged with the duty of slowing the enemy down to give the camp as much time as possible to prepare for an attack. The picket posts were numbered and placed on the approaches to the camp at prescribed distances, anywhere from a few hundred yards out to a mile or more away. Soldiers on picket duty were referred to individually and collectively as pickets, sentinels, or sentries. Mounted pickets were called videttes.

Wayne's camp had four established picket posts during the day of September 20; that evening the number was increased to six, which were placed at the following locations:

Picket #1: "one Mile from Camp near the Paoli"
Picket #2: "1/2 a Mile in the Rear of our Right"

Picket #3: "Immediately on the Right of the Artillery"
Picket #4: "3/4 of a Mile to the Right in front on the Lancaster Road
Picket #5: "One Mile from Camp at the Warren"
Picket #6: "at the fork of two Roads on our left"[2]

Brigade Major Nichols made his inspection rounds of the pickets between 7 and 10 P.M. About 9 o'clock, he discovered that Picket 1, composed of men from the 4th Pennsylvania Regiment and assigned to the Lancaster Road just west of the Paoli Tavern, could not be located. He went to the captain of the guard and asked him if he knew where the picket was. The captain said that he did and led Nichols to the crest of the hill above the Paoli Tavern. Here they found only one sentry; the rest of the men were nowhere to be seen. A sergeant and two men were sent down the hill to the Paoli Tavern to see if the pickets were there; they were not. Nichols and the captain of the guard concluded that the rest of the picket post must have been surrounded by the enemy and taken prisoner en masse.

Returning to camp at about 10 P.M., Nichols went to headquarters to inform Wayne that Picket 1 was missing and that he had reason to believe they may have been captured. Both Wayne and Colonel Hartley were lying down to rest, so Nichols informed Brigade Major, Michael Ryan, of his discovery. Ryan notified Wayne, who, surprised by the news, directed Nichols to find Lt. Col. William Butler, commander of the 4th Regiment, to see if perhaps he had moved the picket. Butler had taken up quarters in a "shead," probably a farm building on the Pearce property near the headquarters; Nichols had difficulty finding him. Once located, Butler informed Nichols that he had not moved the picket post.

Brigade Major Nichols returned to Wayne just before 11 P.M., further convinced that foul play was at work. Wayne asked Nichols some questions about the sentries and how far they were to be extended from the picket post.[3] Then, without explanation, Wayne suddenly exploded at Nichols and told him to "Lie Down and take his Rest." Wayne himself later admitted that "when Major Nichols came back with Col. Butler's answer—I did tell him with some Degree of anger to go to bed—for having"—here "told me a falsehood" was crossed out and changed to "made a Mistake."[4] What Wayne did not bother to tell Nichols was "that that Piquet was Not Carried off at all; between the time that B Major Nichols told me that it was Missing and his Return from Col. Butler—a Light

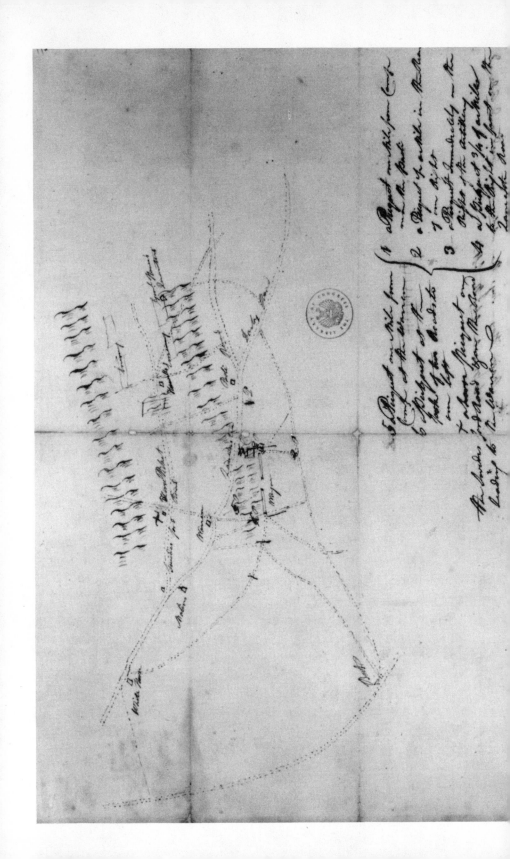

Horse man who I instantly sent to the place where it was posted Returned and told me that he had seen it and all was well."[5]

Much trouble, aggravation, and recrimination would result in the immediate future for General Wayne regarding his mercurial communication habits and his abrupt treatment of Nichols.

In the same late-night hours, Wayne's own brigade major, Michael Ryan, was also busy with pickets and camp security. In response to Mr. Jones's information, Wayne recalled, "I ordered two new Piquets, the One in front on a blind Path leading from the Warren to my Camp [Picket 5]— the Other to the Right and in the Rear [Picket 2],"[6] near Daniel Cornog's house. Major Ryan was sent to carry out the orders

> to have a Piquet placed on a Blind Road which led from the lancaster Road (Near the Warren) to our Encampment. the Guard was to be So posted as to have two Centinels on the edge of the Lancaster road, and to be Mounted by Col. Humpton's Brigade, as Col. Hartley's Brigade had furnish'd an Additional piquet which was sent towards the Paoli.[7]

When Ryan returned, Wayne directed him to reinforce the pickets with twelve light horsemen in the following manner:

> Four were to go with Mr. John Bartholomew "to a Rising Ground Near the Paoli" near Picket 1.
> Two were sent to the newly placed Picket 2 in the right rear of the camp.
> Two were placed with Picket 3 on the immediate right of the camp.
> Two were to remain with Picket 4 on the "Road leading to the Paoli."
> Two were sent to the newly placed Picket 5 near the Warren Tavern.

Wayne also placed a horse picket under Capt. Josiah Stoddard of Sheldon's Regiment on the Long Ford Road at Swedes Ford Road, 1 mile north of the Warren Tavern.[8]

Opposite page: *Manuscript map by Anthony Wayne, October 1777. Wayne drew this map for use at his Court of Inquiry to refute the charge that he was negligent in guarding the camp. It shows the main roads, key landmarks, and the picket positions (1P, 2P, etc.), and includes a descriptive key in the lower right.* LIBRARY OF CONGRESS

While all of these measures were being taken in the American camp, British plans for dealing with their encirclement by rebel forces were put into action. Howe decided to march his army early the next morning toward the Schuylkill River, but not northeasterly toward Swedes Ford as Washington expected. Rather, he planned to move north to Valley Forge and west along the Nutt Road (present-day Route 23) to French Creek. By doing this, he could threaten several targets: the American supply base at Reading, the iron manufactories near Warwick, and the region of Lancaster. Howe could also reverse his march to take Philadelphia and keep Washington guessing as to just where he would cross the Schuylkill.

As for Wayne's force in his rear, Howe decided to launch a surprise night assault to neutralize the threat. Maj. Gen. Charles Grey, headquartered in Howell's Tavern on the Swedes Ford Road at the rear of the British camp, was chosen to lead a select force of British light troops to attack Wayne. Grey's aide, Capt. John André (later famous for his involvement in the Benedict Arnold affair), described the makeup of the force:

> Intelligence having been received of the situation of General Wayne and his design of attacking our Rear, a plan was concerted for surprising him, and the execution entrusted to Major General Grey. The troops for this service were the 40th and 55th Regiments, under Colonel Musgrave, and the 2d Battalion of Light Infantry, the 42nd and 44th Regiments under General Grey. General Grey's Detachment marched at 10 o'clock at night, that under Colonel Musgrave at 11.[9]

The two detachments totaled about 2,000 British troops.[10] Contrary to later legend, *no* Hessian or Loyalist forces were involved in this operation. All of the participating British units had experience as light troops or "special forces." Sir William Howe, himself a light infantry expert, chose the force well. Lt. Col. Thomas Musgrave, commanding the 40th and 55th Regiments, was a light infantry officer formerly with the 64th Regiment of Foot. He was severely wounded in action near East Chester, New York in October 1776.[11] After recovery, he was given field command of the 40th. Musgrave's assignment this night was to march on the Lancaster Road toward the Paoli Tavern to block any rebel movement in that direction; his combined regiments numbered about 500.

Grey's force, the main column, was escorted by twelve light horsemen from Maj. Francis Gwyn's Troop of the Queen's Own Light Dragoons and numbered between 1,200 and 1,500 infantry. For this type of operation, a larger number was unnecessary and might actually jeopardize success. The column was headed by about 500 troops of the 2nd Battalion of Light Infantry, commanded by Maj. John Maitland of the Royal Marines. Following the light infantry was the 44th Regiment, led by Maj. Henry Hope and numbering about 350. Bringing up the rear of the column were two battalions of Scottish Highlanders from the 42nd or Royal Highland Regiment. This unit numbered between 500 and 600 men and was under the command of Lt. Col. Thomas Stirling.

The 2nd Light Infantry Battalion was composed of light companies from thirteen different regiments. These soldiers were well trained in light infantry, or "ranger," tactics. Special missions that required swift movement and stealth were the specialty of light troops. Their uniforms and equipment were modified for the campaign: short red jackets, long canvas trousers or "overalls," light accoutrements, and "round" hats, broad-brimmed felt hats turned up on the left and ornamented with ostrich plumes. These elite soldiers were often posted at the danger points both in camp and in battle: in front of the line of march, on the flanks, and covering the rear of the army.[12]

General Grey ordered the troops to unload their muskets or remove their musket flints so that no British troops would fire; tradition indicates that he was given the nickname "No-flint" Grey for this order. Captain André wrote that "no firelock was to be loaded & express orders were given to rely solely on the Bayonet." He explained, all too accurately:

It was represented to the men that firing discovered us to the Enemy, hid them from us, killed our friends and produced a confusion favorable to the escape of the Rebels and perhaps productive of disgrace to ourselves. On the other hand, by not firing we knew the foe to be wherever fire appeared and a charge [of bayonets] ensured his destruction; that amongst the Enemy those in the rear would direct their fire against whoever fired in front, and they would destroy each other.[13]

Major Maitland, confident of the discipline of his light infantrymen, told General Grey:

The whole of the battalion was always loaded, and that if he would only allow them to remain so, he would be answerable that they did not fire a shot. The General said if he could place that dependence on his battalion they should remain loaded, but that it might be attended with very serious consequences if they began firing. We remained loaded.[14]

The British commanders needed guides who knew the area. Joseph Galloway was the key to providing suitable persons for this task. The names of two persons who served as guides for Grey have thus far come to light. Curtis Lewis, a blacksmith from East Caln Township, was later "attainted of high treason . . . the Cause of his Attainder was his attending a Detachment of the British Army under the Command of General Grey as a Guide to the Encampment of General Wayne."[15] Another guide may have been a deserter from Wayne's force, Pvt. John Farndon of Hartley's Additional Continental Regiment, of whom it "is said he deserted from our Army to the enemy, and piloted some of the bloody Highlanders in the Night to Genl. Waines's Brigade."[16] No specific names have come to light regarding who may have guided Colonel Musgrave.

"Military necessity" added another terror to the darkness of that night for some of the local civilians. As the force moved out, "General Grey's Detachment marched by the road leading to White Horse [Swedes Ford Road], and took every inhabitant with them as they passed along" to prevent any warnings from reaching Wayne.[17] On the Swedes Ford Road about 2 miles west of the British camp stood the Bartholomew family farms. Militia colonel John Bartholomew, who had inherited his father's "old place" south of the Swedes Ford Road, was out of his house that night, guiding the four horsemen sent by Wayne to the hill overlooking the Paoli Tavern near the elusive Picket 1. His brother, Capt. Benjamin Bartholomew of the 5th Pennsylvania Regiment, whose dwelling stood north of the road, was not home either. Ben may have been in the Paoli Camp with his unit or in a hospital recovering from a bayonet wound received at Brandywine. As the British advanced toward Wayne's camp, "It is related that a corporal's guard entered the home of Captain Bartholomew on the Swedesford road and took an aged uncle clad only in his night shirt. He died shortly afterward from the exposure and rough treatment received at their hands."[18]

The night was just beginning.

CHAPTER 13

Near the Admiral Warren Tavern

Saturday Night, September 20, 1777

The main British force left camp about 10 P.M. and stealthily moved westward on the Swedes Ford Road toward the "Moore Hall, or Long Ford Road" (present-day Route 29). Their information placed Wayne's camp somewhere on the wooded heights above the Warren Tavern. In front of this column of 1,200 chosen men was the advance guard made up of English riflemen, probably with the remnants of Ferguson's Corps,[1] a company of light infantry, and twelve troopers of the 16th or Queen's Own Light Dragoons. Under the threat of the death penalty, quiet was ordered.[2] The secrecy and seriousness of this expedition cast a grim mood over the troops.

Ahead at the Long Ford Road, horsemen from Capt. Josiah Stoddard's Troop of Sheldon's Continental Light Dragoons were fanned out on duty as videttes, or mounted pickets. Sometime just before midnight, two of the videttes spotted horsemen on Swedes Ford Road approaching the crossroads. The videttes challenged the horsemen three times and received no response. One vidette then fired his carbine at the figures in the dark; both videttes galloped off at full speed southward on Long Ford Road toward the Warren Tavern and Wayne's camp.

A few hundred yards short of the Warren, one vidette stopped at a fallback position while the other sped on to warn the camp. Reaching the Lancaster Road at the Warren, he turned right and headed west past the tavern, then south up the Road to Chester (Sugartown Road),[3] alerting Picket 5. Continuing up the steep, wooded South Valley Hill, the trooper alerted Picket 6 at "the Crossroads,"[4] then rode on to Wayne's headquarters almost a mile ahead, just east of the Sugartown Road on the rear left flank of the camp.

Horsemen from two troops of Bland's Light Dragoons, commanded
by Lt. Col. Benjamin Temple, were stationed outside Wayne's headquarters. The vidette rode in, quickly dismounted, and entered the headquarters. He notified General Wayne and Col. Thomas Hartley that "he saw a
Body of Horse advancing—that he or another Sentry had challenged
them—that they had refused to answer and were fired at—the Gen[era]l
sent him back for further Inteligence—the Genl. rose up and ordered the
Troops under arms immediately."[5]

Brig. Maj. Michael Ryan related that "Genl. Wayne order'd Me to
Ride Round by the Right and get the Division under arms, at the Same
time order'd Col. Temple to get his Horse[men] Ready."[6]

Back on the Long Ford Road, Lt. Martin Hunter of the 2nd Light
Infantry Battalion noted that "our advanced guard was challenged by two
of the enemy's videttes. They challenged twice, fired, and galloped off at
full speed."[7] The two British maps of the battle note the vicinity of each
place where the American videttes fired. The British column turned left
onto Long Ford Road and headed south toward the Warren Tavern, 3/4
mile away. They were fired upon again by the second American vidette
at his fallback position; this dragoon also took off and disappeared into
the darkness.

When the British reached the Warren Tavern, they were at a loss as to
which way to turn. General Grey's aide, Capt. John André, wrote, "We
knew nearly the spot where the Rebel Corps lay, but nothing of the disposition of their Camp."[8] The guides with the advance troops evidently
were uncertain, too. Later, local tradition erroneously pointed the finger at
Peter Mather, the alleged Loyalist keeper of the Warren Tavern, for guiding the British to Wayne's camp. However, there is no evidence of
Mather's cooperation at all. Mather's daughter, who was eight years old at
the time, recounted years later that "her father was home on that night,
that the British, in their march to surprise Wayne, came to the house and
urged her father to pilot them, but that he positively refused and did not
go, and she added that it was a dreadful night to them."[9] Another local tradition, perhaps from the Bartholomew family, stated:

> Peter Mather, landlord of the Admiral Warren, was pulled from his
> bed and, unclad as he was, forced downstairs and out to a row of
> tall poplar trees in front of the tavern, where there was a crowd of
> civil prisoners coupled together like malefactors and under guard.

The Warren Tavern, circa 1886. Photo by Julius Sachse. After two centuries of operation and the ravages of fire and remodeling, little remains of the original eighteenth century Admiral Warren Tavern (renamed the General Warren Inn after the Revolution). The tavern is still located on the Old Lancaster Road.
AUTHOR'S COLLECTION

Mather was bound to Squire Bartholomew, a man of almost eighty years. Mrs. Mather forced her way to her husband and helped him on with his buckskin breeches.[10]

British accounts mention nothing about Mather one way or the other; they do speak of another unfortunate civilian, the blacksmith at the "Warren Shops" on the Lancaster Road near the tavern. Captain André stated that the British "proceeded to the Admiral Warren, where, having forced intelligence from a Blacksmith, they came in upon the out sentries, piquet and Camp of the Rebels."[11] Lieutenant Hunter corroborated André's statement: "A little farther on the road there was a blacksmith's shop. A party was immediately sent to bring the blacksmith, who informed us that we were close to the camp, and that the picquet [#4] was only a few hundred yards up the road. The blacksmith was ordered to conduct us to the camp."[12] Considering what followed, the blacksmith, whose identity is unknown, actually spared Wayne a total catastrophe.

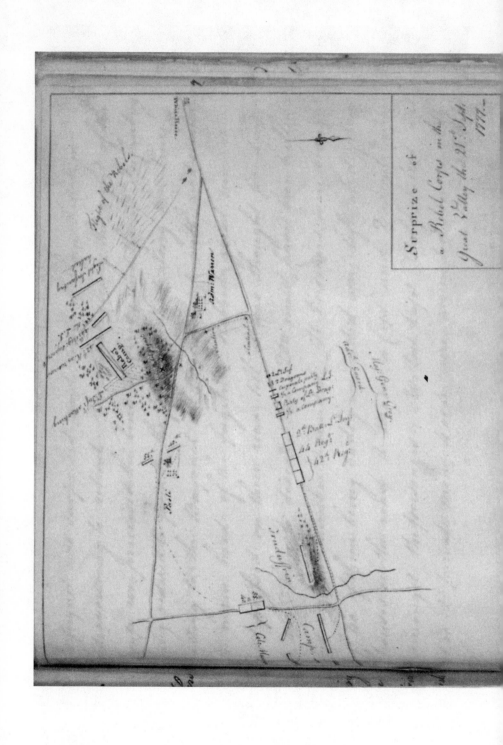

The other British force, the 40th and 55th Regiments under Col. Thomas Musgrave, left the Tredyffrin Camp at 11 P.M., marched up the Road to Jarman's Mill (now Howellville and Cassatt Roads), and moved westward on the Lancaster Road toward the Paoli Tavern. This force was placed so as to block Wayne's escape to the east. Had the blacksmith guided Grey's men up the Road to Chester (Sugartown Road), they would have hit Wayne's troops from the west and probably driven them into Musgrave, thus trapping the Pennsylvanians in a pincer movement.[13] The potential for the annihilation of an entire Continental division was very real and only narrowly averted.

Coerced into cooperation, the blacksmith pointed Grey's force eastward on the Lancaster Road toward the Warren Pass in the South Valley Hill, beyond which lay the upper Long Ford Road. Posted just inside the pass was Picket 4, commanded by twenty-three-year-old Lt. Edward Fitz Randolph of the 4th Pennsylvania Regiment. This picket was composed of the lieutenant, a sergeant, a corporal, and sixteen privates from Capt. John McGowan's Company of the 4th Pennsylvania.[14] Contrary to later insinuations made by their own countrymen, these pickets were alert, as British accounts confirm. In all probability it is likely that they heard the shots fired by the videttes. As the British silently approached, Lieutenant Hunter recalled: "We had not marched a quarter of a mile [from the Warren] when the enemy's picquet challenged, fired a volley, and retreated." According to Hunter's friend Lieutenant St. George:

> We then marched on briskly—still silent—our Company was advanced immediately preceeding a Company of Riflemen Who are always in front—a piquet fired upon us at the distance of fif-

---

Opposite page: *"Surprize of a Rebel Corps in Great Valley,"* manuscript map by Capt. John André. Note that the orientation of the map has N at the bottom. This map clearly delineates the makeup of the advance guard, the location of the two videttes (each marked "a Centinal") who fired, the Admiral Warren Tavern, the "Rebels Piquet" (Picket 4), and the three waves of attack. Close inspection reveals wagons positioned at the rear of the camp and the retreat of American troops and artillery toward White Horse Tavern. Musgrave's force and route of march to the Paoli Tavern are also included. HUNTINGDON LIBRARY

teen yards miraculously without effect—This unfortunate Guard was instantly dispatched by the Riflemen's Swords.

Captain André observed: "The sentries fired and ran off to the number of four at different intervals. The piquet was surprised and most of them killed in endeavouring to retreat."[15] Based on the descriptions given here, the word "surprised" is used in the context of "to come upon suddenly"; the outsentries and the picket were doing their duty, including firing to alert the camp and falling back as the enemy approached.

Lieutenant Randolph and his eighteen pickets valiantly attempted to make a stand, only to be cut to pieces by the British advance guard. The grisly work of bayonets and sabers cost Randolph an eye and nearly his life; the trauma of that night never left him. His granddaughter Julianna Wood recounted:

> He had been on picket duty, and with his comrades was swept away before the overwhelming numbers of the British, who in the darkness of the night came down upon them; he made a narrow escape with his life. Whilst lying on the ground, dangerously wounded, two English soldiers [dragoons] rode by, and looking toward him, one observed to the other, "There is a head that looks as if it had some life in it," and was preparing to shoot when their officer coming up commanded them to desist and save their ammunition—of which they had none too much—for *live rebels,* instead of wasting it on those who were already dead.[16]

Many of the other sentries were killed or severely wounded; plausible local tradition maintains that between four and eight members of this picket were found dead.[17] One private, whose last name is spelled so variously as to indicate illiteracy and possibly a speech impediment, was "so desperately wounded in the head and Shoulder . . . as to Render him Unfit ever doing any duty." Randolph wrote that seventeen-year-old Pvt. George English (or Ingler, Inglirth, or Inglrith) was "on the Lancaster Road, when on a Pickquet Guard under my Command, very badly wounded in the Head, Shoulder, Arm, and Hand. . . . He behaved himself as became a good Soldier."[18]

Back in the main camp, 3/4 mile south of Randolph's pickets and just over the crest of the hill, Wayne's troops were forming up. As Maj. Francis Mentges of the 11th Pennsylvania Regiment recalled:

At about 12 o'clock Genl. Wayne came Riding along in the Rear
of the 2d Brigade Calling out "Turn out my Boys, the Lads are
Comeing, we gave them a push with the Bayonet through the
Smoak." The Troops turned out as quick as Could be Expected
and Formed by Platoons, in less than five Minutes.[19]

Col. Richard Humpton, Wayne's second in command, gave this description:

I was waked by the Noise of a Person calling out, "turn out, turn
out, the Enemy is coming, give them (my brave Lads) Your Fire &
Charge Bayonets" or Words to that purpose—I jumped up &
found it was Genl. Wayne—I asked what was the Matter—He said
the Enemy was very near—I desired Him not to ride along in that
Manner as possibly it might occacion confusion amongst the Men,
to ride back to the Right & that I would get the Men under arms
with all possible speed.[20]

Wayne's aide, Maj. Michael Ryan, rode around the two brigades,
spreading the word to turn out. After reaching the right flank, he rode back
toward the left. There, Capt. Michael Huffnagle of the 8th Pennsylvania
recalled that his commander, "Coll. Brodhead in the meantime came to the
Regiment & said, 'what spunck were we in?' Major Ryan made Answer &
said, 'don't you know that we are surrounded by the Enemy?'"[21]

As the regiments formed a front on the parade, the open area in the
front of the camp, "they faced the great Road [the Lancaster Road]."[22]
Humpton's 2nd Brigade formed on the left, and Hartley's 1st Brigade
formed on the right. The regiments were arranged in the following order
from left to right: 2nd Brigade—Butler's 4th, Brodhead's 8th, Mentges's
11th, and Johnston's 5th; 1st Brigade—Hubley's 10th, Williams's 2nd,
Connor commanding Hartley's Additional Continentals, Grier's 7th, and
Chambers's 1st. To the right of the 1st Brigade was Randall's Independent Artillery Company with four light cannons.[23] About 50 yards to the
right of the formation was a strip of woods, perhaps 20 or 30 yards wide.
On the other side of these woods ran the upper Long Ford Road (present-day Channing Avenue), where Picket 3 under Capt. John Doyle was
stationed. There were fenced open fields on the right of this picket. To
the right rear of the line stood the Bowen farmhouse, beyond which was

a wooded marshy area in the notch between the hills. Both the rear and the front of the camp were covered by thick woods. On the left of the camp were open fields, strongly fenced, all the way to the Sugartown Road and beyond.

Light rain began to fall just as the troops formed. To protect the ammunition, Wayne "in Person Ordered the Whole [force] to take off their Coats and put their Cartridge Boxe's under to save the Cartridges from Damage."[24] Once this was accomplished, Wayne next issued orders for a maneuver to evacuate the camp. Wayne gave the order to "wheel to the right by sub-platoons," a maneuver that would take the infantry from their line facing the front and wheel them into a column of subplatoons, or half companies, facing the right of the camp. The next command, "To the left, face," would have them again facing the front of the camp, only this time in narrow two-man files. From this formation, the regiments could march off either to the right or to the left in a long, thin "column of files." This maneuver sounds complicated, but it was a quick way for troops to move in an orderly fashion through fenced areas, on narrow roads, or on paths through thick woods. Wayne explained the maneuver this way:

> There has been much said and Many Questions Asked about the Disposition made that Night—
>
> . . . when the men were Drawn up on their Proper Parade the Disposition was Perfect for Defence—If to Retreat they had only to Wheel by Sub-Platoons and file of[f] to the Right or Left Occationally [i.e., as the occasion required] whilst some of the Light Troops were formed and Posted to Receive and amuse the Enemy.[25]

They did not have to wait long to find out which direction the British attack would come from or who would be the first to "Receive and amuse the Enemy," as popping gunshots and a volley of musketry issued from Lieutenant Randolph's Picket 4 in front of the right flank, followed by dead silence.

CHAPTER 14

The Paoli Camp

Midnight, September 20–21, 1777

Anthony Wayne, accompanied by Colonel Temple's dragoons, rode across the camp to the right flank, shouting orders to his officers and encouragement to his men. Capt. Michael Huffnagle of the 8th Pennsylvania noted, "General Wayne at this time Road along our Lines and commanded us to turn out & form (said the Enemy were approaching & we should give it to them now) which was immediately Obey'd."[1] As the sound of gunfire from Randolph's picket indicated a British advance on the right flank, Wayne ordered the division to "file off by the left along a Road leading on the Summit of the Hill towards the White Horse—it being the very Road which the Division moved two miles along the Preceeding Evening."[2] This would put the troops onto Sugartown Road north "to the Crossroads on our left" and then onto King Road west toward the White Horse Tavern. At the same time, Wayne ordered Randall's Artillery, which was parked on the right flank near Picket 3, to immediately evacuate by the left. This order was carried out instantly, and the four fieldpieces, together with their ammunition wagons, quickly drove down the rear of the camp toward Sugartown Road. The twenty-five or so commissary and quartermaster wagons, each pulled by four horses and loaded with food supplies, ammunition, or camp equipment, were parked at the rear of the camp. The civilian teamsters hurriedly pulled their wagons into a column and lumbered out behind the artillery.

So far, so good, as the men wheeled by files into a column, the artillery and baggage moved out of camp, and Wayne made further preparations to cover the withdrawal of the Division. The upper Long Ford Road on the right ran from the Lancaster Road (now the Old Lincoln Highway) southward to "the road to the Blue Ball" (present-day Paoli Pike near Warren Avenue). Wayne had placed three pickets on this road: Picket

4, now under attack; Picket 3, immediately on the right of camp, which appears to have been made up of Capt. John Doyle's Independent Company; and Picket 2, "a half mile in the rear of our Right," not far from Daniel Cornog's house. Now Wayne directed the 1st Pennsylvania Regiment, "which always takes the right," to advance into the strip of woods along the Long Ford Road, form a battle line, and slow up the enemy advance.[3]

The 1st Pennsylvania's light infantry company, commanded by Capt. James Wilson, was detached by Wayne and sent out to support the pickets. The light company was placed 300 yards in advance of Picket 3 (vicinity of today's Longford Avenue & West Broad Street). Wilson later recalled, "Genl. Wayne Personally placed me with the Light Infantry, his Orders to me Was, 'Stand like a Brave Soldier and Give them fire,' his Orders I Obeyd as Long as Possible, but the Enimy being too Numerous forsd me to Give Way." When later asked, "How long was ye placed to oppose the Enemy before they came to you at Firing distance?" Wilson responded, "About 8 minutes, & then not above a rod [5$\frac{1}{2}$ yards] distance."[4]

The British advance guard had made quick work of Randolph's pickets. Now they faced a steep, wooded hill where the upper Long Ford Road departed from the Lancaster Road. The surviving pickets occasionally fired as they withdrew up toward Wilson's Light Infantry, posted near the summit. Lieutenant Hunter related: "General Grey then came to the head of the battalion and cried out, 'Dash, Light Infantry!' Without saying a word the whole battalion dashed into the wood . . . guided by the straggling fire of the picket that we followed close up." Lieutenant St. George recalled, "We rushd on thro a thick wood and receivd a smart fire from another unfortunate Picquet—as the first instantly massacred."[5]

Wilson's Light Infantry was surprised and overwhelmed by the attack, as had been Randolph's picket. The British advance was still silent, resolutely moving forward and suffering few if any casualties, all the while driving the rebels before them in confusion. Ahead of Grey's force, the thirty riflemen of Doyle's Company at Picket Post 3 were on the road and in the fenced field that opened up on the British left. Waiting in the woods on the British right were the 200 Continentals of the 1st Pennsylvania Regiment and Gen. Anthony Wayne himself.

As with Randolph's and Wilson's men, the British were nearly on top of Picket 3 before Doyle's men could see anything to fire at. By that time, the British with their bayonets had the advantage in the dark. The experience of Lt. Samuel Brady of Doyle's Independent Company was not one of his more glorious moments:

> Brady was on guard, and laid down with his blanket buckled around him. The British were nearly on them before the sentinel fired. Brady ran, and as he jumped a fence a soldier struck at him with a musket and pinned his blanket to a rail. He tore the blanket and dashed on. A horseman overtook him and ordered him to stop. He wheeled and shot the horseman dead, and got into a small swamp, supposing no one in it but himself."[6]

Wayne wrote to Washington the next morning, "By this Time the Enemy and we were not more than Ten Yards Distant—a well directed fire *mutually* took Place, followed by charge of Bayonet—Numbers fell on each side."[7] Yet the British at this stage still remained silent and had not fired a shot. Most likely what Wayne saw was what Captain André had predicted: a tragic exchange of "friendly fire" in the dark between Picket 3, along with the remnants of Randolph's picket and Wilson's Light Infantry firing at the British advance, and the 1st Pennsylvania firing at the gunflashes of their own comrades "ten yards distant." Col. Thomas Hartley wrote the following day, "Many were killed on both Sides—some times by Enemys and some Times by Friends."[8] The element of confusion was already at work in favor of the British.

Looking back into the camp, Anthony Wayne saw that, as ordered, the division had wheeled by subplatoons and had begun filing off to the left in a column, but for some unknown reason it had stopped and was standing still, about 70 yards away. The time to effect an orderly withdrawal, bought with the lives of the pickets, was growing ever shorter. The American general again sent orders to Col. Richard Humpton, commander of the 2nd Brigade at the head of the column, to move out.

The American picket positions were effectively eliminated by the British advance guard and their own "friendly fire." Now the 2nd Battalion of British light infantry, following the advance guard in a column of files, moved on the double up the upper Long Ford Road in time to see the 1st Pennsylvania Regiment expose its position in the woods by firing a volley. The glimmer of campfires flickered through the woods behind the Continentals, who were now frantically attempting to reload in the dark.

In 1777, a good soldier in broad daylight might load and fire his smoothbore musket three times in a minute; a rifleman might take one to one and a half minutes to load and fire once, as the tight-fitting rifle ball had to be firmly but carefully forced down the rifled barrel with the help of a greased patch of cloth and a wooden ramrod. On a dark, rainy night, with the enemy advancing only a few yards away, reloading time was considerably slower. Lt. Col. Morgan Connor of Hartley's Additional Regiment observed that "the regt. upon the right [was] chiefly riflemen," and Hartley stated, "[Wayne] sent for the first Regement to support the Infantry— Many of these being riflemen." By Wayne's own evidence one officer's opinion was "that forming the 1st Regt. to the Right was Proper—but they were improperly Armed. . . . I shall only Observe that in that Regt. there was Upwards of 200 men[;] 60 of them had Bayonets."[9] The Pennsylvania rifle of that day had two disadvantages: It was slow to load, and it was not designed to hold a bayonet. Darkness all but eliminated the advantage of long-range accuracy. Against bayonets at close range, riflemen rarely had a chance, day or night.

In battle, a trained musketman should automatically remember the sequence for priming and loading: "Handle your cartridge!" (Bring your right hand with a short round to your pouch, slapping it hard. Bring the cartridge with a quick motion to your mouth; bite the top well off.) "Prime." (Shake the powder into the pan—if you can feel the priming pan, if you can get the priming into the pan, if your pan isn't wet with rain . . .) "Shut your pan." (Shut the pan briskly, turn the piece nimbly around to the loading position, keeping both feet in place.) "Charge with cartridge." (Turn up your hand and put the cartridge into the muzzle, shaking the powder into the barrel.) "Draw your rammer."[10]

Again Wayne looked behind him and saw that the column was still not moving. This time he rode over to see what the problem was. Col. Thomas Hartley, commanding the 1st Brigade, which was the rear half of the column, also had no idea why the front was not moving. "The Left Brigade was some Time before they moved. . . . Genl. Wayne a short Space after the orders for moving was communicated to me—passed my brigade towards the Left—desiring us to retreat by the Left and saying the Rear was covered."[11] Orders were sent a third time to Humpton to get the column moving. Wayne rode westward into the dark, seeking the cause of the delay and "all the light horse upon the parade followed the General."[12]

The British light infantry column halted, faced right, and charged bayonets. They let out a throaty *"Huzza!,"* "such a cheer as made the woods echo," and rushed forward into the woods.[13] Caught in the midst of reloading, and faced with this steel-tipped onslaught crashing toward them through the dark underbrush but a few feet away, the 1st Pennsylvania fell back out of the woods pell-mell and ran into the camp, with the British light infantry in hot pursuit. Ahead of them, at the rear of the column and facing the opposite direction, stood the 7th Pennsylvania Regiment, with campfires burning both in front and to the rear of the line, silhouetting and illuminating them in the night. Maj. Samuel Hay of the 7th recalled that due to the light rain, "when on the Parade I ordered them to Secure their arms," which meant that the men were carrying their muskets upside down with the gunlocks secure under their left arms and the barrels pointing downward to prevent rain from wetting the gunpowder. Hay then described what happened:

I wheeled up the Men According to Orders—they were not wheeled up but a few Minutes till there was a sharp fire on our Right, Distant about 70 yards in a stripe of woods. our Backs was then to the firing and I Supposed the left of the line was Marching though the Right could not move. I Ordered the 2 Rear Plattoons of the 7th to face to the Right about [turn completely around] where I saw a number of Men Running up to us which I Supposed to be the 1st Penna. Regt. that was Posted in the Stripe of woods above Mentioned.

they Came up upon our Right and left and by the light of our fires which was both in front and Rear of the line I Discovered the Enemy by their Clothes Close after the infantry. I then Ordered the Plattoons that was faced to fire which they did and Continued to do so for some time which kept the Enemy back untill the Other Plattoons was Moving on Smartly; but the Enemy got up Round us and wounded An officer and some of the Privates on the Parade before we Stired.[14]

While leading the 52nd Light Company into the camp, Lt. Richard St. George witnessed the maneuver described by Hay: "We then saw their wigwams or Huts partly by almost extinguished light of their fires & partly by the glimmer of a few stars and the frightend Wretches endeavouring to form—We then charged." Lt. Martin Hunter recalled, "The enemy were completely surprised, some with arms, some without, running in all directions in the greatest confusion." Here occurred the first recorded British casualties, including Hunter himself: "Captain [William] Wolfe was killed, and I received a shot in my right hand soon after we entered the camp. I saw the fellow present at me, and was running up to him when he fired. He was immediately put to death."[15]

The 7th Pennsylvania took the brunt of the light infantry charge and suffered serious losses. The regimental payroll for September 1777 listed 34 officers, 50 sergeants and corporals, 7 drummers, 5 fifers, and 229 privates, a total personnel count of 325, making this the largest American regiment present—on paper. Of that number, compiled records document 56 killed, wounded, captured, or missing. Major Hay wrote, "Our loss is Coll. Grier, Capt. Wilson & Lieut. Irvine Wounded but non of them Dangerous[ly], and 61 Non-Com[missioned] Officers and Privates Killed wounded and Missing—*which was Just the half of what we then had on the Ground fit for Duty.*"[16] Hay's last remark suggests that much of the regiment was ill or on other duties.

The first wave of the attack, about 500 British light infantrymen, had entered the camp, struck the rear of the stalled column, and surrounded it like a horseshoe. Behind the light infantry, a dozen of the Queen's Own Light Dragoons and 350 regulars of the 44th Regiment of Foot formed into battle line on the Long Ford Road, among the bodies of the fallen Continental pickets, and prepared to launch the second wave.

CHAPTER 15

The Paoli Battlefield

Early Sunday Morning, September 21, 1777

Those soldiers who were able to keep cool heads and stay in platoon formation generally had a better chance than those who broke and ran. The nature of the attack was such that any disciplined, veteran troops might break and run under the same circumstances. The psychological impact of this tactic was calculated to take advantage of darkness and surprise so as to instill panic, confusion, and flight in the defenders. One result of the chaos was the perception that huge numbers of attackers were coming out of the dark. The next day Colonel Hartley wrote about these aspects of the attack:

> Fortune has not been sublime to our Division—The Enemy last Night at twelve oClock, attacked our little Force with about 4000 Men—Horse and Foot—accompanied with all the Noise and Yells of Hell—Our Division was drawn up, but retreating. . . . the Impetuosity of the Enemy was so great—our Men just raised from Sleep, moved disorderly—Confusion followed. . . . The Carnage was very great . . . this is a bloody Month.[1]

The 2nd Brigade, at the front of the column, was still not moving when the British light infantry hit the rear of the 1st Brigade. Wayne had ridden ahead to locate Colonel Humpton, commander of the 2nd Brigade, to find out what the problem was and why his orders were not being carried out.

Some of the British light troops surrounded the 7th Pennsylvania, while others went in pursuit of the 1st Pennsylvania and those from the column who broke ranks and ran in panic. Hartley's Additional Continental Regiment, the unit ahead of the 7th, was also attacked. Some Continentals loaded and fired by platoons, while hand-to-hand fighting erupted in spots.

The British had the advantages of surprise, momentum, and skill, in addition to all being equipped with bayonets. Hartley described the scene:

> The Seventh Regemint having no Front towards the Enemy as well as my own Regiment—were attacked in their flank and Rear & tho' there were attempts made to form them with another Front[,] yet the Enemy were so amongst them that it was impracticable—nor could they retreat regularly, as the left wing had been so long a Moving. Confusion followed—Several men fell on both sides—the Troops in the Rear pressed on those in Front & the Passage on the Left being narrow sacrificed Many of the Troops.[2]

The "Passage on the Left" refers to openings in the fence on the Bowen-Pearce property line at the left side of camp, through which the column was moving out. By piecing together the various accounts, it becomes clear that there were three separate fields and three fences specifically involved in the main battle. The circumstances indicate that these fences were stout, well made, and not easily pulled down.[3] Some pushing and shoving occurred as those in the rear of the column tried to get through the fence openings, only to be blocked by those in the middle who were not able to move ahead because the front was for some reason still standing firm.

A sudden thunderous roar, with loud shouts and a trumpet blast, announced the second wave of attackers. With sabers drawn, the dozen troopers of the Queen's Own Light Dragoons swept across the camp and swarmed around the rear of the shaken 1st Brigade, instilling even more panic. Lieutenant St. George of the British light infantry described "a dreadful scene of Havock—The Light Dragoons came on sword in Hand[.] The Shreiks Groans Shouting, imprecations deprecations The Clashing of Swords and bayonets &c &c &c . . . was more expressive of Horror than all the Thunder of the artillery &c on the Day of action."[4] Three-foot-long saber blades flashed in the firelight, cutting men down and cutting them up. Drum Major Daniel St. Clair of Hartley's Regiment suffered a number of grievous wounds, the nature of which suggest that he was cut up at close quarters by someone on horseback. St. Clair received multiple slashes on his body and head, and lost his left eye and all the fingers on his left hand. The loss of his eye and fingers further suggests that he put up his left arm in a vain attempt to ward off a sword blow to the head.[5]

Previous page: The Paoli Massacre by Xavier Della Gatta, 1782. The 16th Dragoons are in the left foreground, while Continental Dragoons fire pistols over their shoulders as they retreat. In the center, British Lt. Martin Hunter wraps his wounded right hand and Capt. William Wolfe lies dead. Behind the British light infantrymen are five green-uniformed soldiers, possibly British riflemen from Ferguson's Corps. On the right, British troops bayonet Americans in and around the wigwams. The background shows companies of retreating Americans (some firing muskets over their shoulders) with squads of British in pursuit, a wagon being captured and the teamster bayonetted, a fence line, and a volley of gunfire from the 4th Pennsylvania Regiment in the woods covering the retreat. THE VALLEY FORGE HISTORICAL SOCIETY

Left: Private, 2nd Pennsylvania Regiment, by Don Troiani. Although in 1777 standard uniforms and clothing were a rarity in the Continental Army, many of Wayne's soldiers were dressed in a similar fashion to this "Black Irishman" of the 2nd Pennsylvania Regiment. DON TROIANI, WWW.HISTORICALARTPRINTS.COM

Above right: Private, 3rd Continental Light Dragoons, by Don Troiani. Dragoons were important for camp security and communication, as well as for combat. Troopers from the 1st and 2nd Continental Light Dragoons were present at Paoli and wore similar accoutrements. DON TROIANI, WWW.HISTORICALARTPRINTS.COM

Grenadier private, 42nd or Royal Highland Regiment (The Black Watch), by Don Troiani. By 1777, Scottish Highlanders on campaign wore "trews" (trousers) or overalls rather than kilts. Noted for their ferocity in battle, nearly 600 bayonet-wielding Royal Highlanders swept across Wayne's camp without breaking ranks in the third wave of the British attack.

Don Troiani, www.historicalartprints.com

Dismounted Trooper, 16th or Queen's Own Light Dragoon, by Don Troiani. Twelve of the Queen's Own Light Dragoons swept across the Paoli Battlefield with drawn sabers, adding to the terror of the night assault. One American officer wrote, "Our men were much intimidated with the noise of the Enemy's horse." Don Troiani,

www.historicalartprints.com

Anthony Wayne, by Sharples. General Wayne of Chester County was the American commander at Paoli. INDEPENDENCE NATIONAL HISTORICAL PARK

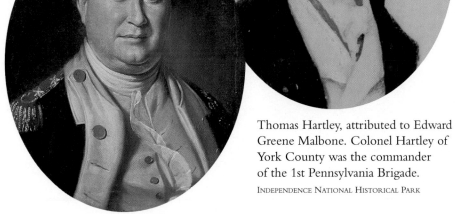

Thomas Hartley, attributed to Edward Greene Malbone. Colonel Hartley of York County was the commander of the 1st Pennsylvania Brigade. INDEPENDENCE NATIONAL HISTORICAL PARK

William Smallwood, by Charles Willson Peale. General Smallwood was the commander of Maryland militia at Paoli. INDEPENDENCE NATIONAL HISTORICAL PARK

Left: Charles Grey. General Grey commanded the British attack at Paoli. Tradition says he was nicknamed "No-flint Grey" because he ordered his troops to remove their musket flints before the attack. AUTHOR'S COLLECTION

Below: Mordecai Gist, by Charles Willson Peale. Colonel Gist commanded a small force of Maryland infantry and artillery at Paoli. MARYLAND HISTORICAL SOCIETY, BALTIMORE, MARYLAND

Above: Thomas Musgrave, by Abbott, circa 1785. Lieutenant Colonel Musgrave's force took position near the Paoli Tavern but did not engage the Americans. A squad of his troops searched Wayne's home, Waynesborough, but "did not disturb the least article." At Germantown, Musgrave successfully defended Chew's House. COLLECTION OF DON TROIANI

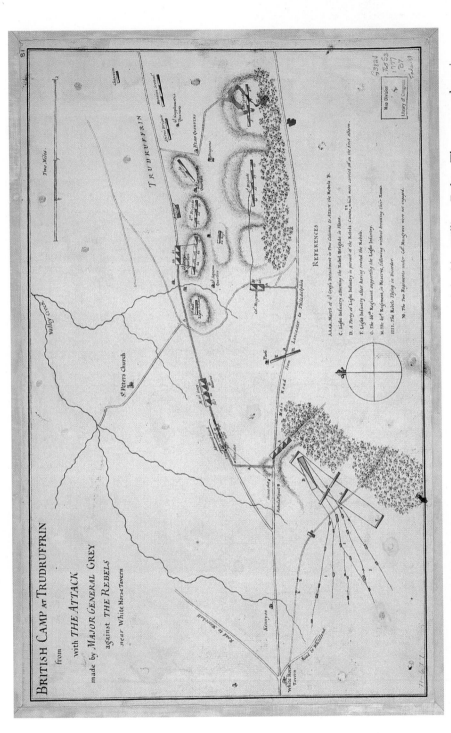

British Camp at Trudruffrin. This original manuscript map was engraved and published by William Faden. The engraved version includes the dates and the notation "drawn by an officer on the spot." The officer who drew the map has not been identified.

"A View of Cheeves [Chew's] House, near Philadelphia, under seige by Washington's army, 3rd [4th] October 1777, and defended by the 40th Regiment under the command of Lt. General Musgrove [Lt. Col. Thomas Musgrave]." This circa 1785 watercolor was used on the medal awarded to the 40th Regiment for bravery and contains a rare contemporary depiction of two British soldiers in campaign uniform (left foreground). One, possibly a dismounted dragoon, wears a peculiar cap or helmet; the other is uniformed in a short jacket and round hat. PRIVATE COLLECTION, UNITED KINGDOM

Paoli Monument. This postcard image, circa 1910, provides a view of the gravesite from the northwest, showing the rail fence of the Bowen-Pearce property line on the left running behind the grave. The tall granite monument and iron fence were erected in 1877 to replace the original stone wall built in 1817. The original marble monument (visible to the right of the granite obelisk) was moved to the south end of the grave. A replica stone wall has since been erected; the granite obelisk has been moved nearby; and the original monument, now encased in plexiglas and nearly illegible, has been returned to the center of the mound and surrounded with shrubbery. The two large cannons in front were made at Warwick Furnace in 1777. AUTHOR'S COLLECTION

British and American soldiers, most of whom probably died in the Paoli Battle, lie buried side by side in the churchyard of the Anglican (Episcopalian) Church of St. Peter-in-the-Valley. AUTHOR'S COLLECTION

Immediately behind the British dragoons came the 44th Regiment of Foot. Another loud "*Huzza!*" rang out, another wall of over 300 bayonets poured out of the woods, another wave of panic swept the stalled column. This attack headed more toward the camp itself, as the rear of the column, already surrounded by the light infantry, further disintegrated or sporadically moved ahead. Royal Engineer Captain Montrésor wrote, "They rushed in and put the whole of the picket to the Bayonet and then huzza'd which further alarmed the main body, however our troops rapidly advanced on their left, which were chiefly in their wigwams."[6] The 44th and the Queen's Own Dragoons moved through the camp to the left of the column and toward the fence on the Bowen-Pearce property line, all the while seizing opportunities to strike at the column and at stragglers fleeing through the camp or into the woods behind it. The chaos of the moment is revealed in Colonel Hartley's description of this phase of the battle:

> After we had gone 200 or 300 yds several Attempts were made to rally the Men—but the Enemy pressing so close upon the left of the Retreat, which was chiefly my Brigade & so many Interuption of Fences that it was impossible to rally Any Men 'till we had got to some Distance from the Enemy—The Men were extremely intimedated with the Noise of the Enemys Horse[.] at the Fences considerable opposition was made by some of the best Men—but many of them suffered.[7]

The 1st Brigade finally pushed through the narrow passage on the left. Some companies formed a battle line along the back side of the fence to cover the withdrawal, while others hurried on in the dark past the 2nd Brigade, which was even yet standing still. Maintaining organization was extremely difficult due to the darkness and confusion, but many officers valiantly exerted themselves in trying to rally and reorganize their troops. In the midst of this fighting, Lt. John Irwin of the 2nd Pennsylvania fell, seriously wounded. At the first alarm, he had stuffed his company orderly book into his waistcoat. Now, his "life was saved by means of this book. It was in his bosom, and received many bayonet thrusts. He was left for dead on the field."[8]

Why was the 2nd Brigade not moving? Wayne later testified that "owing to some Neglect or Misapprehension (which is not uncommon) in Coll Humpton—the Troops did not move until a Second and third Order were sent altho' they were wheeled and faced for the purpose."[9] Until recently, this statement was the only firsthand reference to the halt in print, and it is a recrimination rather than an explanation of what happened. Humpton's description of the situation, heretofore unknown, has come to light from his testimony:

> The Brig[a]de was form'd in as short a time as possible—at least I saw no delay, they remain'd form'd a few Minutes waiting for orders—the Artillery & waggons was driving very fast along our left flank [the back of the camp], being at that time form'd in platoons to the Left, as the Artillery & Waggons greatly incommoded Us either for Action or a retreat I rode to the Left of the Brig[ade] to see if the Fences were down and found a great stopage near the Left of the fourth Regt— . . . Our Artillery & Store Waggons had very little Notice—no Fences laid down or the least preparation made for a sudden retreat.

When later asked by Wayne, "Do you Remember whether the Division moved one mile & a half to the left the evening of the 19th, and whether the Fences were down in that Direction," Humpton admitted that he did, "the evening before the attack, & that the Fences were put down for the wagons & ye rear of the Division but the Front march'd in the road."[10] In other words, the infantry column started moving out by the left front of the camp when the artillery, parked on the right, was ordered to evacuate. The four cannons, followed by the wagons, immediately took off toward the left along the treeline at the back of the camp and through some openings in the Bowen-Pearce fenceline at the left rear.[11] Outpacing the infantry, they drove through other fences (the openings made the previous night) and onto Sugartown Road, where they flew up the road just as the head of the infantry column arrived at the same place. The column halted to let them pass.

Just across Sugartown Road, Col. Adam Hubley "fell in with one of our field pieces (the carriage of which had lost the hind wheels)."[12] In the haste of retreat, the jarring and bouncing of the speeding cannon knocked the wheels off the carriage. The artillery piece broke down in the middle of the road and caused the wagons to jam up behind it, effectively blocking the infantry's escape route for several minutes. By the time Hubley reached this cannon, it had been dragged off the road into a field west of

Sugartown Road; the damage was serious enough to prevent reassembly. Wayne wrote to Washington that "one of the Pecies met with Misfortune near the field of Action which Impeded us a Considerable time," a statement that directly contradicts his later sworn testimony that Humpton's neglect was the cause of the halt.[13]

Lt. Col. William Butler's 4th Pennsylvania Regiment was at the head of the column. From their perspective facing Sugartown Road, the soldiers of the 4th had a thick and very dark strip of woods on their right (no campfires in this area), a fence-lined road in front blocked by a stalled train of cannons and ammunition wagons, with commissary and quartermaster wagons on their left all the way back into camp. The column was trapped, momentarily preventing further orderly movement. One can well imagine the scene that night: shouting officers, swearing artillerymen, skittish horses, and frantic civilian teamsters.

Aides rode up repeatedly, barking orders to move out. Desperate attempts were made to lift, drag, or rehitch the gun, as others worked to pull apart the stout fences on the west side of the road. All the while, minutes ticked as the infantry stood awaiting orders, the shots in the distance coming ever closer. Then, with a blood-chilling roar, the cold steel of a British bayonet charge slammed into the rear of the column, and all hell broke loose.

CHAPTER 16

The Battle of Paoli

Early Sunday Morning, September 21, 1777

B ack in the camp, British troops swarmed through the rows of campfires
and booths, chasing down retreating Continentals and putting them to
the bayonet. A few of the king's men were killed or wounded by gunfire,
but the darkness, rain, and confusion made musketry largely ineffective,
though at times it served to keep some of the attackers at bay. The 10th
Pennsylvania appears to have been the lead regiment of the 1st Brigade and
was near the first fence at the Bowen-Pearce property line when the light
infantry entered the camp. Lt. Col. Adam Hubley, commander of the 10th,
wrote the next day:

> The Enemy in the Course of about Ten Minutes, were amongst
> us, and we were oblij'd to push Bayonets with them, which lasted
> some Considerable time, a number of men fell on both sides. . . .
> We had about 25 Men kill'd, and the Enemy Considerably more
> [sic], as we would give them a volly now and then.—you must
> needs think we were closely imploy'd when we had near 100 Men
> wounded and all with the bayonet or sword. their wounded &c.
> must be very Consid[erable].[1]

The British light infantry, the dragoons, and the 44th Regiment were
fully engaged, chasing their quarry through the camp, into the woods
behind the camp and the fields on the camp's left, battling it out with rebel
platoons, steering clear of volley fire as best as they could. British troops
returning from pursuit in the woods could see the Continentals at the
fence and outflanked them by moving around to the left or right through
the woods. Hubley later testified:

The Enemy were upon us, in our rear, and with their charg'd Bayonets,[.] we push'd forward and got into a field adjoining the One in which we were Attacked,[;] we endeavoured to form Our Men, but found it impracticable, the Enemy being then almost mix'd with us, at the same time calling out, No quarters &c which in my humble Oppinion caused our Men to make a disparate and indeed obstinate stand,[.] a most severe Bayoneting was the Consequence, and after some time our people retired in the third field, and the Enemy, in the field, in which we were first Attacked.[2]

Earlier, some British light troops had gone past the fence in pursuit of stragglers before resistance could be organized there. Now they could double back and hit the rebels at the fence line from the flanks and rear. They could also attack the stalled baggage wagons.

As the battle progressed, organized resistance in the camp soon ceased. The troops at the property line fence fell back in the face of more attackers. Groups of American stragglers took cover in the woods; some hid in the booths, while others, like Lt. Samuel Brady from Doyle's pickets, "got into a small swamp [probably the marshy area in the notch near the Bowen farmhouse], supposing no one in it but himself. In the morning he found fifty-five men in it."[3]

Meanwhile on the upper Long Ford Road, at what had been the right flank of the camp, yet another force—the largest and most terrifying menace of the night—lurked in the shadows and prepared to descend like "a horde o' banshees."[4] Two battalions of the 42nd or Royal Highland Regiment, also known as the Black Watch, formed a double-ranked battle line of 500 to 600 men. Their uniforms were distinctly Scottish but modified for the campaign: canvas or linen "trews" (trousers) replaced the regulation Black Watch plaid kilts (properly called "belted plaids of government sett") and covered the red and white argyle stockings (properly called "diced hose"). They retained their short, red jackets with blue facings, black leather equipment, and "Kilmarnock bonnets," or Highland caps.[5] They were armed with muskets, bayonets, and a reputation for ferocity in battle. The Scots "charged bayonets," let out a screeching Highland war yell, and advanced, keeping their ranks and formation.[6] This was now the third wave of British troops sweeping through the camp, and it was to be a thorough sweep-up. Moving across the battlefield in a solid front, the Royal Highlanders "rushed in upon their Encampment, directed by the light of their fires, killed and wounded not less than 300 in their Huts and about the fires, the 42d. sat fire to them, as many of the Enemy would not come out, chusing rather to suffer in the Flames than to be killed by the Bayonet."[7]

Lt. Martin Hunter of the British light infantry wrote: "The camp was immediately set on fire; the Light Infantry bayoneted every man they came up with; this, with the cries of the wounded, formed altogether the most dreadful scene I ever beheld. Every man that fired was immediately put to death."[8]

On the far left, beyond the flames of the camp, in the midst of the darkness and mayhem, Anthony Wayne was organizing a rear guard to try to cover the retreat. As officers and men struggled to move the disabled cannon off the road, Wayne ordered the 4th Pennsylvania Regiment, the first unit in the column facing the road, to go into the woods on their right and form a battle line. This movement enabled the rest of the 2nd Brigade in the column to move ahead perhaps 100 yards. Colonel Humpton testified:

> Near the Left of the fourth Regt—there I saw Genl. Wayne near the Artillery giving some orders to them, & the fourth regt I believe. He desired Me to go back towards the Right[;] when I got near the Centre [I] found the Right in confusion & retreating with the Left Standing fast, which I have since understood Genl. Wayne orderd'd. by the left standing fast our retreat was greatly delay'd and the greatest part of the Troops put into the utmost Confusion.[9]

The chief aide on Wayne's staff, Brig. Maj. Michael Ryan, was responsible for carrying Wayne's orders to the proper officers. At this juncture, Ryan "assisted the Genl. and several other Officers in attempting to Rally the men in a little Wood. Col. Butler's [4th] Regt. was Rally'd; his light Infantry under the Command of Capt. Fishburn [Benjamin Fishbourne] I assisted in placing."[10] The 4th helped cover the withdrawal of the rest of the column by firing volleys at British troops from the woods. As the king's men closed in, Maj. Marien Lamar of the 4th Pennsylvania shouted, "Halt, boys, and give these assassins one fire!" Capt. Benjamin Burd of the 4th, who commanded "the left Platoon of General Wayne's Division," which headed the column, saw "Lamar . . . bayonetted on horseback a few yards from him."[11] The stricken major fell from his horse, mortally wounded, the

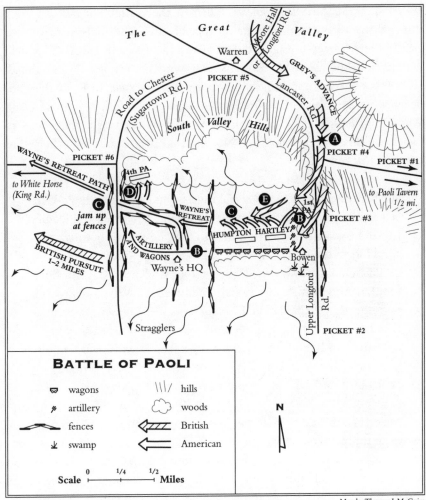

Map by Thomas J. McGuire

Ⓐ *Picket 4 is attacked near midnight by British advance guard.*
Ⓑ *Wayne orders 1st Pennsylvania to cover the right and artillery to evacuate by the left, followed by wagons.*
Ⓒ *Wayne's force wheels into a column and retreats through fence openings, but is delayed by a disabled cannon.*
Ⓓ *Wayne orders 4th Regiment into woods to cover withdrawl.*
Ⓔ *British forces sweep into camp in three waves.*

highest-ranking American soldier killed in the battle. The 4th fell back through the woods and into an open field near "the Crossroads on our Left," where Wayne yet again rallied troops to cover the retreat. This field was north of the camp and east of Sugartown Road. Major Ryan recalled, "There was an attempt Made in an Open field afterwds to Rally them; to no purpose, but about forty Yards from thence on a fork of a Road Genl. Wayne and Myself rally'd a Number of men whom was again form'd to Cover the Retreat."[12] Maj. Caleb North of the 10th Pennsylvania helped to organize this rear guard:

> We Retreated Near Quarter of a mile when I fell in with the General at a Cross Road, who was there forming some men and Desired I would Assist and get some officer to take Command of them: as he would form the Rear Guard there, to Cover the Canon, &c.
> This Guard was [formed?] and Commanded by Captain [Harmon] Stout [10th Pennsylvania] when General Wayne desired me to Ride down the Road Leading towards Chester [Sugartown Road south], and See if the Enemy was Crossing that way which I did and soon Returned Informing him that all was Clear that way. then he Desired I would Ride the Contrary way Towards the Lancaster Road where I would find General Smallwood.[13]

Major North rode off into the night westward on King Road past small parties of troops, some of whom were moving off in good order while others, panic-stricken, fired at or fled from anything that moved. Many who were wounded made their way as best they could, while others were hefted and carried by comrades. At the same time, parties of British light infantry moved about in the dark, causing more chaos. Riding through it all, Caleb North pressed forward with his orders: "Find General Smallwood!"

CHAPTER 17

On the Road to the White Horse West of Camp

Early Sunday Morning, September 21, 1777

Smallwood and the reinforcements, who had been due to appear since early afternoon, still had not arrived. On the morning of September 19, Smallwood was at James McClellan's Tavern in Sadsbury Township (now Parkesburg), about 25 miles west of Wayne's camp. He had been joined the previous evening by Col. Mordecai Gist with 700 men and three iron cannons. "I proceeded on my March to fall on the Rear of the Enemy, in order to harass and obstruct their March . . . and arrived on the 19th at Downing Town on the Borders of their out Posts,"[1] about 12 miles from McClellan's and halfway to Wayne's camp.

The combined force of Maryland militia now numbered 2,100 infantry. The same nagging problems that had plagued Smallwood from the beginning of this assignment continued to hinder him, although his troops finally did receive a supply of proper rations from the commissary storehouses at Downingtown. The condition of the roads—soggy, mired, and rutted—no doubt played a big role in slowing the march and exhausting the men. On the 20th, Wayne sent Col. James Chambers of the 1st Pennsylvania to find Smallwood and act "as a guide to Conduct him into my Rear—where he was expected to Arrive every Moment from two OClock in the Afternoon until we were Attacked."[2]

Time was running out. Colonel Gist related that "on the Evening of the 20th General Smallwood thought it Expedient from the Intelligence he received & Several Expresses to make a forced March toward them." The Marylanders continued their trek "down on [the British] rear within less than two miles [sic], in order to join General Wayne who lay on their Right." This march took Smallwood on the Main Philadelphia/Lancaster Road to the White Horse Tavern, about 8 miles east of Downingtown. Turning right at the White Horse, the militia moved south on the Road to Goshen Meeting (present-day Planebrook Road) and up the long slope of the South Valley Hill.[3]

Just over the summit of the hill, Smallwood's men turned left and headed east on what is now King Road toward Wayne's camp, only 3 miles away. Moving slowly in the dark,

[about] 12 Oclock our Front approached within a Mile of his Encampm[en]t, when we were alarmd by his Camp being surprised and his Army routed, my Guides one of whom [Colonel Chambers] commanded a Cont[inenta]l. Regt. were much disconcerted, and, cou'd or wou'd not point out my Rout[e] further, in this Situation I'd nothing left but to retreat abt. a Mile to an Advantageous Ground I had observed.[4]

Smallwood's statement that "our Front approached within a Mile" of the camp when the firing began places the Maryland militia on King Road approaching the Sugartown Road crossroads. Gist, whose troops were bringing up the rear, wrote, "We were within a mile and a half of the place," giving an accurate description of a column of 2,100 men, along with wagons and three guns, being spread along a road for more than a mile.[5]

The "Advantageous Ground" to which Smallwood retreated was probably the rise of ground where the Chester Road (present-day Route 352) meets King Road. His description of the line of march belied the type of troops he commanded:

Accordingly it was ordered, & the Artillery, Ammunition, Commissarys Stores to precede the Line of March, which was regular, compact and well calculated for defence, in case of attack, outposted by proper flanking Parties, Advanced and rear Guards, in this Position we began the Retreat.[6]

As this militia force was moving west on King Road, something unexpected took place: "We were fired upon by the Enemy." For some of the British light infantry at this stage of the battle, the chase was on, and their enthusiasm was not to be checked. With rebel stragglers on the run and few British officers to observe or identify the culprits in the dark, some of Major Maitland's "bloodhounds" opened fire in violation of their orders.[7] Lt. Martin Hunter stated that before the march, General Grey told Maj.

John Maitland, commander of the 2nd Light Infantry Battalion, to have his men "draw their pieces" and unload. "The Major said the whole of the battalion was always loaded, and that if he would only allow them to remain so, he would be answerable that they did not fire a shot." Describing the pursuit of Wayne's troops beyond the camp, Lt. Richard St. George observed: "For two Miles We drove Them *now and then firing scatteringly* from behind fences trees &c The flashes of the pieces had a fine effect in the Night. . . . [Later, after the dragoon charge,] (no firing from us—& little from them *except now & then a few As I said before scattering shots*)."[8]

The effect of this on the militia was catastrophic. Colonel Gist wrote sardonically, "You will readily conclude that Militia unused to an Attack especially in the Night, must be thrown into some Confusion." Smallwood's comments were a bit more specific:

One of our Men [about] the centre of the Main Body was shot Dead by some of their [British] Stragglers, which threw great Part of our Line in great consternation, many flung down their Guns & ran off, & have not been heard of since, whilst others broke their Order and got into the utmost confusion, the Artillery men & Waggoners cutting their Horses loose and running off with them.[9]

Gist's men were separated from the main body by a few hundred yards. Hearing the shooting ahead, Gist recounted:

I got the Brigade under my Command to form in front, by which time several straglers of Wanes Division retreated to us. This Information made it necessary for General Smallwood to retire leaving my troops to bring up the Rear which we accomplished with a degree of regularity that did them honour.

Then, just when things seemed to have settled down, "A party of the Enemy by this time had got ahead of us and lay in Ambuscade. The firing from them was so close and unexpected that [the militia] immediately broke and left us no possibility of rallying them."[10] But not all of the militia fled at the first sign of trouble, Smallwood reported:

Colo. Johnson, and Major Deakins who made the first Advances in forming the Regiment, to which he belonged, Colo. Marbury

& his Field Officers also kept their Regiment in good order, with these two Regiments I [advanced], & posted them in a field next the Enemys parties, to cover the others. . . . The Enemys parties I imagine retreated upon viewing our Superior number, which perhaps might have been the cause of their not pursuing Wayne—we then regained the Ground above mentioned.[11]

In the midst of all this, Maj. Caleb North somehow found General Smallwood and delivered Wayne's orders "that he Should Retreat to the White Horse—this Message I Delivered Agreeable to his Order."[12]

Smallwood, Gist, and North all narrowly escaped injury or death that night. In the ambush, wrote Gist, "in forcing my way through [the British] line my Horse received two balls through his Neck but fortunately only fell on his Knees and Hams otherwise I must have received the Bayonet or fallen into their Hands." Smallwood confirmed Gist's account:

[We remained] sometime on this Ground but after quitting it our Rear was again Attack'd which put our Main Body & a part of Wayne's Division which had joind it to the Rout; Colo. Gist & myself acting in the Rear, this better to secure our Retreat, was for some time much expos'd, Gists Horse was shott thro the Neck however our Party was brought of[f] safe, except 2 killed and three wounded.[13]

William Smallwood's own close brush with death had a touch of black comedy to it:

After which riding forward with some light Horse to stop our Main Body (in case they [the British] should pursue) to cover the Retreat, the Rear taking us for British light Horse fired a Volley on us within 15 or 20 Foot, wounded several, and killed a light Horseman alongside of me in waiting for Orders—in this confusion several more wou'd have been killed by our own People had I not flung myself from my Horse and called aloud that I shou'd have been glad to have seen them as ready to fire on the Enemy as they now seemed on their Friends. they knew my voice and ceased.[14]

Major North was caught in the same militia volley: "In consequence of a fire from some stragglers, an alarm took place throughout the corps, who commenced a confused and disorderly fire in which one of the Videttes accompanying Major North was killed by his side."[15] The vidette was a trooper from Bland's Regiment of Light Dragoons, recruited in Virginia. The regimental payroll for September 1777 lists "Jones Dean, Private, 6th Troop [Capt. John Belfield's Troop], *Killed by the Militia 20th Sepr.*" Trooper Dean was owed for "one month . . . 8¹/₃ Dollars."[16]

Smallwood and Gist both attempted to regain order and control. Some of the supplies that had been abandoned in the first attack were recovered: "15 Barrels of Flower, and a number of Muskets & some Carbines [that] had been scatteringly flung away by our dastardly Fugitives." General Smallwood attempted to arrange some of his skittish militiamen in a battle line to cover the retreat, but "this Effort, tho' well intended had no other effect than to renew their Panic—in short, nothing was to be seen but flight fear and disorder." Finally, desperate measures were called into play:

> Some few who retained a proper sense of honor I placed in front across the road with Charged Bayonets but this had no Effect; they curl'd round into the Woods & got ahead of this Body—there was nothing left but to order the Retreat to be made to the Red Lyon [about] 5 Miles higher up the Country. this was the only well executed Order of the Night.[17]

Lt. Col. Adam Hubley of the 10th Pennsylvania, having narrowly escaped from the British and rescued a disabled cannon, encountered Smallwood's force near the White Horse Tavern. He testified:

> I retired with the [field]piece to the White horse, and there halted. I found a number of Troops there, and after inquiry found myself Commanding Officer there. I ralyed the men and form'd them after which I went and plac'd several Pickets, about different places. . . . Before I could return to the White horse again, I found, thro' mistakes in Genl. Smallwood's Division, the whole alarm'd, and retiring up the Lancaster road. I again with the assistance of some officers, routed our Men about half a Mile from the White horse[.] Genl. Smallwood then passing, I ask'd what was to be done[;] he desired we would March our Men up the road, about 2 Miles, and then halt.[18]

The Maryland artillery fled with some of the baggage, along with hundreds of militiamen who scattered in all directions. Smallwood wrote, "The Field Officers [colonels and majors] in general behaved firm and well & many of the Captns and Subs [subalterns, i.e., lieutenants and ensigns]; but there are others of the latter two classes who have not been heard of since—and who I believe set the first example in flying."[19] Capt. Thomas Buchanan of the 1st Pennsylvania Regiment stated:

> I was sent forward [by Wayne] to Gen. Smallwood, that lay at the White Horse, to get him to cover our retreat and fix a place of rendezvous, &c. He sent me forward to try to stop as many of his broken troops that had taken the road to Downingtown. On coming near to there, I found where some of his artillery had thrown a field-piece into a limekiln, and had broke the carriage. I went on to Downingtown, and fixed a guard on the road to stop the runaways; got a wheeler and blacksmith to mend the carriage, and went down and put the cannon on the carriage, &c.[20]

The scene of disaster was complete. Nearly 1,000 of Smallwood's men had vanished into the Chester County countryside that night. The embarrassment to the state of Maryland was felt keenly by Mordecai Gist, one of nine survivors of his unit at the Battle of Long Island in 1776. There, his Maryland Continentals had fought like Spartans to save part of Washington's army. Now, to a friend in Baltimore, he wrote bitterly,

> I hope the Governor will exercise his authority by Imprisonment or otherwise of these Miscreants, while the Brave and Virtuous continue with fortitude to encounter the hardships of war untill an Opportunity may offer to return the reflection and disgrace thrown upon the State of Maryland by their unmanly behavior.[21]

Smallwood's disgust with the whole situation is evident in his writings. He wrote to Governor Johnson at Baltimore, "If our wrong headed Assembly cou'd only be here to see these Mens behavior and be a little pestered in restraining and regulating their conduct."[22] Concerning the behavior of some other troops that night, Smallwood's words could have also been sent to London—for very different reasons.

CHAPTER 18

The Paoli Massacre

Early Sunday Morning, September 21, 1777

The Annals of the Age Cannot Produce such another Scene of Butchery," wrote Maj. Samuel Hay of the 7th Pennsylvania, ". . . the Enemy Rushed on with fixed Baynots, and Made the use of them they Intended, so you May figure to yourself what followd."[1] Atrocities took place that night that caused the Battle of Paoli to become known as the Paoli Massacre. Though no documents have been found proving that British troops were specifically ordered by General Grey or their officers to give no quarter (show no mercy) or to commit atrocities, there is substantial evidence that barbaric acts occurred well beyond what was acceptable by the military standards of the day, and not just a few isolated incidents.

James Murray, a British historian who authored *An Impartial History of the War in America* in 1783, made the following observations concerning the "massacre" aspect of the Battle of Paoli:

> General Grey conducted this enterprize with equal ability and success though perhaps not with that humanity which is so conspicuous in his character. . . . A severe and horrible execution ensued. . . . The British troops as well as the officer that commanded them gained but little honour by this midnight slaughter.—It shewed rather desperate cruelty than real valour.[2]

Col. Adam Hubley of the 10th Pennsylvania testified that he heard British troops calling out "No quarters" as his regiment rallied in the second field. He also wrote that "The greatest Cruelty was shewn on the side of the Enemy[.] I with my own Eyes, see them, cut & hack some of our poor Men to pieces after they had fallen in their hands and scarcely shew the least Mercy to any, they got very few prisoners from us."[3]

125

The British did, in fact, take prisoners, as General Grey's aide, Capt. John André, confirmed: "Seventy One Prisoners were brought off; forty of them badly wounded." This suggests that there was no direct order from the high command to commit barbaric excesses or to give no quarter.[4] However, in the mood of the moment, created by general attitudes and fostered by the setting, the usual trauma of battle quickly turned to horror. If soldiers in battle get their blood up and officers are not immediately supervising them, or if some officers look the other way or actively condone such behavior, a frenzy can occur and quickly get out of control. Lt. Martin Hunter made a passing remark in his description of the Battle of Brandywine that may speak volumes concerning the excesses at Paoli: "At this time the whole army were so inveterate against the Americans that they seldom gave any quarter." Another British officer, Capt. William Hale, of the 45th Regiment Grenadier Company, though not present at Paoli, later wrote home about it, "As our Light Infantry gave no quarter very few prisoners were taken."[5]

Murray's analysis of this episode lamented the stain that the Paoli atrocities left on the reputations of both Gen. Charles Grey and Sir William Howe:

> Accidents of this nature falling out in the hands of General Grey or Sir William Howe, carried a worse aspect then if they had happened under the authority of a Vaughan, a Grant, or a Prevost. The professions of liberty which these first gentlemen had so often made, and their former character, as humane and brave men, made any action that had the appearance of cruelty . . . strike the attention of the public more forcibly than any transactions from the hands of those from whom no better things were expected. It was even painful . . . that one of the first and greatest officers in Europe, and a professed friend of the natural rights of man, should so much as be suspected of an action unworthy of his character.
>
> History must do justice to truth and transmit transactions to posterity as they happened. . . . It has much the appearance of inconsistency, for men to disapprove of a war as unrighteous and oppressive, and yet become the principal conductors for it, and leaders in the oppression.[6]

There were many who survived the atrocities, however. Colonel Hubley had a narrow escape, thanks to some quick thinking on his part. The episode would be comical were the circumstances not so tragic:

In this affair I was remarkably lucky. about the Middle of the Engagement, I unfortunately fell in the Hands of some of the British Troops viz: One light Horseman & 4 Infantry. When they took me, I damn'd them for a parcel of Scoundrals, and ask'd them what they meant by taking one of their own Officers, upon which the light Horseman beg'd my pardon, and I desir'd him to follow on, (the four Infantry men fil'd off to the right in the mean time) He came on wth me untill I got him amongst a Party of our Men.[7]

It is difficult to imagine how Hubley, a native Pennsylvanian, was able to pull off this ruse. Did he have a facility with imitating accents or was his native accent close enough to be taken for one of the many British accents? His adjutant, Maj. Enoch Wright, was described a month later—in a deserter description—wearing "a blue regimental coat faced with scarlet, *red plush waistcoat and breeches,* blue stockings, *a small round hat.*"[8] If Hubley was dressed in a similiar uniform, a red waistcoat or jacket and a small round hat could easily give the appearance of a British light infantry officer in the dark. Or perhaps the infantrymen and the dragoon were simply gullible. In the dark confusion of the "second or third field," only dimly lit by the glow of the burning camp a few hundred yards away, a combination of any or all of these factors may have worked to Hubley's advantage.

Regarding the dragoon, Hubley continued:

I then ordered him to surrender, which he refus'd & said he belong'd to our own people, I was afraid he would get off [so] I order'd a fire if he did not surrender which but he refus'd[.] I then ordered him to be shot which was instantly done, and I brought off his Horse, Accoutrements, &c. I was closely Persued but luckily got off safe.[9]

By this time, the jam at the Sugartown Road fence line had cleared, and the front of the column was able to move north on that road toward the King Road crossroads, where Wayne was rallying and organizing the rear guard. Troops were falling back, mostly to the north and west, some in order, others in broken clusters, still others individually, with pockets of British light infantry, light horsemen, Highlanders and 44th Regiment infantry in various modes of pursuit. Some of the British light infantry pursued retreating rebels "for a mile or two from camp," across Sugartown Road and into the fields and woods to the west.

After his escape, Colonel Hubley made his way westward toward Sugartown Road, his ultimate destination being the White Horse Tavern about 4 miles west of camp. In the course of his movement in that direction, Hubley later wrote:

> After passing the third field [the field on the east side of Sugartown Road], in wh[ich] our troops had been shortly before, I fell in with one of our field pieces (the carriage of which had lost the hind wheels [and blocked the road]) and a few men, amongst wh[ich was] a Captain of Artilery. I found, a party of the enemy, Consisting of about 50 men with some light Horse, advancing upon our left but made a halt[.] I there rallied about 60 Men & form'd a rear Guard, ordered another Horse to be hitched to the piece & drag'd it along wh[ich] was done, and brought of[f] the piece. I at this time, whilst we were forming this Guard enquir'd of the men for Genl. Wayne, some of which inform'd me he was at the Cross roads, ralying the Men. These roads are nearby ye field in which we were engag'd.[10]

The artillery captain was Thomas Randall, commander of the independent artillery company attached to the division, who soon had his own experience at the hands of the king's troops:

> Randall, after getting one of his pieces away, was taken [prisoner] while he was anxiously exerting himself for the security of that, and another [gun], which, under the cover of the night, was also got off. On finding himself in their hands, he endeavoured to escape, but the enemy prevented it by knocking him down and stabbing him in eight places. His wounds not admitting of his being carried with them, they left him at a house near the scene of action, and took his parole to return when called for, unless exchanged."[11]

The payroll of this artillery company notes that Capt. Thomas Randall was paroled on September 30; he was formally exchanged in December 1777. A British officer from the 1st Light Infantry Battalion, Ens. George

Inman of the 17th Regiment Light Company, evidently a friend of Randall's from happier times, recorded in his journal: "Near this place [Valley Forge] [the Army] fell in with Genl Waine's Brigade w[hi]ch was cut to pieces. Here I found Thomas Randall . . . badly wounded with Bayonets, he being a Capt. of Artillery in the American Army then attached to Waine's Brigade."[12]

The nature of some of the injuries inflicted on the wounded are the most telling and shocking evidence of the brutality of the night. Capt. Andrew Irvine of the 7th Pennsylvania was later reported as having seventeen wounds in all, most of them minor. Capt. Robert Wilson of the same regiment was stabbed in the side and bashed in the forehead with a "cocknail," a large screw on the gunlock mechanism of a musket. Fife Major Richard Stack, of the 7th Pennsylvania was stabbed thirteen times and taken prisoner; Drum Major Daniel St. Clair of Hartley's Additional Continental Regiment was severely mutilated. Another drummer, John Hutchinson of the 1st Pennsylvania, "received a wound in the thigh with a Bayonet."[13] Musicians were considered noncombatants by tradition in the eighteenth century; to attack them deliberately was considered at the least unprofessional. While it is possible that the darkness and confusion concealed their identity as musicians, the brutal mutilations of Stack and St. Clair, among others, were inexcusable—and highly inflammatory.

Pvt. Jacob Justice of the 7th was "wounded in both legs and his head and rear, thru and then, taken prisoner." Jacob's injuries were so severe that he was originally listed as killed in the payrolls; he was later exchanged and discharged in 1781. William Leary of Philadelphia, a private in the 11th Pennsylvania, was "wounded in [the] hand with sword, Right leg bayonetted, jaw broken by a musket butt." Pvt. John Stead of the same regiment, about thirty years old, was "wounded in fourteen Different Parts of his Body."[14] Another soldier of the 11th Pennsylvania, Pvt. John McKie, hid himself in some bushes and high grass near a fence until his regiment left the field. He was "wrapt up in a blanket, and had under it a blue coat faced with red, which appeared to be the uniform of some Regt. in the Rebel service." Two British light infantrymen of the 37th Regiment, Pvt. Thomas Swift and Pvt. John Williams, later testified that "the Prisoner started up out of the Grass and desired them to look at his firelock, saying that he had not fired a Shot, and upon examining the firelock, they found that it had not been lately discharged. . . ." McKie told the light infantrymen that he was a deserter from the 23rd Royal Welch Fusiliers in 1774 and had tried to desert from the rebel army several times to return to his regiment. "But whilst he was taking off his Cartouch box . . . a Serjeant Murphy came up and wounded him with his bayonet."[15]

The most shocking account of brutality that night came from William Hutchinson, an eighteen-year-old Pennsylvania militiaman from London Britain Township, Chester County. Hutchinson was not present at Paoli; he was stationed at "McClellan's Tavern in the Great Valley" (present-day Parkesburg), 25 miles west of the battle. Many years later, Hutchinson stated:

> The second morning after the Paoli massacre, and whilst we were at McClellan's, a circumstance took place. . . . A Quaker, a stranger, came to our quarters and brought with him a man which he said he had found lying in the woods whose clothes, coat, vest, and trousers were stiff with gore. They would have stood alone when taken off him. He was a Virginian and had shared in the consequences of the massacre; had been singled out at the close thereof as a special subject for the exercise of the savage cruelty of the British soldiers. He told us that more than a dozen soldiers had with fixed bayonets formed a cordon round him, and that every one of them in sport had indulged their brutal ferocity by stabbing him in different parts of his body and limbs, and that by a last desperate effort, he got without their circle and fled. And as he rushed out, one of the soldiers struck at him to knock him down as the finis to the catastrophe; in which only the front of the bayonet reached his head and laid it open with a gash as if it had been cut with a knife. He made, however, his escape, and when brought to our captain, he had laid in the woods twenty-four hours. He had neither hat, shoes, nor stockings, and his legs and feet were covered with mud and sand which had been fastened to his skin by mixing with his own blood as it ran down his limbs.
>
> Our captain immediately dispatched his lieutenant for a physician, who, when he returned, was so fortunate as to bring two with him. We then procured the means of washing and cleansing the wounded man, and upon examining him there was found, as our captain afterwards announced to the men, forty-six distinct bayonet wounds in different parts of his body, either of which were deep and sufficiently large to have been fatal if they had been in vital parts. But they were mostly flesh wounds, and every one

of them had bled profusely, and many of them commenced bleed-
ing again upon being washed. His wounds were dressed, his bloody
garments were burned, and by orders of our captain, he was waited
upon with strict attention until he was able to walk, and then was
by Lieutenant Corry (our lieutenant) taken somewhere not distant
to an hospital, and [I] heard no more of him.[16]

Who was this Virginian, and what was he doing at Paoli? Captain
Stoddard's Troop of Bland's Regiment of Continental Light Dragoons was
from Virginia and was present at the battle, but the description of the soldier's apparel and his story suggests an infantryman. He likely was James
Martin of the 13th Virginia Regiment, whose name appears on the "List
of Wounded from Genl. Wayne's Division at Paoli" made in October 1777
by Surgeon Francis Allison at the Army Hospital in Lancaster. All of the
other soldiers on the list are Pennsylvanians. The regiment's payroll for
September 1777 confirms that "Corporal James Martin, Captain Sullivan's
Company, [was] wounded 21 September."[17] Just why he was at Paoli
remains unknown, although the more far-reaching philosophical answer is
obvious: shedding his blood for his country.

CHAPTER 19

The Great Valley and the Schuylkill River

Early Sunday Morning, September 21, 1777

The ground in the Paoli Camp was littered with the fallen, both living and dead. After less than an hour's fighting, the British troops were recalled to the smoking ruins of Wayne's camp to take an account of losses.

Their losses in the battle had been light; given the darkness and confusion, together with their orders not to fire, which for the most part were obeyed, this is not surprising. Capt. William Wolfe, commander of the 40th Regiment Light Company, "a most Brave & attentive officer," was dead; one unidentified sergeant and one private, Daniel Robertson of the 49th Regiment, were also killed, as well as two dragoon horses. At least two dragoons, two light infantrymen, and three battalion soldiers were wounded.[1] In addition, Lt. Martin Hunter of the 52nd Regiment Light Company was wounded, shot through the right hand. He later wrote:

> The enemy were pursued for two miles. I kept up until I got faint with the loss of blood, and was obliged to sit down. A sergeant of the Company remained with me, and we should have been left behind had not [Lieutenant] St. George missed me after the business was over, and immediately went to General Grey, who halted the detachment until I was found. . . . We had not more than twenty men killed and wounded.[2]

The success of the operation was astounding. In addition to driving Wayne from his camp and possessing the field, Captain Montrésor reported that the British captured "9 loaded waggons with four horses each, and brought off their cattle."[3] Grey's aide, Capt. John André, noted in his journal, "We took eight waggons and teams with flour, biscuit and baggage." In a letter several days later, he wrote:

About 200 killed or wounded remain'd on the field[.] We brought
away near 80 prisoners & of those who escap'd a great number
were stab'd with bayonets or cut with broad swords, as great a
number at least never stopped till they got to thier own homes, in
short this harassing corps is almost annihilated by the loss of that
night & by the subsequent disertions. On our part we had only 7
or eight kill'd & wounded.

We return'd to Camp before day break, with eight or ten waggons & thirty or forty horses borrow'd of General Wayne & having refresh'd the men with some good gin, with which our friends
the Dutch had supplied these gentlemen & which we likewise
borrow'd[,] march'd the next day with the Army quite unmolested
by General Wayne (a Tanner).[4]

The wounded, both British and American, were picked up, placed in
wagons, and taken back to the Tredyffrin Camp, along with the bodies of
Captain Wolfe and the British enlisted men. André wrote that "Seventy-
one Prisoners were brought off; forty of them badly wounded were left at
different houses on the road. A Major, a Captain, and two Lieutenants
were amongst the prisoners." These included Julius Count Montfort, a
French dragoon officer. André further noted, "The Detachment returned
to Camp by daybreak by the Paoli and the road Colonel Musgrave had
marched." This meant that they returned by way of the Lancaster Road
rather than the Swedes Ford Road.[5]

One house where wounded rebels were left was Howell's Tavern,
located on the Swedes Ford Road at the junction of present-day Bear Hill
Road (Route 252) and Howellville Road, "the road Colonel Musgrave had
marched." General Grey had used this tavern as his headquarters; now it
served as a temporary hospital for at least twenty-two of the American
wounded.[6] Another place identified with wounded and dead from Paoli was
the Anglican church of St. Peter-in-the-Great Valley, about 3 miles west of
Howell's Tavern. The church's elderly pastor, the Reverend William Currie,
was a conservative man of the cloth whose commitment to the king as head
of the Anglican Church put him at odds with many in his congregations
and with his own three sons. He lived on Yellow Springs Road, only 2
miles or so from Howell's Tavern and about 3 miles from St. Peter's.

Local tradition maintained that the church was used as a chapel by the
British troops and as a hospital for sick and wounded soldiers. Dead sol-

The Church of St. Peter-in-the-Great Valley, 1999. Photo by Andrew Cordray. Neighborhood tradition holds that this Anglican church was used as both a chapel and a hospital by the British Army during the Tredyffrin encampment, and that British and American soldiers are buried in the churchyard. The church is prominently featured on the 1777 British Camp at Trudruffrin map and is the probable resting place for the British dead from Paoli. AUTHOR'S COLLECTION

diers from both sides were buried in the yard, their graves marked with rough stones. It is both plausible and probable, given the church's proximity, the disposition of its pastor, and the fact that the British did not leave the bodies of Captain Wolfe or the other British dead on the field at Paoli—and buried them *somewhere*—that the British dead are buried in St. Peter's yard. Further evidence of the importance of St. Peter's at the time is suggested by a map entitled "British Camp at Trudruffrin" (see color plate) published by William Faden in 1778. The unidentified British officer who drew the map took great pains to include St. Peter's, which is featured prominently in the center, along with some of the adjacent roads. No evidence has been found indicating whether Reverend Currie knew of or participated in the burial of these soldiers, though such a duty would certainly be in keeping with a devout man of God and minister of the king. Though his Sunday preaching ceased in May 1776, "the Parson continued to baptise, visit the sick, bury the dead, and marry the couples that came to him."[7]

Stories of the terror that night were handed down for generations in the local families. Accounts include visits by British troops, such as that paid to the home of forty-five-year-old Cromwell Pearce, a major in the 5th Battalion of Chester County militia, on whose land Wayne's column had stalled. Major Pearce was not home, but his thirty-seven-year-old wife Margaret was, along with at least two of their six sons, five-year-old Cromwell, Jr., and thirteen-month-old Marmaduke. Years later, Marmaduke's son Stewart wrote:

The British dragoons came to Grandfather Cromwell's house and demanded that grandmother [Margaret] should come to the door. She made her appearance with a babe, Marmaduke (my father) in her arms, and Uncle Cromwell at her side. A brutal soldier, pointing his pistol at her breast, asked for her husband. She replied she did not know where he was. They searched the premises and found a wounded soldier who had obtained shelter there after the battle or massacre. They placed a rope about his neck and led him away to the British camp.[8]

Anthony Wayne's home, Waynesborough, was searched by a squad of soldiers from Col. Thomas Musgrave's force hovering near the Paoli Tavern. On the second day after the battle, Wayne's brother-in-law Abraham Robinson wrote concerning this episode:

I am very glad to see a few lines from you as we have had disagreeable Acco[unts] of the late Night scare, some said you ware killd & others that you ware a prisoner, I was still in hopes of better intilligence; the Night before last a number of the British troops surrounded your House in serch of you, but being disappointed in not finding you they took poor Robert & James—, but behaved with the utmost politeness to the Women and said they only wanted the General. they did not disturb the least Article—there has been several Cannon Shott been heard today in this Neighbourhood. Am very uneasy to hear the Issue—God Bless & preserve you is the sincere prayer of your Brother &c.[9]

It is remarkable that Waynesborough survived through this trying period without destruction, given its location, the reputation of its owner,

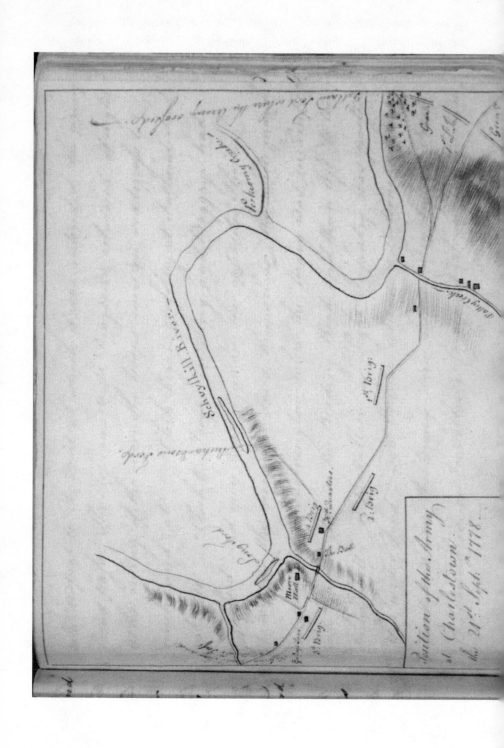

Position of the Army
at Charlestown
the 21st Sept. 1778

the numerous Loyalists in the area, and the fact that it was searched by British troops.

Washington's first notice of Wayne's defeat arrived by way of a courteous note from General Howe, dated September 21:

> There being some wounded Officers & Men of your Army at Howel's Tavern & the neighbouring Houses with whom a Surgeons Mate is left, having Orders to join me on the 23d if not sooner relieved by one of your Surgeons, I am to request you will lose no Time in sending whom you shall think proper for this Purpose, with Directions to give Receipts for the wounded so delivered up as Prisoners of War to be hereafter exchanged.[10]

The polite tone and smooth formal language of correspondence between the commanders in that period was a hallmark of professional conduct. But military courtesy alone was not the reason why Howe was so officious at this moment, nor was it the primary reason for such timely concern about the wounded. Captain von Münchhausen explained two other good reasons for sending the message:

> Very early in the morning a trumpeter was sent off with a letter to General Washington, who was on the other side of the Schuylkill River. The letter informed him that there were more than 100 [sic] severely wounded from Wayne's corps and that it was necessary for him to send surgeons to take care of them, since we had no surgeons to spare.
>
> The main reason for sending this trumpeter off, probably was not only to acquaint Washington with the bad news, but also to have the trumpeter *secure information on the depths of the water* at Val-

---

Opposite page: *"Position of the Army at Charlestown the 21st September 1778 [1777]," manuscript map by Capt. John André. British troops occupied Valley Forge (lower right) on September 18–22. Several hours after the Paoli Battle, Howe's army moved into Charlestown Township and advanced as far as French Creek (upper right). Several Schuylkill River fords are marked: Long Ford on the left, Richardson's Ford in the center, and Fatland Ford on the far right marked with the notation "where the Army crossed."* Huntingdon Library

ley Forge. Giving Washington the news of Wayne's defeat before
he might learn it himself, *might induce him to leave his position and
allow us to cross the Schuylkill unopposed.*[11]

The ulterior motives for this "courtesy" were not entirely lost on the
Continental forces. Capt. Robert Kirkwood of the Delaware Regiment,
stationed 2 miles west of Valley Forge on the left bank of the Schuylkill at
Richardson's Ford, noted in his orderly book on September 21, regarding
orders to Sullivan's Division:

> The General is much Surprised that through the Ignorance of
> Some of our Officers, a British flag [of truce] has Cross'd the River
> and come into our encampment without being Stop'd, the General
> expressly orders that in future no flag from the British army, be
> permitted to Cross the Schuylkill on any pretence. . . .
>   The Brigade Major of Coll. Stones is immediately to repair to
> the Long ford with A Subaltern from Coll. Stones Brigade and
> relieve the one Station'd there, & put him in arrest for permitting
> A Brittish flag to pass the ford into our encampment without being
> examin'd or Stopp'd at the post committed to his Charge.[12]

The route taken by the trumpeter delivering Howe's note was unusu-
ally roundabout. Long Ford was located less than a mile above Richardson's Ford and about 3 miles west of Valley Forge. The shortest and most
direct route from the Tredyffrin headquarters to Washington's camp would
have been north on the Baptist/Valley Forge Road straight to Fatland
Ford. Instead, the trumpeter took that road to the Gulph Road, turned
left, and proceeded to Valley Forge, no doubt notifying Lord Cornwallis of
Wayne's defeat. From here he crossed Valley Creek and proceeded 3 miles
west on the Nutt Road, past the Bull Tavern, and across Pickering Creek
by Moore Hall, then on to Long Ford, where he crossed the river and
passed through the extreme right flank of Washington's army, all the while
protected by a flag of truce. Lt. John Peebles of the British grenadiers, stationed at Valley Forge, observed the trumpeter's route:

> A flag of truce sent out to desire Mr. Washington to bury those that
> were killed last night, and send Surgeons to the wounded—the flag
> came in upon a Camp of theirs about 3 Miles up & on t'other side

the river where *he supposes there were about 3,000*—They have a guard just opposite to us here who ask'd for a truce for ye day, which was agreed to by our Guard, & they chatted to one another.[13]

British intelligence gathering assumed many different forms. By taking this route, the trumpeter was able to view the whole right flank of Washington's position. He also tested the waters and conditions at Long Ford (so named because it utilized an island in the Schuylkill and was several hundred yards long), whereas the British already knew about conditions at Richardson's and Fatland Ford. A Hessian account relates that on the night of September 19, Gen. Sir William Erskine examined Richardson's Ford:

[He was] above Valaisforge at 11 o'clock at night, escorted by a company of Light Infantry and 20 dragoons. The enemy had an outpost of 100 men on the opposite side of the river at that place; they saw him, fired at his troops and lighted up all the houses in the vicinity; the general accomplished his object in spite of it, and found that the river was 1/2 measure deep and had a strong current in that neighbourhood.[14]

Erskine also visited Fatland Ford that same night, according to Capt. Archibald Robertson of the Royal Engineers: "19th . . . Sir William went this night to reconnoitre Fatland Ford. A Negro pass'd over and return'd with only one Shot fired. If Troops had been near a Crossing could have been Effected."[15] The man referred to was probably George Peters, "a Negro Man, [who] came into the King's Army in America on its approach to the Schuylkill River in Sept. 1777—[and] was serviceable in pointing out the Fords in that River."[16]

Washington's headquarters on September 21 was at Thompson's Tavern in Norriton Township, located at the fork of the Egypt Road and Manatawney, or Ridge Road,[17] about 4 miles from Fatland Ford and a good 6 miles from Long Ford. The trumpeter must have taken a long, leisurely look at the American positions during his "tour," for Washington's response to Howe's missive indicates that the American commander in chief did not receive the note until at least midafternoon:

Your Favor of this date [September 21] was received this Evening & agreeable to your request I have sent Doctor [Lewis] Wilson to take charge of the Wounded Officers & Men of the Army under my command who have fallen into your hands at Howels Tavern & the Neighbouring Houses. The Doctor has directions to give a receipt for All that are delivered him, and they will be considered as Your Prisoners.[18]

At 6 A.M., the British Army broke camp at Tredyffrin and marched northward on the Baptist/Valley Forge Road. They followed the same route the trumpeter had taken earlier that morning. As they moved, so did the tales of the previous night's events. At Valley Forge, the commander of the Grenadier Companies of the Guards Battalions, thirty-six-year-old Lt. Col. Sir George Osborn, heard about the battle. To his brother John, the British minister to Saxony, Sir George wrote a few days later:

The affair of Peoli, which has struck more teror than any we have yet had, was conducted by Genl. Gray with the 42nd, 44th and one Battn. of Light Infantry . . . without permitting a man to load. It was a fair surprize in the night and the slaughter was exceeding great. I was ordered the night after to pass the Schuylkill with the Light Company and Grenadiers of the Guards only and was fortunate that our enemy had no inclination to retaliate for their late misfortune.[19]

The terror was not confined to the Americans. In a letter to a friend in England, Lt. Loftus Cliffe of the 46th Regiment confided, "My D[ea]r Jack this was necessary for [our] own preservation, but I am happy that it was not my Duty to see it done."[20] Osborn, however, was mistaken in thinking that Americans had "no inclination to retaliate." As Lt. Martin Hunter of the 52nd Light Company noted, "The Americans ever after Wayne's affair called us 'The Bloodhounds.' I don't think that our battalion slept very soundly after that night for a long time."[21]

CHAPTER 20

The White Horse and Red Lion Taverns

Sunday, September 21, to Tuesday, September 23, 1777

Anthony Wayne was wide awake at the crossroads, covering the withdrawal of his force. He managed to rally a body of troops around the 4th Pennsylvania, which, with one or two cannons, presented a formidable front. He described this to Washington a few hours later: "We then drew off a Little Distance and formed a Front to oppose to theirs—They did not think Prudent to push matters further."[1] As the crossroads lay north of the camp and through a strip of woods, few British troops pushed in this direction; most of the king's soldiers moved in a westwardly direction through open fields and halted just beyond Sugartown Road, with some light infantry pursuing "for a mile or two" as far as the Chester Road (present-day Route 352). Wayne later commented, "[I] Rallied such of the Division as took the proper Route—those who went a Contrary way and out of Supporting distance of the Artillery perhaps Col. Humpton can give the best Acc[ount] of."[2]

Richard Humpton's account describes the retreat across the fields to the west:

The Left [was] Standing fast, which I have Since understood Genl. Wayne order'd. By the left Standing fast our retreat was greatly delay'd and the Greatest part of the Troops put into the utmost Confusion. After we retreat'd a few Miles Col. [Morgan] Connor & my self collect'd about 150 Men with a Number of Officers. We halt'd & took post on a Height 'till Day break & then March'd towards the Lancaster Road.[3]

The tenuous relationship between Wayne and Humpton did not erupt into full conflict until a few days after the battle. Once their own battle was joined, Wayne's descriptions of this phase of the Paoli Battle were vitriolic in reference to his second in command: "The Artillery, Ammunition &ca. were Covered and saved by a Body of Brave troops, which were Rallied and Remained on the Ground more than an hour after that Gentleman [Humpton] had Effected his Escape from Danger tho' perhaps not without Confusion."[4]

Wayne sent several officers, including Brig. Maj. Michael Ryan, Maj. Caleb North, Capt. Thomas Buchanan, and Capt. Richard Willson, toward the White Horse Tavern to try to rally the troops headed in that direction. Either not recognizing or disregarding the full scope of his situation, Wayne momentarily considered launching a counterattack. North and Buchanan delivered Wayne's messages to General Smallwood but to little purpose, for the Maryland militia was hopelessly scattered. Willson stated:

> I fell in with Genrl. Wayne on the Road leading to the white Horse Tavern where I continued about an hour, the Genrl. indeavering to collect what Troops he cou'd at that Place, being about three Quarters of a Mile from the Ground we were attacked on & which might Pass that way on their retreat.
>
> I was then between the hours of one and 2 o'Clock dispatched to the white Horse Tavern to request Colo. Hartly to collect about 500 of the best and most active Men with A Sufficient number of Officers best qualified for the Purpose of returning and attacking the Enemy, and also to inform Colo. Hartley that Genrl. Wayne was on his way to the white Horse and wou'd join him there—
>
> I inquir'd for Colo. Hartly at the white Horse but cou'd not hear of him. I assisted Colo. Hoobly in getting together about 80 Men of the Division which were all that cou'd be then collected.[5]

Earlier, Adam Hubley had rescued the disabled cannon by having it dragged away. He then went down to the White Horse and found himself the senior officer in command. He posted a number of pickets to try to reorganize retreating troops, only to be engulfed by the panic of Smallwood's militia in headlong retreat. Hubley managed to rally some Pennsylvania troops on the Lancaster Road about half a mile west of the White

Uwchlan Friends Meeting House, 1999. Photo by Andrew Cordray. This meetinghouse near the Red Lion Tavern (Lionville) was converted into a Continental Army hospital for the wounded from Paoli and the Valley Forge encampment. AUTHOR'S COLLECTION

Horse, when he encountered General Smallwood himself. He described the proceedings:

> Genl. Smallwood then passing, I ask'd what was to be done. He desired we would March our Men up the road, about 2 Miles, and then halt. Whilst we were on this March, I fell in with Genl. Wayne, [it] was nearly day break, the Genl. & myself then moov'd [back] down the road towards the White-horse, after being down the road some time the General received intiligence of the enemies advancing on our left. The General then gave orders, for our troops to March towards the Red Lion, and there remain until further orders.[6]

The Red Lion Tavern in Uwchlan Township stood across the road from Uwchlan Friends Meeting. In the early-morning hours of Sunday, September 21, the "first day meeting . . . was uncommonly small at Uwchlan Occationed by Thronging of the American Army."[7] The Quakers headed for Uwchlan Meeting encountered the remnants of Wayne's and Smallwood's weary forces trudging, stumbling, and limping toward their meetinghouse, just a few yards from the Red Lion Tavern. Exhaustion—from the alarms, the fight, the flight, the trauma, the confusion in the dark, the march up the long North Valley Hill—would set in at the first halting place. And the condition of the bloodied wounded who were able to escape—limping, carried, dragged along, suffering from saber slashes or horrific puncture wounds created by the 18-inch-long triangular bayonets of the Brown Bess musket—was beyond words. Tradition holds that blood-stains were visible on the floor of the meetinghouse for years afterward.[8]

During the next several hours, troops continued to drift in. Colonel Humpton, who spent the remainder of the night somewhere "on a height" with Col. Morgan Connor and about 150 men, marched at day-light to the Lancaster Road, probably near the White Horse Tavern. Here he met Brigade Major Ryan, "who told Me Gen. Wayne Was at the Red Lyon. I March'd there & found Him & Genl. Smallwood."[9] According to his later testimony, Humpton had no knowledge on September 21 that two warnings had arrived several hours in advance or that a picket was reported missing. The cool professional relationship between Wayne and Humpton continued that morning. It appears that Humpton was oblivious to the fact that anything other than a complete surprise attack had taken place. It also appears that Humpton did not have much of a personal rela-tionship with his subordinate commanders, for he testified that three more days passed before he learned the details of what had transpired concerning the warnings and pickets—and not from Anthony Wayne.

Wayne, however, was unequivocally clear that the attack was *not* a sur-prise. In defense of his actions, after describing the warning from "old Mr. Jones" and the reinforcing of the pickets, Wayne emphatically stated, "This, Gentlemen, don't look like a Surprise—it rather proves that we were Pre-pared either to move off or Act Occationally—when once we were Informed which way the Enemy were Advancing." He further added, "To have made any move previous to knowing that might have been Attended with fatal Consequences."[10] According to Wayne's report to Washington on the morning of September 21, he had "derived every assistence possible" from Colonel Humpton and every other officer. Taken at face value, the letter Wayne wrote that morning does not indicate that anything all that terrible had happened at midnight. This letter is critical, because it is the first official American report to headquarters and analysis of the Battle of

Paoli. It is also Anthony Wayne's view and first perception of what had occurred and contains considerable controversial data:

> About 11 oClock last Evening we ware alarmed by a firing from One of our Out guards—The Division was Immediately formed which was no sooner done than a firing began on our Right Flank—I thought it proper to order the Division to file off by the Left except the [Light] Infantry and two or three Regiments nearest to where the attack began in order to favour our Retreat—by this Time the Enemy and we were not more than Ten Yards Distant—a well directed fire *mutually* took Place, followed by charge of Bayonet—Numbers fell on each side—We then drew off a Little Distance and formed a Front to oppose to theirs—They did not think Prudent to push matters further—
>
> Part of the Division were a little scattered but are Collecting fast—We have saved all our Artillery, Ammunition & Stores—except one or two Waggons belonging to the Commissaries Department—
>
> Gen'l Smallwood was on his march but not within supporting distance[;] he Order'd his people to file off toward this place where his Division and my own now lay—
>
> As soon as we have refreshed our Troops for an Hour or Two, we Shall follow the Enemy who I this moment learn from Major North are marching for Schuylkill—I cant as yet ascertain our Loss—but will make out a Return as soon as Possible, our Dead will be collected & buried this Afternoon—
>
> *I must in Justice to Col's Hartley, Humpton, Broadhead, Grier, Butler, Hubley & indeed every Field & Other Officer inform your Excellency that I derived every assistence possible from those Gentn on this Occasion—*
>
> Whilst I am writing I received yours of the 20th pr. [by] Messrs Dunlap & Leaming with the intelligence you wished to Communicate—It will not be in our power to render you such Service, as I could wish, but all that can you may Depend on being done. . . .

At the bottom of the letter appears the following note: "The two Letters you mention I never Receiv'd—I have Reason to think they fell into the Enemys hands, last Nights Affair fully evinces it."[11]

In his letter, Wayne stated that he couldn't yet ascertain the American losses but would make out a return as soon as possible. To date, this return has not been located. While numerous round-number estimates abound, with most American accounts giving estimates ranging from 200 to 300, only three specific numbers of American casualties have been found in primary documents, but none of these figures come from eyewitnesses.

The first and most comprehensive number comes from Maryland congressman Samuel Chase, who wrote the governor of Maryland from Lancaster on September 25, noting that "in the late shameful Surprise . . . We lost 272 dead, prisoners, wounded & missing in that affair."[12] Where Chase obtained this figure is unknown, but it is possible that he saw a return. This figure seems to be the most accurate total number of casualties, including those wounded, missing, and taken prisoner.

The second specific figure comes from Washington's adjutant general Timothy Pickering, who wrote from the "Camp near Potsgrove" on September 25, "Next day Wayne buried fifty-six of his men, and the inhabitants said the enemy buried twenty-three of theirs, and carried off four or five wagon-loads."[13] This may have been the number sent to headquarters verbally, as no written source has come to light.

The most reliable figure of total dead comes from Col. Adam Hubley, who received the number from an eyewitness, Maj. Caleb North, a good, dependable officer. Hubley referred to the dead found on the battlefield when he wrote from Red Lion to Lancaster on September 21: "[I] sent my Major [North] with 4 of our Horsemen on the field who counted our Dead bodys, the enemy's were taken off, they were inform'd in large numbers." He wrote again on the 23rd, this time with a specific number: "We bury'd our Dead next day in the field of Battle, (52 brave fellows) All kill'd by the sword & Bayonet . . . "[14] Local tradition asserts that one more body was found in the woods a few weeks later and interred where it lay,[15] for a total of fifty-three buried in the battlefield. Whether these were all of the American dead or only those found on the campsite-battlefield is uncertain; tradition holds that eight Revolutionary soldiers are buried at St. Peter's and that at least some of them were from Randolph's Picket Post 4 on the Lancaster Road. British accounts vary widely and give numbers in the range of 200 to 500 rebels killed, but these are certainly gross overestimates.

In the damp early-morning mist in the Great Valley on September 21, a Willistown farmer named Joseph Cox cautiously made his way across rain-soaked meadows and through dank woods to his neighbor's farm. There he paused in horror at the scene before his eyes, a scene that confirmed the dreadful sounds he and his family had heard in the dark a few hours earlier. In the fields of Ezekiel Bowen and Cromwell Pearce, the site of the Paoli Camp, crimson streaks stained the soil around the still, cold forms of what remained of the dead. The hideous condition of some of the remains showed evidence of unspeakable horrors. The air was filled with the sickening stench of death. Trails of dark stains crisscrossed the confused paths of footprints, some with worn shoes remaining stuck in the soft mire,[16] along with scores of dropped muskets, lost equipment, and bits of ragged clothing. Here and there, some of the forms on the ground stirred and moaned. Joseph Cox and other civilians viewing the scene rendered what aid they could, some of them dipping up water with their broad-brimmed hats.[17] The broken fences, the mutilated corpses, the haze and stains and smells of death marked the scene of battle and places of massacre.

CHAPTER 21

The Schuylkill River and Little Conestoga Valley

Sunday, September 21, to Monday, September 22, 1777

The breathtaking panorama of dawn in the Schuylkill Valley greeted His Majesty's troops moving up the Gulph Road and over the ridge of Mount Joy above Valley Forge. From the camp at Tredyffrin, the British Army was in full march for the Schuylkill River by daylight on September 21, but instead of heading for Swedes Ford, where Washington expected to oppose their crossing, Howe's forces swung north to Valley Forge and then headed west toward French Creek without attempting to cross the river. Captain von Münchhausen observed:

> We passed Valley Creek without being opposed by the rebels, whom we could see very clearly. They were wise not to attack us because the heights on which the English grenadiers and four 12-pounders were posted, completely commanded the low terrain on the other side of the Schuylkill.[1]

The spectacular scene included a view of the center of Washington's army, encamped across the Schuylkill on the rise between Fatland Ford and Pawling's Ferry. Lt. James McMichael of the Pennsylvania State Regiment, stationed near Pawling's, attempted to describe the view of the Royal Army from his side of the river in a bit of soldier poetry:

> Just when we came unto our camp, an army did appear,
> They were on an adjacent hill which to us was quite near,
> They travers'd all the hill about, as tho' we were their foes
> And seem'd quite uneasy the secret to disclose.

But we with mirth and jolity did seat ourselves to rest
Upon the hill right opposite, tho' they seem'd quite distress'd.
Then taking Carnaghan's canteen, which had in it some rum,
We took to us a little draught, my rhyme to end did come.[2]

Leading the advance of the British column into Charlestown Township were the Hessian Jägers, both horse and foot. Cap. Johann Ewald traced the army's movement:

About ten o'clock the army passed the defile of the Valley Creek, where Lord Cornwallis was situated on the right bank of this creek. At midday the army crossed the Pickering Creek, where it halted. It set out again in the afternoon and encamped toward evening by the right bank of the Schuylkill in Charlestown Township in Chester County.[3]

The head of the British Army reached all the way to the French Creek Bridge near the junction of the Road to Pottsgrove and Reading and the Road to Yellow Springs (Routes 23 and 113, Phoenixville). The Jägers were posted here, covering the front/left flank of Howe's position, along with the 2nd Light Infantry Battalion, fresh from their victory over Wayne earlier that morning. The Hessian grenadier and musketeer battalions were stationed behind the light troops, with pickets posted at Gordon's Ford on the Schuylkill by the mouth of French Creek, just over a mile upstream from Long Ford and well beyond Washington's right flank.

Two miles back from French Creek was Gen. Charles Grey's 3rd Brigade, encamped south of the Nutt Road near the Road to White Horse. Depending on the direction of travel, this White Horse Road was also known as the Road to Moore Hall and Long Ford, the lower end of the same road used by General Grey to approach Wayne's camp. Grey took up quarters in a small house at this intersection, just a few hundred yards from both Long Ford and Moore Hall.

Howe's headquarters was 1 mile east of Grey's, across Pickering Creek and a few rods beyond the Bull Tavern, where the 4th Brigade was encamped. The 2nd and 1st British Brigades were placed east of headquarters along the Nutt Road toward Valley Forge, while the two battalions of British grenadiers, the Guards and the 1st Battalion of Light Infantry, now the rear of the British column, continued their occupation of the heights at Valley Forge, a little over 3 miles east of headquarters. All together, the army at Charlestown was about 7 miles from head to rear. Capt. Archibald Robertson of the Royal Engineers described the British movements and camp arrangement in relation to the motions and positions of Washington's forces across the Schuylkill:

> At Day Break left the Camp at Tredefferin and march'd to Valley Forge and Extended our left about 3½ miles up the Schuylkill, with 5 fords in our Front at which the Rebels had Posts. We found Sulivan and Sterling on the opposite side with about 6000 men. Washington had march'd the Day before with the Rest of his Army to Guard Sweds Ford to oppose our Passing there, but this Evening join'd Sulivan and push'd a Corps still higher up the Schuylkill to prevent our Turning his Right Flank.[4]

His own army thinly stretched over a 9-mile front, Washington now found himself in yet another of Howe's cat-and-mouse games, the same game Sir William had played so successfully against him at Long Island and Brandywine. This time Washington could not afford to be outflanked again, especially as news of Wayne's defeat arrived. The strategic significance of the Paoli Battle was now painfully apparent: Washington's plan to prevent Howe's crossing the Schuylkill by outflanking him and seizing his baggage with a lightning strike to the rear had been foiled. Worse yet, Paoli had allowed Howe not only to regain the strategic advantage, but also to successfully turn the tables and seize full control of the military situation.

Washington now faced a dilemma: No matter which way he moved, he was going to lose something significant, with Philadelphia lying about 25 miles to his left and Reading 35 miles to his right. If he stayed put, he risked having his army outflanked and possibly trapped against the Schuylkill because of Howe's skill at locating unguarded fords; such an event could well mean a total defeat for the rebels, thanks to the British intelligence network, which was performing so superbly in this campaign. The loss of Philadelphia would be mainly a political and psychological blow; the loss of Reading would be a military blow with potentially fatal consequences to an army whose support system was already weak. Even if Washington proved successful at defending the river fords, the British Army could march westward into the French Creek Valley, destroy the iron manufacturing in that region, and move on to seize Lancaster. From this position of advantage, Howe could then proceed north to Reading and eventually on to Philadelphia, all the while living off a countryside with abundant food, forage, and military supplies. Captain Montrésor noted on the 21st that in the area west of Valley Forge: "We found the houses full of military stores. This country abounds with forage, but the cattle drove off."[5] Howe would also deprive Washington's troops of desperately needed supplies. If Reading proved too far a reach, Howe could turn southeast from Lancaster and move back toward Wilmington, resupply his army from the British fleet, and march on Philadelphia from the south, all the while wearing Washington's army down by attrition and sheer exhaustion. Had Howe chosen to move west, only Wayne's force lay between him and Lancaster.

In spite of their intrepid commander's statements, Wayne's troops were in no condition to move against anyone, least of all the main British Army. The shock of the Paoli Battle was becoming more and more apparent as the day wore on. The loss of officers and men amounted to at least 15 percent; the loss of hundreds of muskets, accoutrements, equipment, food, and supply wagons was crippling. The enlisted men were numb with shock and exhaustion. Some of the officers were feeling discontent, frustration, and anger toward Wayne, while others remained silent or sided with their commander as rumors of warnings received and missing pickets began to spread. Wayne's abrupt treatment of Major Nichols, who had mistakenly reported a picket missing, added to the unrest among those who could recall similiar episodes. Smallwood and Gist were angered and embarrassed by the disgraceful behavior of their men; the Maryland losses by desertion were nearly 50 percent, with less than five battle casualties. And everyone was fed up with the lateness and perpetual shortages of the inept Commissary and Quartermaster Departments. Washington's reaction to the supply situation concerning Wayne and Smallwood was noted in a Commissary Department letter from Ephraim Blaine to William Buchanan on September 24:

> Last night I received the inclosed by Mr. McGarmont which has given me great uneasiness, [I] am astonished Mr. Gast did not furnish the necessary supplys before he left General Smallwood. His Excellency has had the Accounts and is very much displeas'd. . . .
>
> Genl. Wayne and Smallwood has been much distress'd for the Necessary supplies for their People, [I] suppose you have heard of

their being surpriz'd in the night by the Enemy, and a good deal worsted; The number of our loss not properly ascertain'd, but Considerable.[6]

Wayne's command, now amounting to less than 1,500 troops, with considerably fewer qualifying as "effectives," together with 1,100 of Small-wood's Marylanders, many of whom were unarmed, remained at Red Lion all day on September 21. Rumbles of thunder in the late afternoon heralded the approach of the last storm of the summer of 1777. Prudently reconsidering his thoughts of marching after the British, Wayne decided to keep his diminished force at the Red Lion and Uwchlan Meeting for the night.[7] At dawn the next morning, Anthony wrote to his wife Polly at Waynesborough:

> The Enemy made a hard push to Carry us the night before last—I sent off the Artillery and Chief part of the troops puting two Reg-iments with the Light Infantry to receive them and to Cover the Retreat of the Others—which we happily Effected with some loss—the Enemy did not Suffer less—and thought prudent to halt.[8]

Wayne and his troops were soon on the march, but not toward another direct encounter with the British. Instead, they headed 14 miles northwest on the Little Conestoga Road to David Jones's Tavern on the Ridge Road (present-day Route 23) near the Little Conestoga Creek, just over the line in Berks County and a good 20 miles west of the British Army. Col. Richard Humpton remembered, "The Next Day [September 22] we Marched for Jones Tavern about three Miles from Reading Furnace—there I think it was the Genl read me a Letter which he proposed sending to His Excellency . . . "[9] This was the same letter that contained Wayne's first report of the Paoli Battle and in which he praised all of his officers, includ-ing Humpton, for their assistance.

Located in Caernarvon Township, David Jones's Tavern was founded by and named for the father of Lt. Col. Jonathan Jones, a long-serving officer formerly of the 2nd Pennsylvania Regiment. Colonel Jones had served with Benedict Arnold in Canada in 1775 and with Wayne at Three Rivers and Fort Ticonderoga in 1776. He resigned from the army in April 1777 due to severe illness. During the previous winter, he had fallen wounded and lay buried in deep snow for nearly a day; the snow actually

Jones's Tavern, circa 1910. Photographer unknown. Now a private residence, David Jones's Tavern served as a temporary hospital and encampment ground for Wayne's force September 22–24, 1777. From here, Wayne rejoined the main army at Trappe and Col. Thomas Hartley accompanied the wounded to Reading.
TRI-COUNTY HISTORIANS, MORGANTOWN, PA.

saved his life and kept him from freezing to death. Now Jones was conva-lescing at home, attempting to rebuild his health.[10] Whether the fact that he was a comrade in arms or that the Jones and Wayne families had long connections, having known each other since the 1720s, played any role in Wayne's decision to go there is unknown.

When retracing the routes taken by the participants in this campaign, one cannot help but be struck by the distances covered on foot, by horse, and by wagon through difficult terrain. The rolling countryside is pleasant to see but exhausting to traverse, especially for soldiers lugging equipment and erratically fed on poor rations. On this first day of autumn, the weather announced the new season with sunshine, high-flying clouds, and chilly, biting winds. With roads either muddy or dusty, fluctating tempera-tures, and radical changes of conditions, the strain of incessant marching took its toll. Even troops hardened to the rigors of soldiering found the pace exhausting, and the march must have been a grueling ordeal for the wounded. Maj. Samuel Hay of the 7th Pennsylvania, writing to Col. William Irvine, described the scene near Jones's Tavern after the troops arrived and the wounded were established in camp:

> The 22d I went to the Ground to See the wounded[;] the Scene was Shocking, the Poor Men groning under their wounds which was all by Stabs of Baynots and Cuts of Light Horsemens Swords, Coll. Grier is wounded in the Side by a Baynot Superficily Slanting towards the Back Bone, Capt. Wilson Stabed in the Side by a Baynot and in to the Body but not Dangerouss, as it did not take Either the Guts or Belly[;] he got also a Bad Stroak on the Head with the Cock Nail of the lock of a Musket. Lieut. Andr. Irvine was Run through the fleshey part of the Thigh with a Baynot, they are all Lying Near David Jones Tavern, with Capt. McDowell which I left with them to Dress and take Care of them and I hear they are all in a fair way of Recovering.[11]

There were Continental Army hospitals in Reading and Lancaster, among other places, but the wounded from Paoli were in several widely separated spots miles from either location. At General Howe's request, Washington had sent Dr. Lewis Wilson to Howell's Tavern to look after the wounded prisoners left there and at the neighboring houses. Wayne may have left some of the wounded at Uwchlan Meeting and Red Lion, while he took others with him to Jones's. From there, they could be sent to either Reading or Lancaster. In addition, farmers were picking up wounded men in the neighborhood of the battle and transporting them to wherever they could find American troops. One, Corp. James Martin, was found by a Quaker farmer two days after the battle somewhere near the scene of action. The farmer took the pitifully wounded soldier all the way to McClellan's Tavern in Sadsbury Township, over 25 miles west of the battlefield.[12]

One of the wounded soldiers taken to Reading was twenty-five-year-old Pvt. James Reed of Capt. Thomas Church's Company, 5th Pennsylvania Regiment. Reed had joined Col. Anthony Wayne's 4th Pennsylvania Battalion at York in January 1776. He served in "the Battle of the three rivers and Several Scrimages in Canada" in 1776 and was wounded at New Brunswick, New Jersey, in June 1777. Reed returned to duty and fought at Iron Hill, Delaware, "and Brandewine and Pioly in Pennsylvania," where he was badly wounded. He was taken with the others to Jones's Tavern, from which he was sent to the army hospital at Reading. Reed survived and was discharged from the army at Reading Hospital in November 1777. The rigors of war and British bayonets and medical attention were unable to bring Reed down: He died in Moon Township, Beaver County, Pennsylvania, in 1846, sixty-nine years after Paoli. He was ninety-four years old and was probably the last American survivor of Paoli.[13]

The senior surgeon of the Army's Middle Department, Dr. Francis Alison, was "ordered to the Ship tavern in Chester County, to remove the wounded of General Wayne's Division massacred at the Paoli, to the town of Lancaster."[14] Some of the casualties presumed dead and left on the field by the British were picked up by local people and taken to the Sign of the Ship, located 1 mile west of Downingtown.[15] One such soldier was also named James Reed, a twenty-one-year-old private of the 10th Pennsylvania. Born in County Antrim, Ireland, in 1756, Reed emigrated to Chester County, Pennsylvania, in 1774. He joined the Pennsylvania militia "Flying Camp" in 1776 and served five months, only to be taken prisoner at Fort Washington on Manhattan Island in November 1776. He was held in New York for thirteen weeks, part of which time he was confined to the "prison hulks," cut-down ships used as prisons that were notorious for overcrowded, brutal, and filthy conditions. Reed was finally paroled and, being a "true Revolutionary," promptly enlisted for three years in the Continental Army, a parole violation that would merit death were he captured and recognized. Joining Capt. Robert Sample's Company of Adam Hubley's 10th Pennsylvania Regiment, Reed once more put his life on the line for his new nation:

> At a place called Paoli on the Lancaster Road the Americans were surprised and put to the bayonet and [he] was left for dead with numerous bayonet wounds, was afterwards found & taken to the Sign of the <u>Ship</u> on the Lancaster Road and continued weak and feeble till after the close of the war—and wholly unable to rejoin the army.

Fifty-six years later, after the federal government finally approved a comprehensive pension plan for Revolutionary War veterans, seventy-seven-year-old James Reed, in dire personal circumstances, applied for a pension. An examining attorney wrote:

Reed has evidences to satisfy any one who sees him that he has seen hard service somewhere. He is covered with scars evidently the marks of bayonet wounds—some of which have disfigured him very much—He is a man of Piety & strictly & morally honest—but very poor & subsists principally upon the charities of his neighbors.

If the evidences now presented to the [War] Department are deemed Sufficient—I sincerly hope he may receive a speedy return—for whatever his adopted country does for him to reward him for his Sufferings must be done Soon or the chance will come too late.

For his services, a grateful nation awarded James Reed the sum of $80 per year, with back payments to 1831 totaling $240. Reed died at age eighty on July 3, 1836, one day short of the sixtieth birthday of the United States.[16] As an old revolutionary from Ireland, his story may be summed up by an old Irish revolutionary saying, *Lá ar bith feasa:* "Any day now . . . "

CHAPTER 22

The Schuylkill River Fords

Tuesday, September 22, to
Wednesday, September 23, 1777

General Howe seemed to be in no hurry to make a push on Philadelphia; if he could defeat Washington by maneuvers and attrition, all the better. The weather had improved splendidly since the "equinoxial gale" of the 16th and 17th, and autumn greeted the Royal Army this morning with bright skies, cold winds. and a touch of frost.[1] From "Headquarters CharlesTown 22d Septembr. 1777" came this warm acknowledgment in the General Orders:

> The Commander in Chief issues his perticular thanks to Majr. Genl. Gray, The officers and men of the detachment Under his Command, that Yesterday Morning Surprised a post of the Enemy; thier Steadiness in Charging With Bayonets without firing a Single Shot not only proves thier Spirit & Discipline but also thier Conduct & Evident Superiority over the Enemy, The Gallant Charge made at the same time by the Detachment of Dragoons does them great Honour.[2]

That same morning, British military observers noticed movements across the river in the Continental camp. Washington's army appeared to be shifting upriver toward their right in the direction of Reading. This was indeed the case, as Washington wrote to President John Hancock, now in the city of Lancaster, on September 23:

> [On September 19–20] I immediately crossed the Schuylkill above them and threw myself full in their Front, hoping to meet them in their passage or soon after they had passed the River. The day before Yesterday [the 21st] they were again in Motion and marched

rapidly up the Road leading toward Reading. This induced me to beleive that they had two objects in view, one to get round the right of the Army; the other, perhaps to detach parties to Reading, where we had considerable Quantities of military Stores. To frustrate those intentions, I moved the Army up on this side of the River to this place [camp near Pottsgrove], determined to keep pace with them.[3]

Washington feared a repeat performance of Howe's flanking march at Brandywine. The head of the British line of march was at French Creek Bridge, already more than a mile above Washington's right. According to Howe's aide, Captain von Münchhausen, the American commander's decision to move up the river was also prompted by the news of the Paoli defeat: "It is reported that Washington, upon receiving word of the defeat of General Wayne, retreated from his position to the right along the Schuylkill, to the region of Reading, and that he left only 500 men to observe our movements."[4] Orders to Gen. John Sullivan were issued from headquarters at Thompson's Tavern at 8 P.M. on September 21, directing him to use his division as a screen for the army's movement. By the morning of the 22nd, the Continental forces had shifted away from the river fords, leaving only "a small Pickett at each Fording Place as a party of Observation" to keep an eye on Howe's movements.[5]

Wondering just what these American maneuvers might mean, Howe decided to see what sort of response he would get from Washington if he attempted to move toward Reading or cross the Schuylkill. At 7 A.M. on September 22, Howe sent Gen. Sir William Erskine on a reconnaissance patrol up the Road to Pottsgrove and Reading (present-day routes 23 and 724) with mounted and dismounted Hessian Jägers, part of the 2nd Battalion of British Light Infantry, and one squadron of the 16th Light Dragoons. An hour earlier, Capt. Johann Ewald departed with a force of twelve mounted Jägers, eighty foot Jägers, and fifty Hessian grenadiers, heading to a village in Pikeland Township "which lay in the rear of the army." About 8 A.M., Ewald skirmished with a small party of American troops that "placed itself behind the houses and fences and fired several shots." The rebels vanished into the woods when the Jägers advanced quickly toward them. Ewald then made some interesting discoveries:

> I passed the village, which consisted of perhaps forty or fifty buildings but had been completely deserted by its inhabitants. I deployed

on the other side behind the hedges or walls and searched through the village, where I found a blown-up powder magazine and a rifle factory, in which several thousand pieces of fabricated and unfinished rifles and sabers of all kinds were stored. . . . I then ordered everything smashed to pieces, set fire to the factory, and marched back.[6]

The powder magazine, located "a mile from French [Creek] Bridge,"[7] was Peter De Haven's Continental Powder Mill on French Creek, established by Congress to produce gunpowder for the Continental Army. De Haven had also established the Public Gun Lock Factory and the Public Gun Manufactory to manufacture musket parts and other related hardware for the Pennsylvania State Board of War and Committee of Safety. The scope of manufacturing evidently included swords and blades of various types; the works also made intricate gun lock mechanisms and assembled finished muskets.[8] These enterprises were located a mile or so east of the present-day village of Kimberton.

The powder mill had exploded back in March 1777, possibly the result of sabotage. De Haven reported to the Committee of Safety that "Wee are very Supspities [it] has bin Don by Mr. Peck or his Men." Col. Peter Grubb, a local militia officer, was allegedly seen at the mill "somewhat in Drink; he Damned the Powder Mill, and told Col. Dewese, Let us Blow it to hell, Which I thought Was a very odd Exprestion."[9] The report proved groundless. Given this episode, it is not surprising that Colonel Dewees was reluctant to allow his Valley Forge to be used as a military magazine. This may also explain why Dewees requested guards to be placed at the forge in April 1777.[10] Additionally, the ironmaster expressed serious reservations about making his ironworks a military target in case of invasion but was reassured that all supplies would be moved well before an attack. Now Dewees's worst fears were being realized as were De Haven's, who had written to the Supreme Executive Council on September 10: "Wee have got sum information that thare is part of Mr. How's army within four miles of Downins Town, and I believe they intend for our Magazene, and we are in a very poor situation for defending it. I should be very glad if you would send a proper Gard for this place."[11]

This guard consisted of local Pennsylvania militia, who "fled into the wood so hastily that not a single man was caught" when approached by Ewald's Jägers. At the magazine, the Hessians found "1 ton of powder, 100 muskets and a great many intrenching tools."[12] The destruction of De

Haven's manufactories completed, Captain Ewald's force moved back to the French Creek Bridge "to cover General Erskin's withdrawl, who had gone 2 miles on the other side of same to reconnoitre the whole district."[13] The heart of both the state of Pennsylvania's and the Continental Congress's ordnance and munitions manufacturing capacity, the French Creek Valley, now lay open for the taking.

Howe still had his eye on Philadelphia, and Washington's withdrawal upriver toward Reading was the perfect opportunity to seize the largest city in North America with a minimum of losses. At 5 P.M., Crown forces crossed the Schuylkill River simultaneously at Gordon's Ford on the left and, 6 miles downstream, Fatland Ford on the right. With supporting fire from four Hessian fieldpieces and one or two British guns, about 200 Hessian grenadiers under Captain von Westerhagen and Captain Schimmelpfennig, together with 20 mounted and 60 dismounted Jägers under Captain Lorey and Captain Wreden, crossed Gordon's Ford and drove away the Americans stationed on the left bank. They found that the ford "was not very wide and only 1½ feet deep, with a hard bottom and an island in the middle. But the rebels had put up a small abatis [obstruction], which would have to be cleared away before cannon and wagons could cross."[14] At Fatland Ford, with Richard Swanwick of Charlestown Township as a guide, Sir George Osborn led the light infantry and grenadier companies of the Guards Battalions across the Schuylkill without firing a shot.[15] The water at this ford was 3 feet deep or, as Lt. John Peebles put it, "up to a Grenadier's breetches pockets."[16] Securing the area below James Vaux's mansion, Fatland, Osborn and the Guards opened the way for Howe's army to cross the Schuylkill and seize Philadelphia.

The crossing at Gordon's Ford was intended only as a feint; the Hessians were recalled back to the right bank just after dark, and the whole army was issued the following orders:

> The Troops order'd to be under Arms by the rising of the Moon which was between 8 & 9. [The order of march:] The 1st & 2d Light Infantry, Queen's Dragoons and Rangers to lead the Column. The Regiments to march by, & follow them on their right—British Grenadiers—Guards—4th & 3d Brigades—Stirn's Brigade—Hessian Grenadiers & Yagers—1st & 2d Brigades— Genl. Grant to give orders about the Baggage. The Heavy Artillery at the Head of the 3d & 4th Brigades.[17]

Most of the troops did not actually move until after midnight. The 2nd Battalion of Light Infantry had to march all the way from their position near French Creek in order to be in place at the head of the march across the Schuylkill. Grenadier Lieutenant Peebles noted, "We march'd between 1 & 2 OClock in the morning . . . & cross'd the Sckuylkill at Fat land ford. . . . The Troops took up ground as they arrived, made fires, & dryed themselves."[18]

From somewhere near the top of Mount Joy, a Chester County soldier observing British movements by the light of a waning moon noticed the fires made by Howe's troops as they left their camp at Charlestown and Valley Forge to cross the river. Maj. Caleb North of the 10th Pennsylvania, the officer who had returned to Paoli to count his slain comrades and help bury them, was again out on reconnaissance duty for Wayne.[19] The fires he saw were not those described by Lieutenant Peebles of the Royal Highland Regiment. What North saw was a huge conflagration along the Valley Creek that lit up the slopes of Mount Joy, illuminating the rushing waters of the Schuylkill and filling the valley with embers and smoke.

William Dewees's Valley Forge was on fire, together with the storehouses and all of the Continental Army supplies for which the British Army had no use. The dwelling houses in the vicinity were largely spared, including Isaac Potts's small, elegant house near the mouth of the Valley Creek. Streams of golden sparks shot high into the starlit night as the billowing flames silhouetted the last of His Majesty's troops moving out of the Great Valley region.

CHAPTER 23

Southeastern Pennsylvania

Late September to Early October 1777

Philadelphia witnessed the triumphal entry of the Royal Army on September 26, three days after it crossed the Schuylkill. Howe finally achieved his goal of seizing the rebel capital through a series of maneuvers, leaving Washington high up in the country at Faulkner's Great Swamp in New Hanover Township near Pottsgrove. The Crown Forces occupied Germantown on the 25th; Lord Cornwallis took possession of the city the next morning. The good news for the Continentals was that Reading and the French Creek Valley were spared; the bad news was that the British now held Philadelphia, which opened the floodgates for criticism of Washington's handling of the situation, even by some of his most loyal supporters.

On September 23, Maj. Caleb North returned to the camp at Jones's Tavern and reported the British Army's motions at Valley Forge to General Wayne. North's immediate superior, Lt. Col. Adam Hubley, wrote to his friends in Lancaster:

> I'm this Moment inform'd, the Enemy, have cross'd Schuylkil; That very little resistence was made by his Excellency. indeed, no Musketry was made use of at all. His Excellency, by Account, it seems, had his reason for suffering them to cross in this manner. We have no particulars respecting this matter yet, but dare say shall be able to let you know more about it.[1]

Later that evening, a thoroughly disgusted Gen. William Smallwood wrote to Governor Johnson from Jones's Tavern, detailing the Maryland militia's "march of folly," their disgraceful behavior at Paoli, and the "strange Infatuation" of the army's maneuvers:

Genl. Howe Yesterday Morning crossed the Schuylkill within two Miles of the left Flank of our Army without Opposition . . . it's said an Opposition was not intended. strange Infatuation: they seem to have nothing to do but push forward and of course we run away. It's to be lamented that human Nature is subject to so much Degeneracy but I will drop the subject; I can't think of it with patience.[2]

Col. Thomas Hartley wrote to Lancaster from "Camp Johnses Tavern Little Cannestogoe, Tuesday Eveng," with mixed feelings of loss, optimism, and determination:

These are the Fortunes of war; the little Checks we meet with tend to make the Survivors Soldiers and States Men; and God knows we want both Statesmen and Generals some times.—Our Worthy commander in Chief feels for his Country—he is sorry to loose an Inch of Ground. but the loss of Citys may some Times be the Salvation of States—

. . . last Year when we had no Army—we did not sink under our Calamities—we roused like Men—this I hope will again be the Case—Shallow Politicians and weake Constitutions have suffered us thus to be struck in the Vitals—better Days I doubt not will attend America. . . .

In our Division we are considerably weakened—but shall to Morrow march in Search of the enemy—push forward your [Lancaster militia] Force—and assist in expelling the Insolent Invaders from our Country.[3]

Anthony Wayne expressed his views on the state of affairs in a letter written September 29, after he rejoined the main army near Trappe. By that time, the simmering discontent among the division officers concerning Paoli had come to the surface, and tempers were running high. Wayne's anger and frustration with the turn of events, his injured pride, and his passion for the cause are evident in his letter:

I am not of the Cabinet—you can not therefore expect that I should be Acquainted with any of our Movements Previous to their taking place,—possibly all may be for the better—but I am so hurt by our Conduct of late—that I can't reflect one single moment without much pain.

Our Gross eaters, lion talkers, Lamb like fighters, (who say that the Province is not worth Defending) may hug themselves up in the Security of their Persons at the Sacrifice of the first City in America—but then will not some Other City in some Other State flourish,—there is Comfort for a Christian. . . .

I believe it will be found that Mr Howe passed the River almost in the face, & not out of View of our Grand Army—& that without the least Opposition. . . . I have now done with a Picture, over which I wish to draw a vail,—until our Arms produce one more lovely—which I don't in the least despair of—Provided our Great and good Genl. follows the Impulse of his own Judgment and Heart.[4]

In Washington's defense, Hubley later commented, "I dare say his Excellency is censur'd, by many, for his conduct in this matter. But wise Men—will suspend their Judgements. Time . . . will convince the World, he did it for the best." Maj. Samuel Shaw wrote, "Here, again, some blustering hero, in fighting his battles over a glass of madeira, may take upon him to arraign the conduct of our general, and stigmatize the army as cowards . . . [but] should we miscarry, posterity would execrate, and the world call us fools."[5]

The criticism did not come from military people only. John Adams, who had fled Philadelphia on September 19 along with most of Congress, had his own thoughts regarding Washington's decision making. From Trenton on September 21, writing in his diary about the man whom he had nominated as commander in chief, Adams confided:

It was a false alarm which occasioned our Flight from Philadelphia. Not a Soldier of Howes has crossed the Schuylkill. Washington has again crossed it, which I think is a very injudicious Maneuver. . . . By some Deception or other [Howe] will slip unhurt into the City. . . . Oh, Heaven! grant Us one great Soul! One leading Mind would extricate the best Cause, from that Ruin which seems to await it. . . . One active masterly Capacity would bring order out of this Confusion and save this Country.[6]

Mr. Adams proceeded the next day to Bethlehem along with some other Congressional refugees who were gradually making their way toward Lancaster, carefully staying wide of the contending armies. Adams's fellow delegate from Massachusetts, James Lovell, foolishly returned to Philadelphia. "My evil genius tempted me back into this Sodom after I had breakfasted yesterday morning with the other night fugitives at Bristol," he wrote in a letter. Lovell had left some personal belongings and also intended to meet some friends; instead, "to this vile place I returned, and in the last evening had my pocketbook stolen with 260 dollars" in the London Coffee House at Front and Market Streets. The Congressman concluded: "Be as favorable as you can about my want of care among pick-pockets. . . . I am plaguing myself and ruining my wife and children here."[7]

Nearly 40 miles west of the city, Wayne and Smallwood broke camp at Jones's Tavern on September 24 and began marching east toward Trappe to rejoin the main army. Col. Thomas Hartley went to Reading along with the wounded from the Paoli Battle. The next morning, Hartley had breakfast with John Adams and other congressmen. The conversation turned to recent events, as Adams noted:

> Rode this Morning to Reading, where We breakfasted, and heard for certain that Mr. Howes Army had crossed the Schuylkill. Coll. Hartley gave me an Account of the late Battle, between the Enemy and General Wayne. Hartley thinks that the place was improper for Battle, and that there ought to have been a Retreat.[8]

Henry Laurens of South Carolina later wrote, "At Reading I learned of General Wayne's false step, a second hindrance to our driving the Invaders out of the Country." Laurens's criticism was levelled not only at Wayne:

> Upon the whole the blunder of General Sullivan in the battle of Brandywine & the unpardonable negligence of General Wayne have reduced the American States to the present dilemma. If the former had been as Wise as he is allowed to be brave the latter would not have been disgraced by a Surprize when he ought to have been upon his Arms nor should we have heard any more of General Howe but his hurrying fragments of Regiments & Men on board his fleet.[9]

In the long term, Congress needed to get a more realistic picture of the Continental Army, its condition, and its capabilities. At that moment, it was better for their own well-being that the Congressmen steered clear of the two armies—especially their own.

Tensions were mounting among some of the Pennsylvania Line officers as the remainder of Wayne's command, together with Smallwood's and Gist's militia, moved through the hilly townships of northern Chester County toward Parker's Ford, 16 miles east of Jones's Tavern. The main Continental Army was at Camp Pottsgrove, strung out for miles on the rolling terrain of New Hanover and Pottsgrove Townships, with headquarters at the home of Frederick Antes. Around noon on September 25, Wayne and Smallwood arrived at Trappe, 6 miles below the main camp. Col. Richard Humpton later testified that it was on the march from Jones's Tavern where he first learned from Col. Benjamin Temple of Bland's Light Dragoons that Wayne had received warnings in advance of the Paoli attack, "which I scarcly could believe as I never before then had heard any thing of the Matter, on My Mentioning this, Major Nicolls of Col. Hartley's told Me that He had acquaintied the Genl. that a Picquet was Missing."[10]

Sometime between leaving Jones's Tavern and the morning of the 27th, a confrontation took place between Anthony Wayne and Richard Humpton, whom Wayne later referred to as "the prosecutor." Humpton was supported by a significant number of officers. Furious over having his judgment questioned, and feeling betrayed by a cabal of disloyal subordinates, Wayne fired off a letter to Washington, demanding an inquiry:

> I feel myself very much Injured until such time as you will be kind Enough to Indulge me with an Enquiry into my Conduct Concerning the Action of the night of the 20th Instant—
>
> Conscious of having done my duty I dare my Accusor's to a fair and Candid hearing—dark Insinuations and Insidius friends I dread—but from an Open and avowed enemy I have nothing to fear.
>
> I have no other mode of showing them forth to Open view, but through your means, I must therefore beg an Immediate Enquiry.[11]

One of the remarkable qualities of George Washington's leadership was his ability to maintain grace under pressure. He carried an enormous weight of responsibility at that moment: the discouraging loss of Philadelphia after an exhausting four weeks of maneuvering; criticism heaped on him from all quarters by legions of "experts"; a fatigued and footsore army, poorly fed, inadequately armed, and badly supported by an incompetent supply system; generals removed for a variety of reasons, leaving great gaps in the administrative structure; a local population largely indifferent to the cause. Then there was the burden of the human cost: hundreds of deaths from sickness and battle; thousands of wounded, maimed, and sick; desertions and sell-outs conspiring to destroy the army. Now Washington's most audacious and hot-tempered commander was embroiled in a serious internal leadership crisis with his subordinates, faced with a growing rift that threatened to finish what the British had started at Paoli.

Through his aide Tench Tilghman of Maryland, Washington responded to Wayne's letter immediately, which may have helped cool down the volatile Pennsylvanian:

His Excellency commands me to acknowledge Yours of this morning and to assure you that upon the first convenient opportunity you shall be gratified in your Request for an enquiry into your Conduct in the Affair of the 20:th~Genl. Sullivan is still waiting for an enquiry into his Conduct in some late Affairs and one Court may determine both Matters. If the Army lays still tomorrow the General says he will endeavour to have it done.[12]

The battle lines were drawn. Maj. Samuel Hay of the 7th Pennsylvania, whose regiment had suffered the brunt of the attack at Paoli, wrote to Col. William Irvine on September 29: "The officers of the division have protested against Gen Wayne's conduct, and lodged a complaint and requested a court martial, which his Excellency has promised they shall have. This has brought down his pride a little already."[13] As the larger events of the war played out, the army did not lie still the following day; Wayne would have to wait for his day in court.

On September 28, the Continental Army shifted camp to Pennibacker's Mill (present-day Pennypacker Mills) on the Skippack Road, about 30 miles northwest of Philadelphia. Over the next several days, Washington edged his army closer to the main British camp at Germantown, hoping to seize an opportunity to attack. By October 2, the stage was set for an all-out assault on the Crown Forces, which Howe had foolishly spread very thin. Wayne and his officers would have to vent their frustrations on the king's men; the Pennsylvania troops were only too happy to oblige.

The British light infantrymen on outpost duty at William Allen's house, Mount Airy, knew all too well that Wayne's troops were out for blood. From "Camp Near Beggars Town Octobr 2d 12 Midnight," Lt. Richard St. George of the 52nd Regiment Light Company, 2nd Light Infantry Battalion, referred to "the nocturnal bloody Scene" of Paoli when he wrote:

> They threaten retaliation, vow that they will give no quarter to any of our Battalion. We are always on the advanced Post of the army—our Present one is unpleasant. . . .
>
> There has been firing this Night all round the Centrys—which seems as if they endeavour to feel our situation—I am fatigued & must sleep—Coudst <u>Thou</u> sleep thus? . . . No more than I. . . . I wake once or twice. . . . My Ear is susceptible of the least Noise.[14]

The British Army intelligence network was still functioning splendidly, as St. George intimated: "Mr Washington by the accounts of some come in to day is Eighteen miles distant with his Main Body—they also say He intends to move nearer us to try the Event of another Battle." It would be an event that St. George would never forget.

CHAPTER 24

At the Battle of Germantown

Saturday, October 4, 1777

A t dawn on October 4, as a gray fog enveloped the streets of Philadelphia, the boom of distant cannon fire echoed through the city. On
the Germantown Road near the outskirts of the city, a blue-coated German officer on horseback heading for town heard the cannon shots at
about 5:30. He paused, glanced back in the direction of Germantown,
then spurred his horse on to a gallop toward Second Street. Capt.
Friedrich von Münchhausen of General Howe's staff was carrying a message that morning from Sir William Howe to Lord Cornwallis. He has-
tened to Cornwallis's headquarters on South Second Street, notified the
slumbering earl's aides of the gunfire, then rode back on the double toward
the growing rumble of battle.[1]

The first cannon shots that von Münchhausen heard were fired by two
Royal Artillery 6-pounders stationed at Mount Airy, Loyalist William Allen's
country mansion on the Germantown Road at Beggarstown. Located 2
miles north of the main British camp in Germantown, this picket post was
manned by sentries from the 2nd Battalion of British Light Infantry, commanded by Maj. John Maitland of the Royal Marines. The light infantry
camp 400 yards away on Mount Pleasant was posted so as to give the main
camp plenty of warning in case of a rebel attack. After several nights of
harassment by American patrols, the "day of wrath" finally arrived in earnest.

Continentals from the 6th Pennsylvania Regiment, part of Gen. Thomas
Conway's Brigade, advanced in the murky dawn up the Germantown Road
from Chestnut Hill and the Cresheim Valley. These Pennsylvanians were not
present at Paoli; nevertheless, they were eager to give the "Bloodhounds" a
payback for the "nocturnal bloody Scene." Their approach was a chilling
replay of the British advance at Paoli: With fixed bayonets and a troop of
Continental light dragoons armed with drawn sabers, Conway's troops qui-
etly approached the British pickets with the intention of surprising and
silencing them without firing a shot. Alert British light infantrymen spotted

their movement up the Germantown Road, however, and gave fire with their muskets; then the blasts of two Royal 6-pounders alerted the main camp and announced the attack all the way to Philadelphia.

In another eerie similarity to Paoli, the 2nd Battalion was encamped in "wigwams" in the fields on both sides of the Germantown Road at Mount Pleasant. Lt. Martin Hunter observed: "It was a very fortunate circumstance for us that we had changed our quarters two days before from the houses in Beggarstown to wigwams outside the town, for I am certain, had we been quartered in the town the morning we were attacked, we should all have been bayonetted." The light infantry men were well aware that they were singled out for the vengeance of the Pennsylvania troops. Their response to the attack was rapid: "On the first shots being fired at our piquet the battalion was out and under arms in a minute; so much had they in recollection Wayne's affair that many of them rushed out the back part of the huts." The sky lightened for a few minutes, only to darken again with cloud cover and ground fog. After firing a few volleys, the British pickets fell back to Mount Pleasant and rejoined the battalion, which "did not consist of more than three hundred and fifty men, and there was no support nearer than Germantown, a mile in our rear."[2] They steadied themselves with the cool confidence of elite veterans prepared to make a stand.

Conway's four Pennsylvania regiments led the American column on the Germantown Road. They fanned out on the road itself and behind the houses on the immediate right and left. Following Conway's Brigade was Gen. John Sullivan's Division of Maryland and Delaware troops, who moved to the right of the road and formed a battle front. Next came Wayne's two brigades, who quickly and eagerly deployed to the left of the high road. As Conway advanced in the center and Sullivan's force lumbered forward on the right, Wayne's troops on the left thrust ahead toward the light infantry with cold determination. The British "heard a loud cry of 'Have at the Bloodhounds! Revenge Wayne's affair!' accompanied by a volley." Lt. Martin Hunter saw his friend Richard St. George, who had saved him at Paoli, topple over as a musket ball smashed into his skull. The grievously wounded officer was carried off the field on the back of Corp. George Peacock.[3] The "Bloodhounds" returned the volley, let out a loud "*Huzza!*" and charged Conway's men with bayonets. The Americans fell back, re-formed, and counterattacked. The light infantry again charged and drove Conway back, only to discover that "two columns of the enemy had nearly got round our flanks." The 2nd Light Infantry Battalion "was so reduced by killed and wounded that the bugle was sounded to retreat; indeed, had we not retreated at the very time we did, we should all have been taken or killed."[4]

Wayne's Pennsylvanians were not taking prisoners; they descended on the British light infantry, intent on revenge. Wayne wrote, "Our People Remembering the Action of the Night of the 20th Sepr. near the Warren— pushed on with their Bayonets—and took Ample Vengeance for that Nights Work." He claimed that the Pennsylvania Line officers "Exerted themselves to save many of the Poor Wretches who were Crying for Mercy—but to little purpose." Wayne noted that "the Rage and fury of the Soldiers was not to be Restrained for some time—at least not until Great Numbers of the Enemy fell by our Bayonets."[5] The attack was so severe that the British light infantry lost all semblance of order, broke ranks, and ran for their lives.

Lt. Loftus Cliffe of the 46th Regiment was on picket duty near the light infantry when the attack began. He described the effects of Wayne's "Rage and fury" on the 2nd Battalion and on his own regiment:

> We were a good distance on the right of the light Infantry, moved towards them and see them quite broke, flying like Devils, we heard the word "Stop, Light Infantry, stop!" which made us wait expecting they would rally, when a Devil of a fire upon our front & flank came ding dong about us, we had but 60 men, could not cope, were obliged to fly, for the first time I ever saw the 46th turn, but alas it was not the last that Day. . . . [On] all sides of us was the hottest fire I ever heard.[6]

General Howe and his staff came riding up the Germantown Road and found the light infantry in headlong retreat. "Seeing the battalion all broke, he got into a great passion and exclaimed, 'For shame, Light Infantry! I never saw you retreat before. Form! Form! it is only a scouting party.'" As the American forces advanced into view, a round of grapeshot hit a chestnut tree near the British commander. Lieutenant Hunter gloated:

> I think I never saw people enjoy a discharge of grape before, but really all the officers of the 2nd Battalion appeared pleased to see the enemy make such an appearance, and to hear the grape rattle about the Commander-in-Chief's ears, after he had accused us of running away from a scouting party. He rode off immediately full speed.[7]

Captain von Münchhausen galloped the 5 miles from Philadelphia back
to Germantown. He rode toward the sound of the heaviest gunfire, "since I
knew that the General would always be where the firing was heaviest." He
rode through Germantown to the northern end of the village, where he
met Howe and the rest of the staff, "and was astounded to see something I
had never seen before, namely the English in full flight."[8]

One mile south of the 2nd Battalion's camp was Col. Thomas Musgrave's 40th Regiment of Foot, posted at the entrance of Germantown.
Howe had placed the 40th here specifically to support the light infantry
outposts in case of attack. The 40th's camp was located behind Chief Justice
Benjamin Chew's country house, Cliveden, a substantial gray stone mansion that had served as Musgrave's quarters. Musgrave "saw the light
infantry . . . falling back toward him, whereupon he detached half his regiment forward to support the retreating troops."[9] The fleeing light infantrymen notified the 40th that the Pennsylvanians were giving no quarter.
Upon being further informed that Wayne's troops were already in the 40th's
camp behind Chew's house and nearly had the regiment surrounded, Musgrave ordered the other half of his unit into Cliveden. About 100 to 120
British soldiers barricaded themselves inside and turned Cliveden's "massy
walls" into a formidable fortress. Wayne's and Conway's troops fired a few
vollies at the house, then moved beyond it to attack the main British camp
1 mile farther on.[10]

At this point, realizing what surrender would mean for them all, Musgrave told his troops:

> That their only safety was in the defence of that house; that if they
> let the enemy get into it, they would undoubtedly every man be
> put to death; that it would be an absurdity for any one to think of
> giving himself up, with hopes of quarters; that their situation was
> nevertheless by no means a bad one, as there had been instances of
> only a few men defending an house against numbers; that he had
> no doubt of their being supported and delivered by our army; but
> that at all events they must sell themselves as dear as possible to the
> enemy.[11]

The 40th held on for nearly two hours, through a severe artillery bom-
bardment, first from the front and then from both front and rear of the
house. Repeated infantry assaults were repulsed; attempts to burn the house

down were thwarted by the musket fire and bayonets of the British, who frustrated each rebel strategy to drive them from Cliveden by fire and sword. The "no quarter" behavior of the Pennsylvanians in the opening attack gave Musgrave's troops the resolve to stand firm against overwhelming odds.

The stubborn determination of the British to hold Cliveden at all costs created great confusion in the American lines. It caused troops to shift, countermarch, collide with, and fire at each other in the fog and smoke; it also prevented the Continental reserves from joining the attack on the main British camp. Finally, with ammunition spent and confusion in the fog conspiring to foil Washington's battle plan, the American attack suddenly fell apart, and the Continentals withdrew piecemeal into the battle haze. Musgrave was finally relieved at Cliveden by the 3rd British Brigade, commanded by Gen. Charles Grey, the officer who had led the attack on Wayne at Paoli.[12]

The Continental Army withdrew nearly 25 miles to Pennibacker's Mill (in present-day Schwenksville). Washington lost over 1,000 men killed, wounded, and missing in the three-hour battle at Germantown; British losses were half that number. Near Whitemarsh Church, Wayne's troops helped cover the army's withdrawal. Wayne described his role in these terms:

> Genl. Howe for a long time could not Pursuade himself that we had run from Victory—but the fogg clearing up he Ventered to follow us. . . . I, at this time was in the Rear and finding Mr Howe Determined to push us hard . . . we gave him a few Cannon Shot with some Musketry—which caused him to brake and Run with the Utmost Confusion—this ended the Action of that day.

Wayne's bravery in battle was always remarkable:

> My Roan Horse was killed under me within a few yards of the Enemies front and my left foot a little brused with one of their Cannon shot but not so much as to Prevent me from walking— my Poor horse Recevied one Musket Ball in the breast—and one in the flank at the same Instant that I had a Slight touch on my left hand—which is Scarcely worth Mentioning.[13]

In an already exhausting campaign, the Continental Army's march to and from Germantown set a record of physical endurance that few soldiers wished to repeat. The army began marching at 6 P.M. on October 3rd; the battle commenced at 5:30 A.M. and lasted until midmorning. Lt. James McMichael of the Pennsylvania State Regiment reported that he arrived at "Pennybecker's Mill" at 9 P.M. "I had previously undergone many fatigues, but never any that so much overdone me as this. . . . I had marched in twenty-four hours 45 miles, and in that time fought four hours, during which we advanced so furiously thro' buckwheat fields, that it was almost an unspeakable fatigue."[14]

The next day, in the General Orders, Washington made the following statement:

> The Commander in Chief returns his thanks, to the Generals and other officers and men concerned in yesterday's attack, on the enemy's left wing, for the spirit and bravery they manifested in driving the enemy from field to field. . . . The enemy are not proof against a vigorous attack, and may be put to flight when boldly pushed. This they will remember.[15]

Regarding the behavior of Wayne's troops at Germantown, Col. Adam Hubley of the 10th Pennsylvania wrote:

> Altho it may be, & indeed is call'd cruel by the Enemy, the Treatment they receiv'd from our Division, but Justice call'd for retaliation, and we paid in the same Coin that we received on the bloody Night, on which our Division was surpriz'd. I must confess, our people shew'd them No quarter and without distinguishon put their Bayonets, thro' all ye came across, at the same time reminding them of thier Inhumanity on that Night. It was a very remarkable Circumstance that the same troops, who engag'd us on that Night, also engag'd us in this Battle, so that our behavior to them is still more justifiable, in short as in our Division we neither give nor took quarters. And Our Division, with Genl. Sulivan & Conway, have the Generals public thanks, for this Manly behaviour.[16]

Although Germantown was an American defeat, Anthony Wayne, soon to face a very different battle, summed up his satisfaction with the performance of his troops by writing, "Upon the Whole it was a Glorious day."[17]

CHAPTER 25

Camp Towamencin and Camp Whitpain

October 1777

The smoke from the Battle of Germantown had barely dissipated when preparations began for the inquiry into Wayne's conduct at Paoli. The army rested at Pennibacker's Mill until October 9, when they moved down the Skippack Road and established camp along Skippack Creek in Towamencin and Skippack Townships. That same day, Washington lost yet another general officer, Brig. Gen. Francis Nash of North Carolina, who had been critically wounded by a cannonball at Germantown. On October 10, Nash was interred with full military honors in the Mennonite burial ground at 10 A.M. At high noon the same day a convicted deserter, John Farndon of Hartley's Additional Regiment, was hanged until sunset from a gallows "erected for that purpose at the artillery park." Camp scuttlebutt had it that "he deserted from our Army to the enemy, and piloted some of the bloody Highlanders in the Night to Genl. Waines's Brigade."[1]

The next morning, Anthony Wayne sent General Washington the following information:

> The Charge exhibited against me is—"that I had timely notice of the Enemies Intention to Attack the troops under my Command on the Night of the 20th Ulto. and notwithstanding that Intelligence I neglected making a Disposition until it was too late either to annoy the Enemy, or make a Retreat without the utmost Danger and Confusion."
>
> I must Request your Excellency to Order the Officers Concerned in Support of this Charge to Attend with their Evidences— at the time and place— where you'l please to Order the Court of Enquiry to sit—which I beg may be the soonest Possible.[2]

Washington wasted no time; that same day, October 11, the notice for Wayne's Court of Inquiry went out from "Head-Quarters, Toamensing":

> The Court of Inquiry, of which Lord Stirling is President, [along with General McDougall, General Knox, Colonel Spencer, and Colonel Clark,] now sitting at the President's quarters, is to inquire into the conduct of Brigadier-General Wayne. . . . The President will give notice when the Court can enter on the inquiry, and when the parties and evidence are to attend.[3]

Lord Stirling's quarters were at the "House of Houfer."[4] The court was held October 13 and 14. The evidence given at the inquiry provides the most important and detailed eyewitness descriptions of what actually happened at Paoli.

A total of sixteen Pennsylvania Line officers testified at the inquiry. On the first day, seven officers gave their evidence; five were cross-examined by Wayne and two were questioned by McDougall. The second day, nine officers gave testimony, of which four were cross-examined by Wayne and five were questioned by Stirling. Of all the officers who testified, only four, Humpton, Hay, Huffnagle, and Ross, made specific statements censuring Wayne's conduct, with one more, Mentges, appearing hostile to Wayne. The other officers gave straightforward statements detailing what they recalled of the night. Some of these statements were lengthy; others were barely more than a few brief sentences. These eleven statements neither praised nor condemned Wayne, but rather dispassionately submitted the facts of the case.[5]

Wayne mainly focused his cross-examination on the time elapsed from when the men were first ordered to form up and then wheeled and on how long they stood in column without moving. He also quizzed the officers on the dispositions of regiments made to cover the retreat. Three of the officers were asked by McDougall and Stirling how far the British camp was from Wayne's camp; they cited varying distances ranging from 1½ to 3 miles.[6] Finally, nine of the officers addressed the issue concerning the missing picket reported by Brigade Major Nichols and Wayne's behavior towards the major. Five, including Nichols, had known about the picket situation before the battle; all but one, Col. William Butler, were from the 1st Brigade. It was Butler's regiment that had provided the picket in question. In his cross-examination, Wayne specifically asked Nichols where the picket was located, and then asked him point-blank, "Do you know whether that picket was taken off by the enemy?" Nichols responded, "They were not."[7] Wayne provided the court with a map detailing the location of the pickets, the main roads in the area, and the position of his camp relative to the British camp.

On October 15 at 10 A.M., having heard the testimony of all the officers concerned,

> The Court met according to adjournment and proceeded, to the Consideration of the Evidence before them~They then formed their opinion, which they desired their president to deliver to the Commander in Chief, a Copy of which Signed by the members, is to be Lodged with the evidences, in the Custody of the Adjutant General.[8]

Regrettably, vigorous research has yet to locate the written opinion of this court, in Washington's Papers, Adj. Gen. Timothy Pickering's Papers, or elsewhere. This is truly unfortunate, as it would provide a vital missing piece to the story of Wayne's trial. Though the inquiry's exact finding remains unknown, whatever was written did not vindicate Wayne's conduct to his satisfaction, and its effect on the hot-tempered Pennsylvanian was evidenced by the vitriolic blast with which he condemned the proceedings.

Even before Wayne knew the inquiry's official finding, he believed that the court's officers had paid little attention to his version of the events, as evidenced in his letter to Washington on October 17:

> Altho' I am Confident that your time is Necessarily taken up on the most Important buisness—yet my own Honor and Character Induces me to Request your Perusal of the enclosed Defense . . . however the Gentlemen who Composed the Court of Enquiry may have Determined—yet so Consious am I of having done my Duty—that I am very Desirous of having my Conduct brought to the Decision of a Genl. Court Martial if the lest doubt Remains on your Excellencies mind with Reguard to it.
>
> I don't know what the Opinion of the Court was—nor have I any Copy of the Evidences—or my own Defence—excepting this which I beg may be Return'd.[9]

The Continental Army suffered from a shortage of just about every necessity in that period, including paper. Some of the letters of Col.

Thomas Hartley and Col. Adam Hubley were written on scrap paper, and many of the muster rolls and payrolls were cramped onto pathetically small pieces of paper. This may explain why Wayne at that time had only one copy of his defense and asked Washington to return it.

After learning the findings of the Court of Inquiry, Wayne fired off a long and bitter letter to Washington on October 22, in which he detailed what he saw as flaws in the testimony and in members of the court:

> I must Acknowledge that the Opinion of the Court of Enquiry has given me both pain and Surprise—Surprise to find Gent'n go on the most ["false and" was crossed out here] Erroneous ground in two facts from which they seem to found their Opinion i.e. with Reguard to the Distance [of the British Camp], and the Carrying off of one of the Piquets—
>
> the Distance between the nearest part of the Enemy's Camp and where I lay was near 4 miles [which] was greater than from their Camp to the fat Land ford and Richardson ford on Schuylkil being the very fords at which Genl. Howe's Army passed—Consequently had I been farther Distant it would have put it out of my Power to Comply with your Excellencies Orders—i.e. to harass their Rear but this the Court seem to have lost sight of and may have mistaken the Distance.

Thus far, Wayne maintained restraint in his evaluation of the evidence. His anger and suspicions that a conspiracy to discredit him was at work first revealed themselves in his refutation of the "missing picket" report:

> but With Regard to the Piquet I am almost tempted to believe it could not Altogether be a Mistake—Sir it is notorious that that Piquet was not Carried off at all. . . . A Light Horse man who I instantly sent to the place where it was posted Returned and told me that he had seen it and all was well—when M[ajor] Nichols came back with Col. Butlers answer—I did tell him with some Degree of anger to go to bed—for having ["told me a falsehood" was crossed out here] made a Mistake—
>
> this Circumstance I literally Related to the Court—I find they paid no Credit to my Assertion—however the Officer of that Piquet will be able to set this Matter in a Clear point of view.

Unfortunately, the testimony of the officer of Picket 1 has not been located, if indeed it was recorded; his identity remains unknown. Wayne continued to berate the proceedings:

> they have also (when very Manute [minute] for Other Circum-
> stances) forgot to mention one Or two Reasons for my taking and
> Remaining in that Position [Smallwood's anticipated arrival and
> the British march to the Schuylkill]. . . . However they Perhaps
> did not think Proper to pay any Reguard to any Assertion of
> mine—yet they might have given some Credit to Genl Small-
> woods own Letter . . . [and] the Enemies Actually Marching—
>   they Effect to give me some Credit for taking off the artillery
> and for <u>Attempting</u> to Rally the Troops <u>after being Routed</u>—they
> don't say that the Artillery was on the right when the Attack was
> actually made . . . they don't say that I remained with the troops
> on the right which were posted . . . nor do they say that I actually
> did Rally a body of the Troops and Remained with them on the
> Ground for a full hour which effectually Covered the Retreat of
> the Greatest part of the Division And of all the Artillery.

At this point in the letter, though not in his defense testimony, Wayne made a passing reference to the ultimate cause of the delay that resulted in the blocking of the column's evacuation route, the immediate "mechanical" reason for the disaster at Paoli: "altho one of the [artillery] Pecies met with Misfortune near the field of action which Impeded us a Considerable time."

In his defense testimony, Wayne attributed the delay to "some Neglect or Misapprehension in Col Humpton (which is not uncommon)." He stated a second time in his testimony, "the Neglect or Misapprehension of Col. Humpton, had Detained the Division too long." But Humpton was not the immediate target of Wayne's venom in this letter to Washington, but rather someone on the Court of Inquiry—Lord Sterling, who had lost three guns at the Battle of Short Hills in June and several pieces at Brandy-wine in September.

> These Circumstances and facts were in full proof before them—
> [crossed out: "but they forgot to mention them—Indeed they
> have"] but perhaps they did not think them worth mentioning—
> they were not of the Criminal kind [crossed out: "unless it be a

crime to make a disposition and Cover a retreat in the face of
every Difficulty and Danger—whilst an other Gentleman Officer
in open day light and Almost on every Occation has given up his
Artillery besides expressing something bordering on A Surprise."]

The letter closed with an appeal to Washington's sense of honor and a
request for a full court-martial.

After this State of facts which I pledge my Honor as a Soldier and
a Gentleman to give full and Ample proof of, I appeal to Your
Excellencis own feelings whether I can be easy under so severe
and unjust a Charge—I must therefore beg An Immediate tryal by
a Genl Court Martial—["or an Officers Court of Enquiry" was
crossed out here] Your Compliance will much Oblige your Excel-
lancies Most Obedient and very Humble Servant.[10]

Washington faced a very serious management crisis at this moment.
Since early summer, his Continental command structure was deprived of five
generals for one reason or another: Arthur St. Clair, Benjamin Lincoln,
William Smallwood, Prudhomme DeBorre, and Francis Nash.[11] Two others,
Adam Stephen and John Sullivan, were faced with impending inquiries. Sullivan was actually facing two inquiries; his recall after Brandywine was stopped
only by Washington's pleading with Congress not to remove the only remaining general in that division.[12] Now his most bellicose, active field commander, stung by the Paoli defeat, the criticism from some of his own officers,
and the inquiry's finding, was asking Washington for a general court-martial.

The court-martial of Brig. Gen. Anthony Wayne was held three days
after this letter was written. Five generals, five colonels, and three lieutenant colonels sat on the court, with Gen. John Sullivan as president.[13]
The proceedings were held in the president's quarters at the "Camp near
Whitemarsh" (Camp Whitpain, now Ambler) on October 25, 26, 27, and
30. The weather appropriately reflected the mood of the moment: the first
grim day of clouds, fog, and drizzle was followed by two dark, violent days
of howling wind and relentless rain that intensified as a slow-moving
"Nor'easter" engulfed the region. By the 27th, a waterlogged Royal Engineer captain, John Montrésor, wrote from the flooded British batteries near
Fort Mifflin, "At Night a mere Tempest;" he could easily have been describing what was transpiring at Wayne's Court Martial.[14]

Intensive research has located Wayne's defense testimony, written in two full versions, with fragments of a third surviving; regrettably, the full official records of this court-martial have yet to be found. Inexplicably, no other information about this trial, even in oblique references or passing comments, has been located in the papers of the court officers.[15] A document labeled "To the Printers 2nd Novr. 1777 Determination of a Genl Court Martial" contains several rough drafts of Wayne's testimony. The writings contain the same level of vituperative commentary found in the letter condemning the inquiry. The first paragraph here was later edited:

["The action of the Night of the 20th Sepr. near the Warren—has been variously and very Erroneously Represented—and the Conduct of Genl Wayne [words illegible] placed in a very unfavorable point of view by men equally Devoid of P[——] as they are of truth and Bravery/Honor. . . . But after the Expiration of five Weeks (during which period the tongue of Slander was not Idle). . . ."]

the Action of that Night has caused much Speculation—the tongue of Slander has not been Idle—But however Sanguine some Gentlemen were in their Attempt to Detract from the Merits of the Genl. and Worthy Officers and Soldiers of his Division (who with unparalleled Bravery stood the bayonet of the Enemy—saved all the Artillery and Effected an honorable Retreat) In the face of Every Dificolty and Danger) they find themselves Egrideously Deceved in Pressing a Charge which could Proceed but from the Worst of Motives and the Worst of Hearts.

Taking any criticism of his judgment as a malevolent personal conspiracy against him, Wayne continued his defense with an indirect indictment of the Court of Inquiry: "I am happy Enough to bring my case before a Court of Whose Honor and Impartial Judgment I can not have the least doubt."

The defense testimony proceeded with a detailed description of events as Wayne saw them. In response to the charge that he had received timely notice of the enemy's intention to attack, Wayne cited the information given him by "old Mr. Jones" between 8 and 10 P.M., which he quickly discounted with the statement, "this could not be deemed a Sufficient Notice upon any Military Principle." Taken at face value, Wayne was absolutely right: Information from an elderly civilian who heard it at a tavern from a servant who overheard British soldiers talking about it is certainly questionable, even though Wayne knew both the servant and the old man personally. Curiously, Wayne had immediately sent out additional horse patrols in response to this "insufficient" warning. Wayne failed, however, to mention the warning given by Col. John Bartholomew, the local militia officer who had supper with him before 6 P.M. and who gave warning of an impending attack. Bartholomew's credentials were impeccable. Two officers, Thomas Hartley and Morgan Connor, witnessed this at supper, and Hartley wrote about it at 6 P.M. Bartholomew's warning could be deemed more than sufficient notice by sheer prudence.

After citing all of the precautions taken and how he had ordered the men to form up on parade, Wayne stated, "This Gentlemen don't look like a Surprise—it rather proves that we were Prepared either to move off or Act Occationally." He explained that he had given the orders for retreat and that he had personally moved the 1st Pennsylvania and the light infantry off to the right and formed them in the strip of woods, with the light infantry advanced 300 yards; this was done to buy time for an orderly evacuation. Wayne himself and all the light dragoons in camp were present on the right as the British advanced. He emphasized, "If this was making no Disposition—I acknowledge I know not what a Disposition is." In describing Humpton's failure to carry out his orders, Wayne observed, "Here I have a fair field for Recrimination were I so Disposed—I shall wave the Subject and beg leave to Read the Orders which I rec[eived] from his Excellency from time to time."

Having thus laid out the particulars of the situation as he saw them and the orders from Washington, Wayne made his plea to the court:

> In the eyes of Gentlemen and of Officers I trust I stand Justified for the part I took that Evening . . . let me put a Question—Suppose after all these Repeated Orders from His Excellency—and the Arrival of Genl Smallwood I had Retreated before I knew whether the enemy Intended to Attack me or not . . . would not these very Gentlemen have been the first to default me—would not His Excellency with the Greatest Justice have Order'd me into Arrest for Cowardice and Disobedience of his Repeated Peremptory and Pointed Orders—would I not have stood Culpable in the eyes of the World—would I not Justly merit either immediate Death or Cashiering—I Certainly would—what line could I follow but that one that I did? what more could be done on the Occation than what was done?

I hold it needless to say more on the Occasion—I rest my Honor & Character—which to me is more Dear than life—in the Hands of Gentlemen—who when Deciding on my Honor will not forget their own.

The verdict of the court-martial was rendered on November 1, 1777:

The Court, having fully considered the charge . . . are <u>unanimously</u> of opinion that General Wayne is not guilty of the charge exhibited against him, but that he on the night of the 20th ultimo did everything that could be expected from an <u>active, brave and vigilant officer,</u> with the orders which he then had. The Court do acquit him with the highest honor. The Commander in Chief approves the sentence.[16]

Thus on November 1, 1777, did the official military record close on "Wayne's Affair." Wayne was vindicated; later that day, perusing his papers, he came across a letter he had written September 29. The note was filled with frustration about Howe crossing the Schuylkill and anger over the loss of Philadelphia. Having just finished the trial of his career, he added a note at the bottom that indicated his exhaustion: "I am too much out of Order to say more."[17]

A week after the court handed down its decision, Col. Daniel Brodhead of the 8th Pennsylvania Regiment wrote to the division commander, Maj. Gen. Benjamin Lincoln:

I have long Wished to write you. . . . Yet through the Alternate want of Pen, ink, Paper & Convenience, I confess this is the first Letter I wrote you. . . . Since you left us your Division has suffered greatly and that chiefly by the Conduct of Gl.—W. Most of the officers are unhappy under his Command and as to my own part I have had very little satisfaction since the Command devolved on him.[18]

Wayne and his officers had to move on, as the more immediate and much larger problems of maintaining the war effort demanded their attention. Private feelings and personal grudges needed to be put aside for the sake of the public service. Brodhead wistfully closed his letter to Lincoln: "The officers of your Division will be exceedingly rejoiced to hear from you. . . ."

CHAPTER 26

Chester County, Pennsylvania

1777–1817

The Battle of Paoli has been described by various names. "Last night's affair" was the first recorded name, Anthony Wayne calling it that in his letter to Washington the following morning. Lieutenant Martin Hunter recorded that rebel troops shouted "Revenge Wayne's Affair!" at Germantown. The most famous and enduring name has been the Paoli Massacre, since it occurred less than 2 miles from the Paoli Tavern, a well-known landmark. Lieutenant St. George was the first to use the word *massacre* in association with the engagement. When describing the attack on the pickets, he said, "We . . . received a smart fire from another unfortunate Picquet—as the first instantly massacred." Yet, as many reliable historians have been careful to point out, it was not a massacre in the strict sense of a large-scale indiscriminate slaughter. While atrocities were indeed committed, most of Wayne's force escaped unharmed. Sir George Osborn made reference to "the affair of Peoli," and Congressman Henry Laurens described it as "General Wayne's false step." Other names abound: Capt. John André's map is titled "Surprize of a Rebel Corps in the Great Valley." William Faden's engraved map labels it "The Attack made by Major General Grey against the Rebels near White Horse Tavern." In his testimony, Capt. George Ross called it "the Action at the Warren." Capt. John McGowan, in writing a certificate of disability for Pvt. George English, termed it "The Payola Batle or Sticking Night."

Although they did not participate in the battle, several Hessian officers wrote reports about Paoli to their superiors. Maj. Karl Baurmeister wrote that Grey's troops "attacked their right wing with the bayonet. His men deployed so fast that they massacred it." Baurmeister further noted that "many threw away their muskets. . . . In the daytime General Howe sent troops of dragoons to the place . . . with orders to destroy all the enemy's abandoned muskets—which numbered about one thousand."[1] While this number is probably exaggerated, it indicates that a great quantity of muskets were left behind. Many of these were dropped by Maryland militiamen, whom Smallwood reported as "daily losing their muskets." In addition, hundreds of shoes, blankets, knapsacks, canteens, cartridge boxes, hats, and all types of clothing littered the field; Congressman Samuel Chase of Maryland wrote, "About 500 of Genl. Waynes Division lost their [shoes] & their Blankets in the late shameful Surprise. . . . Our Militia behaved very ill, many of them were run quite off with[out] their Arms."[2] Local civilians went out the next day to help gather and bury the dead, and tend to the wounded who were left for dead and take them away for medical attention. No doubt most of the equipment and clothing was picked up over the next few days by local people and disposed of, utilized, or stored. On November 3, Gen. John Armstrong of the Pennsylvania militia issued the following order:

> Captain David Denny [Colonel Gilen's Battalion] is hereby Authorized to take with him as many of the Militia of Chester County, or others as he Shall think Convenient, and proceed to [Brandywine Battlefield] and also to the place & neighbourhood where General Wayne was lately attacked in the night—At each of these places . . . Captain Denny will make diligent Search for, and Collect . . . all such publick Stores, Arms, Acoutrements, Kettles, Salt, Blankets—Hydes, Axes &c. &c. As have been left by either Armies. . . .
>
> Such of the inhabitants as have taken care of and without reserve shall readily yield up to the said Captain Denny . . . and shall acquaint him where any such publick Stores are held or Secreted, he will pay at a reasonable rate for their Service—And Such as Shall be found defrauding the publick by Secreting, imbezelling or converting to their Own private use or emolument any of the publick Stores whatever may expect to be considered as enemies to their Country and treated accordingly.[3]

The "52 brave fellows" who were "bury'd . . . next day in the field of Battle" were gathered in a central location on the Bowen-Pearce property line, the scene of some of the fiercest fighting, and interred in a trench about 12 by 60 feet. The soldiers were placed in two rows of twenty-six.[4] "While they were engaged in the act of burying the dead a number of

British officers rode up and viewed the grounds, but did not interfere with them."[5] The burial was done with great care, as afterward noted:

> The very visible marks of attention . . . bestowed on [the burial] by a few . . . fellow citizens. . . . The grave has been dug north and south, and the bodies regularly laid east and west. The hats, shoes, clothing and armor [accoutrements] of the gallant, though unfortunate wearers, have been consigned to the grave with them.[6]

The mound created by the interment was marked some time after with a heap of stones. The Paoli battlefield quickly returned to its former peacetime use as farm fields.

Maj. Gen. Anthony Wayne, hero of the Revolution and of the Northwest Territory, died in December 1796, before he could return home to Waynesborough. He was buried at Fort Presque Isle (present-day Erie), hundreds of miles from Paoli. Having committed his life to the service of his country, and suffering from numerous ailments, wounds, and injuries acquired in that service, the fiery Patriot characteristically requested, "Bury me on the hill, at the foot of the flagpole."[7]

On July 4, 1817, as Revolutionary War veteran James Monroe prepared to move into the newly rebuilt White House, burned by the British in 1814, another generation of veterans, who had clashed with the "old foe" during the War of 1812, met and resolved to take responsibility for a neglected gravesite in Chester County. This grave was located on the line between the former Bowen farm (owned by the Griffith family since 1804) and the Pearce family farm, the boyhood home of Col. Cromwell Pearce, the heroic commander of the 16th U.S. Infantry Regiment in the War of 1812. Pearce was five years old when the Paoli Battle took place; now back in Chester County after the war, he was elected high sheriff in 1816. Another distinguished comrade-in-arms, twenty-six-year-old Maj. Isaac Barnard of the 14th U.S. Infantry, was a newly minted West Chester lawyer who became sheriff's counsel and deputy district attorney.[8] Together with former district Congressman and militia surgeon William Darlington, the veterans mobilized Barnard's local militia unit, the Republican Artillerists, and began a movement to mark and preserve the grave of the Paoli soldiers.

The artillerists passed resolutions on July 4 and wasted no time organizing the effort, for they wanted to dedicate the memorial on September 20, the 40th anniversary of the battle. They consulted with local Revolutionary veterans to get their views on how the grave should be marked; the veterans approved the placing of a marble monument similiar to the monument over Anthony Wayne's remains at St. David's Church.[9] Within a month, preparations were well under way.

In early August, Isaac Barnard was in Philadelphia searching for a monument. Funds were short, but Barnard was determined to do the best he could with what was available. He located a simple classical monument of white marble, consisting of a pyramid mounted on a pedestal, resting on a plinth of Pennsylvania blue marble. Barnard asked a stone merchant, Richard North, to inquire about it for him. North replied on August 16:

> I have recd your favour . . . respecting the Marble Monument you saw when in this City. I have agreeably to your request made enquiry as to price and find the person will not take less than $175 as it now stands.
>
> The Cap I think can be repair'd but it must have a new Bace, The Die or sollid part must also have some repairs, which altogether I think would cost from 30 to 35 Dollars—the Bottom plinth is about 3 feet square and the person who owns it says a foot thick, but it is sunk in the Ground[;] the Die about 3ft 11 high and 1ft 8In square, so that the whole higth will be about 8.ft 4 or 5In—The wieght altogether I think will be about 36 or 37 hundred Gross—
>
> If you wish to take in the whole expence you should alow for Boxes as it would be unsafe to take it in a waggon without. The Letters or Inscription would be 3 Cents a Letter & half price for Blacking which together would be 4.5 Cents each Letter.—The Boxes will cost about 8 Dollars—I have now given you the particulars as near as I possibly can.[10]

The monument was "finished under the direction of the celebrated [William] Strickland," the prominent neoclassical and Greek Revival architect of Philadelphia.[11] In addition to Barnard, Darlington, and Pearce, a work party including Isaac Wayne, son of Anthony Wayne, and Gen.

William Brooke of the Pennsylvania militia, along with "a few respectable citizens of the neighborhood," rolled up their sleeves to prepare the site:

> They proceeded to dig the foundation for the monument, and soon discovered that for the better security of the superstructure it would be advisable to disinter that portion of the relics of the patriotic soldiers which occupied the dimensions of the foundation. . . . . The principal parts of the bones of four bodies were raised, and a repository being formed in the center of the foundation, they were again carefully committed to the earth.[12]

A group effort was required to complete the work in time for September 20, so the Republican Artillerists pitched in and finished a stone and lime wall enclosure 65 feet long, 20 feet wide, and about 4 feet high, with a gate in the middle of the western wall.[13]

The dedication ceremonies were held on September 20, 1817. At 10 A.M. at Paoli Tavern, the Republican Artillerists mustered over 400 soldiers from several local militia regiments. The troops paraded in uniforms resplendent with row upon row of braid and buttons, whitened crossbelts, and glittering breastplates, their heads topped by tall, black shakoes of felt and polished leather profusely decorated with gleaming badges, tasseled cords, plumes, and pom-poms.[14] Revolutionary veterans, who were specially invited to attend the proceedings, must have been impressed by the current military fashions as they recalled the sorry assortment of mufti with which they had had to make do so often. At 11 A.M. the troops moved out in a solemn military procession and headed west over the Lancaster Turnpike. Some of the old soldiers marched in the procession, which moved past the site of Picket 1 and down the hill to the Warren Pass, where Randolph's Picket 4 had received the first shock of battle and where the first blood had been shed. They proceeded past the blacksmith shop, whose proprietor had been forced to show the British the way to camp, and halted at the Warren Tavern, where the British column had stopped to gather information on the whereabouts of Wayne's position. At 1 P.M., the march moved on to Sugartown Road, the route a Continental vidette had taken with the first warning of the British advance. The line of soldiers advanced up the long hill, turned left near the spot where a disabled cannon had blocked Wayne's escape route, and marched on to the gravesite, scene of the battle's heaviest fighting.

As the procession entered the field, the music played "The Dead March in Saul." The local press said there was a great crowd. "The very trees were animated by the adventurous boys, who had ascended them to witness the ceremonies. The old were there, telling the young 'the tales of other times.'" At the monument, "upon the top of a lofty oak, waved the American flag."[15] The guests of honor included Isaac Wayne, the general's son, and the eighty-two-year-old Reverend David Jones, former chaplain of Wayne's 1st Pennsylvania Brigade. Jones had served with Wayne during much of the Revolution and was a survivor of the Battle of Paoli. He had also served in the Northwest Campaign of the 1790s and volunteered as a chaplain during the War of 1812 at age seventy-seven.[16] A fellow 1812 veteran, twenty-six-year-old Maj. Isaac Barnard, delivered the formal address at the dedication:

A Period of forty years is this day compleated since a number of our brave Countrymen fell a sacrifice near this spot in the cause of American Independence. The soil which was consecrated by the remains of these warriors has lain neglected & exposed without a single stone to indicate to the passing traveller where slept the champions of our Country's freedom. In a few short years the place of their interment would have been involved in doubt & uncertainty[;] fruitless would have been the zeal of the patriots who might have sought at a future day to designate the ground which wraps the followers of the gallant Wayne.

Barnard then gave a brief but animated account of the general circumstances of the war and the battle itself, and condemned "the indiscriminate and dreadful Carnage . . . which will forever stain the character of the British arms and consign to eternal infamy the name of Grey and his Midnight assassins." He called to mind those who were "wantonly butchered" in "this atrocious slaughter," now formally called the Massacre of the Paoli. Then Major Barnard reminded his listeners why they were there:

These men who fell far from their homes and their friends were deposited in one Common grave in this retired & sequestered spot and here we raise this Monument as a standing record of our gratitude for their services & respect for their Memories—to honor those who have nobly fallen to obtain the liberty and blessings which we now enjoy is a high and sacred duty—and to perform this duty we have now assembled and it is a source of delightful pleasure to see present on this occasion so numerous & so respectable a body of our fellow Citizens[.] This pleasure is greatly heightened by viewing among the number so many of the surviving Patriots of the Revolution who shared in the Sufferings of their fallen Companions.

In the presence then of this united assemblage we will now Compleat the monument to departed worth.[17]

At this point, the Monument Committee performed the official act of completion, "adjusting the pyramid which crowns the monument." The pedestal was inscribed on all four sides with words composed by Dr. William Darlington. The front inscription on the west side reads: "Sacred to the Memory of *the Patriots* who on this Spot fell a Sacrifice to *British Barbarity* during the Struggle for *American Independence* on the Night of the *20th of September 1777.*"

Once the pyramid was in place, Reverend Jones rose to speak, assisted up to the rostrum by Major Barnard and J. Pearce, Esq. The elderly pastor was "a tall, soldierly looking figure," though, in contrast to the braided, high-collared coatees and plumage of the military, "he always wore the cue, the cockade hat, the breeches, the knee-and-shoe buckles; in short, the dress of a gentleman of 'ye olden time.'"[18] Jones spoke eloquently, giving an eyewitness account of the battle and relating his own experiences of that night. Unfortunately, his words have not survived. Following his remarks, the troops fired a few vollies, after which the Republican Artillerists fired a twenty-gun salute with their "elegant brass field piece" to honor those who fell at Paoli.[19] With the thunder of the cannon echoing through the woods, the ceremonies concluded.

After the crowd dispersed and the troops marched away, only a grass-covered mound and a gleaming white marble monument, protected by a whitewashed stone wall, remained to indicate "where slept the champions of our Country's freedom" who fell at Paoli in 1777.

Epilogue

Dramatic events often take on a life of their own and lose nothing in the telling except the truth. Many early-nineteenth-century authors produced flowery, romantic accounts of the Revolution, frequently taking great liberties with historical facts to create popular lore. Later in the century, numerous Victorian-era historians produced weighty tomes of authoritative verbiage, reinforced with carefully selected quotations from old writings; often these works were lavishly bound and enhanced with imaginative illustrations. Victorian history writing was much like Victorian architectural remodeling: filled with additions, embellishments, improvements, and corrections. Often a core of facts provided the basis for flights of fancy and imagination.

As the country grew, and as powered printing presses and inexpensive paper revolutionized the spread of information, the demand increased for popular literature that highlighted heroism, betrayal, glory, shame, or national pride. Much of this work was quoted repeatedly by writers well into the twentieth century, even though little of the information was documented. Thus interpretations for generations to come were based on the creative imaginings of this era, the fact that the material appeared in print seemingly giving it authenticity.

Fortunately, some nineteenth-century historians, though sometimes dismissed as "mere antiquarians" by their peers, reacted to the general trends of Romanticism and Victorianism by collecting and publishing the primary materials for the sake of their historical value and for scholarship. Their efforts saved countless papers from loss and made them available for future study, though not always without prejudice. These history writers sometimes edited or "laundered" the papers, particularly those that were less than flattering to popular heroes. Because of all this, it can be difficult to sort out fact from fiction.

Lafayette's visit to America in 1824 sparked an immense interest in the Revolution, which was sustained by the Semicentennial of 1826. Renewed national awareness of the veterans from the War for Independence was awakened by the realization that the starry-eyed French teenager whom Washington had treated like a son was now a dignified, elderly man in his late sixties. Everywhere he went as "The Nation's Guest," Lafayette was greeted with celebrations, receptions, brass bands, and long-winded dignitaries. Amid the crowds were wrinkled, weathered faces that lit up in his presence; eyewitnesses noted Lafayette's animated reaction when encountering his old comrades-in-arms. He made a point of meeting as many of them as possible, and when circumstances permitted, he reminisced with them about their shared experiences. Lafayette wrote, "I have found more old soldiers of the Revolution than I had expected, and it has been sweet to see what memories I had left in their hearts."[1] As the fiftieth anniversary of the war approached, some of the aging survivors of the Revolution began to write down their experiences or publish their personal papers.

In 1832, Congress passed the comprehensive Veterans' Pension Act for all Revolutionary War veterans and their widows, with some restrictions. To prove their eligibility, if they could not produce discharge papers, applicants were required to provide a narrative of their services. By the 1840s, most of the Revolutionary generation was gone or in its last decade. Pennsylvania, which had provided an estimated 15,000 soldiers during the Revolution, listed less than 1,500 pensioners in the census of 1840; their median age was close to eighty. As they passed on, much of their history passed with them; their personal papers sometimes were lost or destroyed shortly after their death, as was the case with some of the people involved at Paoli. Pension applications that contain narratives of common soldiers' services are frequently the only records of their experiences. As historian John Dann wrote in his groundbreaking book, *The Revolution Remembered,* "The military pension records, now kept at the National Archives, contain some of the most valuable, yet least explored, sources for studying the American Revolution."[2]

The historiography, or history of the history writing, of the Battle of Paoli is a melange of fact, fiction, gothic horror, and legend. The battle's unusual circumstances provided much fertile ground for fertile imaginations, resulting in numerous colorful accounts that have little or no basis in fact. One early source describes a bloodthirsty Hessian sergeant bayoneting hapless barefoot rebels "like so many pigs" until blood ran out the touch-hole of his musket.[3] There is no evidence of Hessian involvement at Paoli, however, even in the detailed reports of Hessian officers who recorded the most minuscule patrols and minor skirmishes involving their men, yet this account has been repeated ever since its publication in the 1850s. Many versions of the Paoli Massacre incorrectly state that because it was referred to as a "surprise," Wayne's troops, including the sentries, were asleep when the British entered the camp, and the redcoats (and/or Hessians) sprang on them suddenly, stabbing them into their final slumber. These inaccuracies have been parroted time and again, even in the face of published primary accounts from both sides that indicate otherwise.

Anthony Wayne himself has been a favorite topic of Paoli legends, sometimes in blind defense of the hero, more often at the expense of his tarnished reputation. Views of Wayne have tended to polarize into either an avenging angel from heaven or a mad dog of war from hell; in fairness to the real person, all speculation or opinion must take a proper place relative to the facts. Some of the tales are laughable: One story tells of Wayne turning his coat or cloak inside out to show a red lining, thus enabling his escape; a variation of this absurdity has him actually taking command of the Royal Highland Regiment and ordering it to cease attacking![4]

Another persistent myth charges Wayne with drunkenness in camp and/or at the Paoli, the Warren, or the White Horse Tavern. One version claims that Col. Richard Humpton ran to the Paoli Tavern while the battle was in progress to summon Wayne to his duty; others suggest that it was Humpton who was drunk, along with the sentries. A book published in 1930 claimed that the accounts of Paoli are so confusing because *everybody* was drunk—officers, soldiers, and teamsters—and goes so far as to say that "they danced around like a troop of circus clowns" during the attack.[5] To be sure, Anthony Wayne was a hard drinker in a hard-drinking age, but not one primary account provides any supporting evidence of his being drunk at Paoli. How much of his mercurial behavior could be attributed to alcohol consumption is mere speculation; other important factors, such as age, physical condition, personal disposition, sleep deprivation, and stress, also played key roles in his leadership performance. Had there been so much as a suggestion of drunkenness at the time, Wayne's detractors certainly would have used it against him at the inquiry and court-martial, for drunken behavior in officers was not tolerated, especially in relation to a military catastrophe. The explanation for the omission of the charge of drunkenness at the court-martial, according to the Prohibition-era account, was that all were guilty of intoxication, so it was not brought up for fear of self-incrimination.[6] Inconveniently for this argument, army documents record that after Wayne's acquittal, Gen. Adam Stephen was cashiered from the service primarily due to drunkenness.

The Paoli gravesite is another topic of oft-repeated fallacy. The most enduring myth regarding its location is that the land where the massacre occurred was owned by a Tory named Griffith who refused to allow rebels to be buried on his property. A variation of this states that the neighbors who buried the soldiers refused to bury them in Tory soil, so they were moved to the Pearce property. To begin with, the grave is located in what was approximately the middle of the battlefield. The camp was located mostly south of present-day First Avenue between Warren Avenue and Wayne Avenue. The fighting swept through this whole area and was especially heavy at the Bowen-Pearce fence lines (Wayne Avenue) and at other fences west toward Sugartown Road. Sporadic fighting took place west of Sugartown Road as far as today's Hickory Lane, with light British pursuit as far as Chester Road (Route 352). The Griffith property ran north to south approximately from modern Monument Avenue to the southern edge of the Malvern Prep woods, and east to west from Warren Avenue to Wayne Avenue.

Land records show that the Griffith family did not own the property until 1804, when they bought it upon the death of Ezekiel Bowen, who had owned it since the 1760s. At the time of the battle, Bowen's land was technically owned by Richard Mason, a Philadelphia merchant, who had acquired it in early 1777 from Bowen. In April 1778, Bowen was again the owner, suggesting that the property had been in receivership. Bowen's whereabouts in 1777 are undocumented, but chances are that he and his family still lived on the farm. His politics led him to take the oath of allegiance to the United States in 1778, and he is listed as a member of the Willistown militia in 1780.

The probable reasons for the gravesite's location is that it was central and it was the scene of heavy casualties due to the fence along the property line. The grave actually straddled the property line, so the Griffith family ceded 10 perches of land in the 1820s to place the grave entirely on the parade ground site.

The legends extend to characters in the region. In the 1830s, an ancient Scottish warrior by the name of Andrew Wallace was a familiar sight to the locals as he wandered the roads of Chester County. Sergeant Wallace was a veteran of the French and Indian War, the Revolutionary War, the Northwest Territory Campaigns of the 1780s and '90s, and the War of 1812. He claimed to have been born in Scotland about 1730 and to have fought in the Battle of Culloden in 1746 for the Young Pretender "Bonnie Prince Charlie." His pension application states that he enlisted in the Continental Army in April 1776 at the Turk's Head Tavern (West Chester) as a soldier in Capt. Thomas Church's Company, Col. Anthony Wayne's 4th Pennsylvania Battalion. The 4th Battalion became the 5th Pennsylvania Regiment the following year, and Wallace stated that he became a sergeant; the regimental payroll for September 1777 lists him at that time as a private in Church's company. He also claimed that at Brandywine, "he bore from the field Genl. Lafayette who was there wounded," though this would have placed him several miles from his regiment. Wallace was present at Paoli and "narrowly escaped the savage brutality of the foe by taking refuge in a cluster of chesnut oak sprouts."[7] In a later interview he claimed that an unnamed brother of his was killed at Paoli. By the 1830s, Sgt. Andrew Wallace supported himself with his soldier's pension and by wandering through the county selling cards printed with his portrait and labeled "the last survivor of Paoli." He died in New York in 1835, reportedly at the age of 105. Though Andrew Wallace was a Paoli survivor, he was not, as he sincerely believed, the last. How much of his life's story in the 1830s was real and how much was imagination is unknown, but Army records confirm that Andrew volunteered to serve his adopted country for nearly thirty years, and he deserves a place in the story of independence.

Col. Caleb North, the officer of the 10th Pennsylvania Regiment who returned to Paoli the morning after the battle to count and help bury his fallen comrades, died at his home in Coventryville, Chester County, in 1841 at age eighty-eight. North held many positions of responsibility in his life, including sheriff of Philadelphia County. For more than twenty years, he served as president of the Pennsylvania Society of the Cincinnati, the oldest American war veterans' organization, composed of Revolutionary War officers and their male descendants. George Washington was the society's first president; Anthony Wayne was the first and most honored president of the Pennsylvania chapter. (Ironically, on the society's charter member list next to Wayne's name is none other than that of Col. Richard Humpton.) North was also a charter member and the last surviving Pennsylvania Line officer of the Revolution. Unfortunately, his personal papers were burned shortly after his death.[8] Although North was the last surviving American officer of Paoli, he was not the last survivor of the battle.

Two participants at Paoli share the distinction of being presently documented as the last survivors, one an American private, the other a British officer. Pvt. James Reed of the 5th Pennsylvania Regiment, badly wounded at Paoli, died in Moon Township, Beaver County, in 1846 at age ninety-four. Little else is known about him except what was written in his pension application. The British officer was Lt. Martin Hunter of the 52nd Regiment Light Company, who was shot through the left hand at Paoli, the only British officer wounded in the attack. After seeing much service in America, he later rose to the rank of general in the British Army and served in India under Lord Cornwallis. In his declining years, at the insistence of his children, Hunter wrote down his recollections of service; thus much of his life story has survived for the record. With all of the conflict he witnessed over the years, he wrote that Paoli was "altogether the most dreadful scene I ever beheld." He died at Medomsley, England, in December 1846 at age eighty-nine.

The history of the Battle of Paoli is best summed up in the words of Chester County's most famous soldier, Anthony Wayne, himself an expert at spinning yarns: "Col. Johnson will give you a picture of our Army,—after making the Proper Allowance's for Embelishment it will be near the truth."[9]

Court of Inquiry Documents

Document 1: Order of Witnesses and Testimony

At a Court of enquiry held at the House of
Houfer in Camp the 13th of Octor. 1777—

By order of His Excellency General Washington to enquire into the charge against
Brigadier General Wayne,—

Vizt. That he had timely notice of the Enemy's intention to attack the troops under his
Command on the night of the 20th Ulto. And notwithstanding the intelligence, he
neglected making a disposition, untill it was too late, either to annoy the enemy or make a
retreat without the utmost danger and confusion.

Present
Major General Lord Stirling, President
Brigadier General McDougall
Brigadier General Knox
Colonel . . . Spencer
Colonel . . . Clark

Lieut. Colo. Butler delivered in his Testimony, as in the paper marked .A. read in the
presence of Genl. Wayne in open Court.—

Major Hay delivered his testimony, paper B. which was read & he crossexamined as
indorsed on the back of that Paper.—

Lieut. Colo. Connor delivered in his testimony, paper .C and crossexamined & marked
on the back of that Paper.—

Brigade Major Nichols delivered in his testimony paper D.—

Lt. Colo. Butler crossexamined by Genl. Wayne as indorsed on A.—

At the request of Genl. Wayne, Colo. Hartley produced his testimony, the paper marked E.
Major Ryan did the same, paper F.

Capt. Wilson also gave in his paper .G.

The Court adjourned till tomorrow Morning 10 oClock.
Octobr. 14th 1777—
The Court met according to adjournment.—

Capt. McGowen's testimony was received & crossexamined H.

Colo. Brodhead, gave in his testimony & was crossexamined by Genl. Wayne I/J.

Capt. Hoffnagles Evidence mark'd K.

Gen'l Wayne said that as this Evidence was mere matter of opinion & hearsay he did not chuse to ask him any questions.—

Major Mentges evidence marked L.—and crossexamined by Genl. Wayne—

Capt. Ross evidence marked M.

Lieut. Colo. Hubley's evidence marked N.—

Capt. James Wilson marked O.—and crossexamined.—

[Colonel Humpton marked P.]

Major North . . . Q

The Court adjourned till tomorrow morning ten oClock—

Octobr. 15th 1777—

The Court met according to adjournment and proceeded, to the Consideration of the Evidence before them—They then formed their opinion, which they desired their president to deliver to the Commander in Chief, a Copy of which Signed by the members, is to be Lodged with the evidences, in the Custody of the Adjutant General.—

[Signed] Stirling

Alex. McDougall

H Knox

Oliver Spencer

J. [?] Clark

(Wayne Papers, Volume I, HSP)

Document 2: Testimony of Lieut. Col. William Butler, 4th Pennsylvania Regiment

[Paper marked "A"]

Lt. Col. Butler's Testimony

With Questions and answers—

As I am Cal'd on By this Honorable Cort to Give information Reletive to general Wayne's Conduct on the Night of the Surprise 20th of Septr. Last—My Evidanse Can Be of no use to the Cort as What I Lernt Was from the Mouths of other Gentlemen. Nor Was it My Business to pry into the Orders the General had Recieved. Coll. Humpton Told me the General had Been inform'd the Enemy wou'd Attack us that Night. Major Nickle [Nichols], Came and Waken'd me & Told me he Blieved one of our Piquets was Taken of[f]. I asked him if he had Acquainted the General. He told me he had & the General Told him to go & Take his Rest. What Ever Plan the General had Lay'd Eighther [either] for a Retrait or to Attack the Enemy I was never mad[e] Acquainted With, therefore knows nothing further

13th Octr. 1777   Wm. Butler, Lt. Col. 4th P. R.

Questions put to Colo. Butler by Genl. Wayne

Question. do you reccollect how long the division was wheel'd before they mov'd?

Ansr. I think about four minutes.

Questn. do you recollect aftr the right was broken Whether I posted Your regt. to cover the retreat?

Ansr. I do.

Ques—Do you remember at What time the Artillery pasd?

Ans—While I was forming the Infantry.

Questions put to Colo. Butler by Genl. McDougall

Questn how near was the enemy encamp'd to General Waynes divisin the evening preeeding the attack?

Ans—I think about two miles.

Question Was the position of that part of the enemies army which lay nearest to You known the evening before the attack?

Ansr. Yes. view'd by Genl. Wayne[,] myself and others.

Question. Was the front or flanks of General Waynes division nearest the enemy?

Ans—The right flank lay obliquely nearest the enemy.

Questn. Was there any thing in the nature of the Ground that oblij'd Genl. Wayne to take that position? With his flank obliquely to the enemy?

Ans—the ground would admit of no other position.

(Force Papers, Library of Congress)

Document 3: Testimony of Major Samuel Hay, 7th Pennsylvania Regiment
[Paper marked "B"]
Major Hay's Testimony

On the Night of the 20th of Septr. Last when General Waynes Division lay—Near the Admiral Warran, between the Hours of 12 & 1 Oclock in the Morning Major Nichols Came to the Booth where I lay and Made a Noise which awaked Myself and Some Other Officers which was lying therein and Order'd us to get the Regiment under arms Immediately for the Enemy was coming out and was very near[.] We Immediately all got up and had the Men under arms in a few Minutes[;] they faced the great Road [Lancaster Road] and the 7th Regiment to which I belong was on the Right of the line where I Expected the Enemy would come first[.] While the Men was getting under arms it Began to Rain[;] when on the Parade I ordered them to Secure their Arms they Stood so I think about 15 minutes or Very near that time during which time I heard some Single Shotts go off which I supposed to be the Centries of our Picquetts[.] Majr. Nichols Came along again and Said we were to Retreat from the left of the line by Sub Platoons, I wheeled up the men According to Orders[;] they were not wheeled up but a few Minutes till there was a sharp fire on our Right[,] Distant about 70 yards in a stripe of woods[.] our Backs was then to the firing and I Supposed the left of the line was Marching though the Right could not move[.] I Ordred the 2 Rear Platoons of the 7th to face To the Right about ["to the right about, face," the command to turn completely around] where I saw a number of Men Running up to us which I Supposed to be the 1st Penna. Regt. that was Posted in the Stripe of woods above mentioned[.] they Came up upon our Right and left and by the light of our fires which was both in front and Rear of the line I Discovered the Enemy by their Clothes Close after the Infantry[.] I then Ordered the Plattoons that was faced to fire which they did and Continued to do so for some time which kept the Enemy back untill the Other Plattoons was Moving on Smartly but the Enemy got up Round us and wounded An officer and some of the Privates on the Parade before we Stired[.] we Moved off as fast as we could untill we fell in with the Other Plattoons which had Moved off some Distance. but the Enimy getting in amongst us threw us into Confusion[.] from what I have Related I am of Opinion some Disposition should have been taken to Annoy the enemy or for the Safety of Our own Troops Especially as I was told by Majr. Nichols that General Wayne had Notice of the Enemies Coming out One Hour and a half Before they Came.—those Reasons Induced Me to think General Waynes Conduct that Night Blameable.

Sam. Hay Majr.

Octr. 13th 1777

7th Penna. Regt.

Question 1st By General Waine to the Wittness.

How long did your regt. stand wheel'd in Sub Platoons after Major Nichols ordered the regt. to march off[?]

Answer[:] 4 or five minutes before the fireing began in the rear, which was the right before they wheeled.

[On the back of Wayne's Plan of Encampment is written:] *Major Hay says, the whole were faced and ordered to march of[f] by the left.

(Force Papers, Library of Congress)

Document 4: *Testimony of Lieut. Col. Morgan Connor, Hartley's Additional Regiment*
[Paper marked "C"]
Colonel Connors Testimony

The following is what I know of the charges brot. against Gen. Wayne respecting his Conduct on the Night of the 20th Septr.—

I Suped in Company with Genl. Wayne, Colo. Hartley & Col. Brodhead, there was also a Mr. Bartholomew of Chester County in Company Who Sayed he believed the Enemy wou'd attack us that night,—the reasons he gave for Such an opinion I do not recollect[.] A little before night an old Man of the Neighborhood of our then encampment enquired for General Wayne. the General being gone out Col. Hartley & myself asked his business, &c. I think the Substance of his information was as follows, That one of his neighbours had been in the enemy's Camp that day, and that he heard them (the enemy) say they wou'd attack General Wayne that night, that they wou'd have done it the night before if he had not changed his ground. Genl. Wayne Soon after returning, this was inform'd him as before recited—About 10 o'Clock Captn. Nichols then acting as Brigade Major having been ordered to Visit the picketts, (there being no field officer appointed to that duty) reported that he cou'd Not find the advanced pickette 'tho he had examined all the ground near the place the pickette was originally posted at between eleven & twelve o'Clock a light horseman inform'd Genl. Wayne that he believed a body of the enemy were advancing up the Swede's ford road, that he had fired upon them but they did not return the fire. Genl. Wayne ordered him back to make farther discoveries, and desired the troops may be put under Arms with all expedition, Which was I believe generally Complied With[.] Soon after the division got under Arms a firing began upon the right, I believe from our pickett next to the Camp and Shortly after from the regimt. upon the right of the Brigade I belong to[.] The regimt. I commanded [Hartley's ACR] being in the Center of the Brigade[,] I saw nothing of [the] General Since he first Came to the parade until he passed by me coming from the right of the Division Where the firing was[.] When he gave orders for the troops to move by the left by half platoons, upon Which our Brigade Wheel'd & March'd, but the regt. upon the right being chiefly riflemen soon gave Way, and the Brigade upon our left not moving at the Same time We did, from What Cause I don't know, one Brigade pressing upon the other and the enemy by this time falling upon our rear, a rout ensued, all the light horse upon the parade followed the General—The foregoing is the Substance of What I at present can recollect of this Matter.

Morgn. Connor Lt. Colo.

Questions to the witness by Genl. Wayne

[Question] Do you recolect at what time in the evening of the 20th Sepr. I returned to Camp.

Answer He belives soon after dusk.

Question Do you know whether after the retreat began there was a regt. of the Division on the left proper of the Division to Cover the retreat.

Answer He heard there were.

Question Do you [know] whether the 1st Pena. Regt. the light infantry & light Dragoons were march[ed] into a Cops[e] of Wood on our Proper right, to receive the Enemy.

Answer He heard the Commanding [officer] Say that he was ordered by Genl. Waine to form to Front the Enemy as they advanced.

Question Did you See Me and other officers Endeavor to rally the Troops after they had broke & passed the regt. formed to the left

Answer He did.

Question When did the artillery retire from the right

Answer He thinks Immediately after the fireing began on the Picket.

Question Do you know of orders being given to the division to march from the left by Sub Plat[oons] before the Firing began on the right

Answer Does not recollect he did.

(Peter Force Papers, Library of Congress)

Document 5: Testimony of 1st Brigade Major William Nichols
[Paper marked "D"]
Major Nichols's Testimony

W. Nichols being Call'd to declare What he Knows Respecting the intiligence he gave Genl. Wayne the Evening of the 20th September, Saith that he Went between the Hours of 7 and 10 oClock to Visit the Centrys and found they Ware Not placed as he had Ordered[.] he Came to the Capt. of the Guard and Asked him if he Knew any thing of the Detachment of the Guard Which he had Ordered Out Which Consisted of one Sub[subaltern, i.e., lieutenant or ensign] one Sergt., one Corpl. and 16 Privates[;] he answered he did[.] he Asked him to goe and shew him Where they Ware, Which he did and Upon going to the place found one Centry Only Which Was Posted agreeable to the Orders he had given[,] that he and the Capt. of the Guard with one Non Commissioned Officer and 2 or 3 men Advanced Along the Road Towards the Paoli and found Not One Centry[,] that they Stopt there and Sent the Non Commissioned Officer With One Man Down the Hill Toward the Paoli[.] they Returned and Made Report that they Saw Not a Man—W. Nichols and the Capt. of the Guard Agreed that the Enemy had Surrounded the Officer as he Marchd With his Guard and Carryed them off[,] as the first Centry Was placed Right, that he then Went and Informed Genl. Wayne that he had Reason to think one of the Piquets Was Carryed off by the Enemy[,] that he had Reconoitered the Ground Where they Ware Ordered & Could Not find them. the Genl. Seemed to be Surprised and Ordered him to goe to Colo. Butler and enquire if he had Moved the Guard Which he did [i.e., Nichols went to Butler]. Colo. Butler Informed him he had not Seen them[;] he then Returned and Informed him What Colo. Butler Said. the Genl. then Asked him Some Questions Respecting the Centries[,] how far they Extended and Afterwards Told him to Lie Down and take his Rest. he Lay Down and After Lying Some short time was Wakened and Ordered to get the Brigade Under Arms.

W. Nichols

Interrogatories to Major Nicholas by Genl. Wayne—

[Question] Where was the picket place'd which You allude to?
ansr.—It was order'd to be plac'd a mile to the right of the front.

Questn. on what road?

ansr. on the Lancaster road.

Questn Was that the road by which the Enemy approach'd?

anr. In my opinion the Firing was that way.

Questn Do you know whether that picket was taken off by the enemy?

Ansr They were not.

Questn Do you remember any thing of the first Pensylvania Regt., Light Infantry and light horse, being march'd and form'd to the right to receive the enemy?

Ansr I heard of the first regt. but not of the infantry or horse.

Quest did you see or hear of any of the light horse being wounded with Swords?

Ansr I did not.

Quest do you know whether any of the light horse were order'd to patrole the roads upon the information of old Mr. Jones?

Ansr—I met two going upon the Lancaster road on that business.

Quest how long was the troops wheeld by Sub plattoons in order to file off by the left before the firing began on the right?

Ans—I cannot recollect whether they were wheel'd or not before Firing was begun.

Quesn do you remember Carrying orders along the line to march off by the left?

Ans—I do.

Questn had the Artillery pas'd at that time?

Ans—I think they were passing.

Questn do You remember any thing of seeing me or other officers endivng[endeavoring] to rally the troops?

Ans—I did.

Quest—Did You retire by the boot [tavern] or by the White Horse [tavern]?

Ansr: By the Boot.

General McDougall ask'd the evidence

Questn. How near was the enemy encamp'd to General Wayne's division the evening preceding the attack?

Ans—I suppose it might be about three miles.

Questn: Was the position of that part of the enemies army which lay nearest to you known the evening before the attack?

Ans.—I do not know.

Questn Was the front or flanks of Genl. Waynes division nearest the enemy?

Ans.—The right flank was, nearest the enemy.

Question at What time of night was it When you first inform'd General Wayne of your suspicion that the enemy had carried off the Paket[picket]?

Ans.—I think between nine and ten oClock.

Question At What time was it that the General desir'd you to lay down and take Your rest?

Ans.—I Suppose it might be an hour after I inform'd him of my suspicion.

Questn at What time was the attack made?

Ans.—I think between 12 & 1 oClock

Quesn Were any & what troops form'd When the enemy first made their attack.

Ans—the first Pensa. Regt.

(Force Papers, Library of Congress)

Document 6: *Testimony of 1st Brigade Commander Colonel Thomas Hartley*
[Paper marked "E"]
Col Hartley's Testimony:

General Wayne on the 19th of Sepr. in the Afternoon changed the Position of his Troops on understanding the Enemy intended to attack us, and took Post on some high Ground above the Warren Tavern on the Lancaster Road. the Right of his Division towards Philada. In Part of the Front was a small wood and a Corn Field—on the Right a small wood and some open Fields—there were Roads passing the Flanks—the Right about two miles distant from the Enemys Encampment—

Genl. Wayne in the afternoon of the 20th of Sepr. desired Coll. Humpton and myself to examine some Roads and Ground to the Right or rather in the Rear of our then Encampment as a Passage by which he said he belived he should shortly afterwards move the Troops—we viewed the Ground with him.

Genl. Wayne rode out afterwards with some Gentlemen—as I understood towards Genl. Smallwood or to reconnoitre—I remained at our Quarters.

In the Evening Mr. Bartholamew came up, and spoke of the vicinity of the enemy and their Numbers—an Old Man of the Name of Jones also visited us. he said he came to see Genl. Wayne to tell him he had been down at the Paoli where he had seen a Servant or some other Person who had been in with the Enemy, where the Soldiers had told him, that they would attack Genl. Wayne's Party that Night. that they would have done it the Night before had he not changed his Ground. Mr. Jones was for returning Home but I persuaded him to stay till the General came to his Quarters—Genl. Wayne came to his Quarters a little after Dark according to my Recollection. When he received the foregoing Information from Mesrs. Bartholamew and Jones—Mr. Bartholamew insinuated that our Situation was a little Dangerous—

Pickets ware placed on the several Roads—and I sent Major Nicholl to forward them to their several Posts—Major Nicholl acted as Brigade Major to me at that Time— & was very industrous and assiduous that Night—

Some Time after Genl. Wayne and myself had layn down Major Nicholl came in and sayd one of the Pickets had been carried of[f]—but I do not exactly recollect the Conversation that afterwards happened between the General and him.

Between elven and twelve oClock a Light Horse Man came in and sayd he saw a Body of Horse advancing—that he or another Sentry had challenged them[,] that they had refused to answer and were fired at—The Genl. Sent him back for further Inteligence[.] the Genl. Rose up and ordered the Troops under arms immediately—

I got my Brigade paraded & formed according to the former Front. we were some Time under arms when the Horseman returned & the Enemy advanced—There was a Picket about 100 yds. From our Right & the Light Infantry about 30 or 40 in Number under Captain Wilson were disposed of rather more advanced along the Road which the Enemy were advancing on—Genl. Wayne was to the Right with the [light] Horse. he sent for the first [1st Pa.] Regement to support the [light] Infantry—Many of these being riflemen. This Regiment being nearest to support—But previous I believe (a small Space of Time) to the Moving of this Regiment the [light] Infantry had been fired on—Orders came that the Troops should move by Sub Plattoons—which was done in the remainder of my Brigade & they were ready to move of[f] to the Left—

The artillery was in Motion towards the Left—orders came to my Brigade that the Division was to move of[f] by the Left. The Left Brigade was some Time before they moved to the Left—Genl. Wayne a short Space after the orders for moving was communicated to me—passed my brigade towards the Left—desiring us to retreat by the Left and saying the Rear was covered.

The Enemy, soon afterwards advanced—the first [1st Pa.] Regiment came before them in Disorder—the Seventh Regemint having no Front towards the Enemy—as well as my own Regiment [Hartley's Additional Regiment]—were attacked in their flank and Rear & tho' there were attempts made to form them with another Front yet the enemy ware so amongst them that it was impracticable—nor could they retreat regularly, as the left Wing had been so long a Moving—

Confusion followed—Several Men fell on both Sides—the Troops in the Rear pressed on those in Front & the Passage on the Left being narrow sacraficdd Many of the Troops.

After we had gone about 200 or 300 Yds. several Attempts were made to rally the Men—but the Enenemye pressing so close, upon the left of the Retreat, which was chiefly My Brigade & so Many Interuption of Fences that it was impossible to rally Any Men 'till We had got to some Distance from the Enemy. The Men were extremely intimedated with the Noise of the Enemys Horse[.] at the Fences considerable opposition was made by some of the best Men—but many of them suffered.

I understood from Genl. Wayne during the Day of the 20th of Sepr. that he certainly expected Genl. Smallwood would join him—almost every Minute & was in the same Expectations, 'till The Attack was made upon us.

Two Persons had been sent to Genl. Smallwood to show him the Way[,] the last was Coll. Chambers. Genl. Smallwood was it seems but a short Distance from us when we were attacked.

Genl. Wayne being acquainted with the Country chose the Ground himself—whereon we were attacked.

The foregoing Facts are true according to the best of My knowledge.

Thos. Hartley Coll.

Commg. First Brigade   Genl. Waynes Division

[no cross-examination or questions]

(Force Papers, Library of Congress)

Document 7: Testimony of Brigade Major Michael Ryan, Wayne's Aide
[Paper marked "F"]

I had been out of the Genls. Quarters about Some Business[.] On My Return in the Evening, the Genl. order'd me to have a Piquet placed on a Blind Road which led from the lancaster Road (Near the Warren) to our Encampment. the Guard was to be So posted as to have two Centinels on the edge of the Lancaster road, and to be Mounted by Col Humptons Brigade, as Col. Hartley's Brigade had furnish'd an Additional piquet which was sent towards the Paoli. When I return'd after Seeing the Guard March'd off Genl. Wayne order'd Me to get 12 Horse immediately Ready to be Dispos'd of in the following Mannr.[:] 4 were to go with Mr. Bartholomew to a Rising Ground Near the Paoli to watch the Enemies Motions[,] 2 were to remain as Videts with the piquet on the Road leading to the Paoli[,] 2 with the Piquet on the Blind Road above Mentioned[,] 2 with a Piquet on a Road leading to the Lancaster Road from our Right, and the other 2 on a Road we had reconoitred that day which led Round to the Paoli,[.]

About an hour after those videts were Sent off, Major Nichols inform'd Me that he could Not find the advance Piquet which was placed on the Paoli Road,[.] I immediately acquainted Genl. Wayne with it, and he desir'd Major Nichols to enquire of Col Butler where he had Posted the Piquet,[.] Sometime after[,] Major Nichols return'd and ask'd Me to let a Young Gentleman Sleep with me. the Gentleman was hardly in bed when one of the Videts Brought intelligence of the Enemies being advancing, Genl. Wayne ordar'd Me to Ride Round by the Right and get the Division under arms, at the Same time order'd Col. Temple to get his Horse[men] Ready.

I rode from Right to left of the Division twice to have the Troops form'd, they were told off in platoons[,] the officers properly placed, was then order'd to desire the Artillery to get as quick as possible to the left of the Division. Genl. Wayne Sent Me with orders to wheel by Sub Platoons and March by the left, which orders I deliver'd as I rode along the line to the left,[.] the Troops were wheeld but it was Some time after before they Mov'd,[.] there was likewise orders given that the Men should put their Cartridge Box's under their Coats to keep them from the rain.

Genl. Wayne and the Light Horse, the 1st Regt. and I believe part of the 7th Regt form'd on the Right to Receive the Enemy[.] I after they were forced assisted the Genl. and Several other Officers in attempting to Rally the Men in a little Wood. Col Butlers Regt. [4th Pa.] was Rally'd[;] his light Infantry particularly under the Command of Capt. Fishburn [Benjamin Fishbourne] I assisted in placing. There was an attempt Made in an Open field afterwds to Rally them, to no purpose[,] but about forty Yards from thence on the fork of a Road Genl. Wayne and Myself rally'd a Number of Men, whome was again form'd to Cover the Retreat,[.] from thence Genl. Wayne Sent me to the White Horse, to Collect what troops went that Way and to desire Genl. Smallwood to form his Men at that place,[.] As to the timely intelligence Mentiond, I was Not present when it was given, but I was afterwds inform'd by an officer[,] I believe by Col. Hartley, That a Servant Boy at the Paoli Told Mr. Jones he heard a Soldier Say we were to be attack'd that Night

M. Ryan B. Major

Questions put to Major Ryan by Genl Wayne

Question—do you Know the reason why the troops did not move off according to orders after they were wheeled for that purpose?

Ansr. I do not know altho' I delivered both orders at the same time.

Question how long was it from the time they wheeld for the purpose before they mov'd?

Ans between 5 & 6 minutes.

(Force Papers, Library of Congress)

Document 8: *Testimony of Captain Richard Willson, Hartley's Additional Regiment*
[Paper marked "G"]

On the Night of the 20th September after the Division under the Command of Genrl. Wayne had been <u>attacked</u> and was retreating I fell in with Genrl. Wayne on the Road leading to the white Horse Tavern where I continued about an hour. the Genrl. Indeavering to collect what Troops he cou'd at that Place, being about three Quarters of a Mile from the Ground we were attacked on & which might Pass that way on their retreat[.] I was then between the hours of one and 2 o'Clock dispatched to the white Horse Tavern to request Colo. Hartly to collect about 500 of the best and most active Men with A Sufficient number of Officer[s] best qualified for the Purpose of returning and attacking the Enemy, and also to inform Colo. Hartley that Genrl. Wayne was on his way to the white Horse and wou'd Join him there—I inquir'd for Colo. Hartly at the white Horse but cou'd not hear of him. I assisted Colo. Hoobly[Hubley] in getting together about 80 Men of the Division which were all that cou'd be then collected.

Richard Willson

[no cross-examination or questions]

(Force Papers, Library of Congress)

Document 9: Testimony of 2nd Brigade Major Captain John McGowan
[Paper marked "H"]

The Evidence of Capt. McGowan

The Evidence of John McGowan, Captn. 4th P. Regt. is as Follows[:]

that on the Night of the 20th of September last at Pealioa Camp Commanded by Genl. Wayne—that between the hours of 12 and one oClock on Said Night that Genl. Wayne Came in person and Called at Lt. Colo. Butlers Shead and told the officers that was in Said Shead to Get our troops under arms as soon as possible and tell them off as they Were told in the Evening before, and also told us that the Enemy Was advancing—Imeadiately to the Right of our Camp We heard a few Shotts then our Right Wing began to Retreat and put the Left Wing in Confusion.

Jno. McGowan

[On the back of the above testimony is written:] that the Division was formed in Sub' platoons, wheeled to the left and Stood in that position for near a Quarter of an hour before they Moved. that he was acting that Night as Brigade Major to the Brigade Commanded by Col. Humpton, and at the time of the orders arriving for Wheeling to the left he was absent by order of Lt. Col. Butler & gone to give orders to a party of Militia [probably Smallwood's] near them.

that he Rallied Col. Humptons Brigade four times that Night before they came to the Second fence.—

[no cross-examination or questions]

(Force Papers, Library of Congress)

Document 10: Testimony of Colonel Daniel Brodhead, 8th Pennsylvania Regiment
[Paper marked "I/J"]

Colonel Broadheads Evidense

On the evening of the 17th [should be 18th] Sepr. last, Genl. Wayne's Division recd. Marching Orders about 4 oClock in the afternoon[;] the Division was in Motion and Marched towards the Enemy,[.] at about 2 oClock in the Morning we arrived within two Miles of the Enemy, and lay on our Arms untill about 10 oClock when the Genl. informed us the Enemy were Advancing & Ordered us to Retire, which we did to a piece of high Ground about 1½ Miles to our Rear,[.] there we remained without any material Occurrence that Day, and in the Evening were Ordered to make Fires & take Rest.

We lay at that place untill the next Evening [Sept. 19th] when we received Orders to March to the Rear about two Miles, which we did, but about 7 or 8 oClock in the Evening the Genl. desired me to follow the Troops & order them back to the Same Ground, which I did & returned with them,[.] Nothing material happened During the Night nor the next Day [Sept. 20] 'till four oClock[.] We then Rec'd Orders to prepare for a March. Accordingly the Division formed but the weather being Cloudy and threatening Rain we were Ordered to build Booths to secure our Arms & Ammunition & go to Rest.

The next morning between the Hours of twelve & one oClock the Enemy made an Attack on our Right, immediately after the Alarm was given, and the Artillery which was on the Right Retreated,[.] the second Brigade Received Orders to Form and were drawn up in a line with the fires[.] the Enemy then appeared in front but did not immediately attack,[.] the second Brigade received no orders to March untill the Artillery and the greatest part of the first Brigade had past it[,] when I understood we were to Retreat from the left[,] upon which I rode to Col Butler & desired him to retreat from the left[,] soon after which a general pushing [of] Bayonets insued[,] and after Rallying the Troops twice we were in the greatest Confusion[,] being Oblidged to Retreat over a Number of Fences near one of which I recd. A small wound and being dismounted fell in the Rear.

Daniel Brodhead
Col. 8th Pena. Regt.

Questions put to Colo. Broadhead by Genl. Wayne

Question. do you remember what time in the eveng I return'd from reconoitring the 20th?
Ans—I think after dark but do not exactly remember the time.
Question. Do you remember a Mr. Jones giving the information[,] of any horse being order'd to patrole and an additional number of Pickets being order'd to be placed[?]
Ans—I Remember the Horse being order'd to patrole, and I think the pickets were order'd to be strengthened. this happen'd I think about 8 oClock in the evening.
Question How long do you think Mr. Jones was at my Quarters before I return'd?
Ans—I do not know, as I was not present when Mr. Jones first Came.
Question—At What time of night did the Videt Alarm us of some people approa[c]hing who would not answer him When Challeng'd?
Ans—at twelve oClock.
Question how long after this do you think before the division was under arms?
Ans—not more than a quarter of an hour—
Questn. What kind of Weather was it?
Ans—Cloudy and I think raining a little.
Questn. was there or was there not then any cautions given to the men respecting the ammunition?
Ans.—I do not know.—
Questn. Was the division wheeld any time previous to their march'd [marching?]
Ans—Yes they were wheel'd to the left. And stood waiting orders to move—
Question: do you know whether there were orders given for their wheeling to the left?
Ans—There were orders.
Question How long did they stand in that position previous to their marching?
Ans I think about ten minutes
Question did you know of any troops being form'd to our right to receive the enemy?
Ans—I do not know.
Question What distanc do you think our Quarters were from the enemies encampment that night?
Ans I believe about a mile and a half or two miles—

Lord Stirling Questions to Colo. Broadhead—

Quest. did you know of any intelligence the Genl. receive[d] that evening of the enemies intention to attack?
Ans—Mr. Jones inform'd Genl. Wayne that a certain person whom Genl. Wayne knew had been into the enemies Camp and heard the Soldiers say that they intended to Attack Genl. Wayne that night.

(Force Papers, Library of Congress)

Document 11: Testimony of Captain Michael Huffnagle, 8th Pennsylvania Regiment
[Paper marked "K"]

Capt. Huffnagle's Evidence

Being Call'd as an Evidence to Support the charge against Brigadier Genl. Wayne concerning the Action near the Paoli on the Lancaster Road do declare as Followeth[:]

That on the night of the 20th of Septr. Last the Division under the Command of Genl. Wayne was alarm'd of the approach of the Enemy Betwixt 11 and 12 oClock at night. General Wayne at this time Road along our Lines and commanded us to turn out & form, (said the Enemy were approaching & we should give it to them now) which was Immediately Obey'd. the Enemy had then drew near us,[.] Coll. Brodhead in the mean time came to the Regiment & said what spunck we were in,[.] Major Ryan made answer & said don't you know that we are surrounded by the Enemy.

in or about the expiring of ten Minutes the firing began on the right of the Division. The Enemy by this time were advancing upon our flanks with Charg'd bayonets. we not being in a disposition to oppose the Enemy were obliged to Retreat which was in great Confusion.

The officers in General being Immediately afterwards Inform'd, that Major Nichols had Given General Wayne Notice some time before the Action that one of our Picquets was taken off[.] the General Answer'd by ordering him to go to his Rest. & at this time the firing began on the right. We neither had orders to fire upon the Enemy, or to Retreat untill General Wayne's Brigade [the 1st Brigade] Broke through us in great Confusion. from these Circumstances we had Reason to Judge that there was timely Notice Given to General Wayne of the approaching of the Enemy and we not being alarm'd nor posted in a place able to make any oppossistion and in Consequence of Major Nicholas [Nichols's] Information Gave us Room to Censure the Conduct of General Wayne.

Mich. Huffnagle Captn.

8th. P. R.

[Notation on the Court of Inquiry list:] Genl. Wayne said that as this Evidense was mere matter of opinion & hearsay he did not chuse to ask him any questions.—

(Force Papers, Library of Congress)

Document 12: Testimony of Major Francis Mentges, 11th Pennsylvania Regiment
[Paper marked "L"]

Major Mentges evidence

Being Caled upon as an Evidence to Support the Charge Laid against Brigadier Genl. Wayne., Concerning the affair of the 20th Ultimo.—

I do declare upon my Honour that I did not hear of any other orders of Genl. Wayne,[.] at about 12 O'Clock Genl. Wayne came Riding along in the Rear of the 2d Brigade Calling out ["]turn out my Boys, the Lads are Comeing[,] we gave them a push with the Bayonet through the Smoak,[."] The Troops turned out as quick as Could be Expected, and Formed by Platoons, in less than five Minutes. Orders came to Wheel to the left, and there they Stood without Movement, the Right of the 1st Brigade being Attacted in about 4 Minutes, and Retreated before we Mov'd from our Ground. The Artillery Moved at the Same time in Rear of us and being lead by Genl. Wayne, our Brigade Marched off from the left.[,] and being Immediately pushed by the Enemies. Notwithstanding the Brigade Marched in good order through the 2d Field, and then Came in Confusion. Also no Disposition of Defense nether of Retreat has been made to prevent the Surprise of the Enemies, Whereof the Genl. was Informed off by Major Nichols, 3 Hours before the Attack.

Camp the 14 8bre[October] 1777

F MENTGES Maj.
11 P. Regt.

Questions to Major Mentges by Genl. Wayne

Ques do you know of the 1st Regt.[,] the light infantry & light horse being form'd on the right to receive the enemy at the time the division had orders to Wheel & march by the left?

Ans. I do not know any thing about it—

Questn. do [you] know of the 4th regt. of your own brigade being form'd upon the left to favor the retreat?

ans. I do not—

Question by Lord Stirling

Question before the alarm was given, had you heard of any intelljance of the enemie's intention to attack the Camp that night?

A: I had not.—

(Force Papers, Library of Congress)

Document 13: Testimony of Captain George Ross, 11th Pennsylvania Regiment
[Paper marked "M"]
Capt Ross Evidence

Being Call'd as an Evidence to Support the Charge Against Brigadier Genl. Wayne Concerning the Action at the Warren on the Lancaster Road. do declare as Followeth—

That on the 20th of Last Sep. 1777 the Division under the Commd. of Genl. Wayne Was Alarm'd of the Approaching of the Enemy betwixt 11 and 12 Oclock at Night,[.] General Wayne at this time Road along our Lines and Commanded us to form Which was Immediately Obey'd: the Enemy had then drew near us, in or About the Expiring of 10 Minutes the firing began on the Right of the Division. The Enemy by this time was Advancing upon Our flanks With Charg'd bayonets,[.] We not being in a Disposition to Oppose the Enemy, Was Obliged to Retreat—Which was in great Confusion—

The Officers in General being Immediately Afterwards Inform'd that Major Nichol's had Given General Wayne Notice some time before the Action. that One of Our Picquets was taken off, the General Answered by Ordering him to Go to his Rest[.] from these Circumstances we had Reason to Judge that there was timely Notice Given to General Wayne of the Approaching of the Enemy. And we not being Alarm'd Nor posted in a place Able to make any Opposissitions, And in Consequence of Major Nichol[s's] Information.[,] Gave us Room to Censure the Conduct of General Wayne.

Geo. Ross
Captn. 11. P. R.

Lord Sterling

Ques. before the alarm of the approach of the enemy did you hear any thing of the enemies intentin to attack You that night?

Ans. I did not.

(Force Papers, Library of Congress)

Document 14: Lieut. Col. Adam Hubley, Jr., 10th Pennsylvania Regiment
[Paper marked "N"]
Lt. Col. Hubleys Evidence
On the Evening of the 17th [should be 18th] Septr.—Genl. Waynes Division received marching orders,—about 4 o'Clock in the Afternoon, we mooved off. and about 2 or 3 oClock in the Morning arrived within 1½ Miles from the Enemies Encampment.—we Continued on this Ground, and lay on our Arms untill about 10 oClock same Morning.— We then received intiligence of the Enemies Advancing towards us. Genl. Wayne gave orders to the Division, to retire about one or two Miles, upon, some heighths.—we accordingly moov'd, & took post on the same—nothing matterial happening, that day, we were ordered to make fires, & take rest in the evening.—

We lay at that place nearly all next day [Sept. 19], towards evening we mooved off in the rear of this Encampment about 1½ Miles[.] The same Night, we received orders, to return to our former ground & take post for that Night, which orders were executed.—we Continued on the ground that Night, and next day [Sept. 20] untill about 4 oClock,[.] we then received orders, to get ready for a March, and accordingly the Division form'd, But the Weather threadning with rain[,] Genl. Wayne gave orders for the Division, to make Booths, &c. in order to secure their Arms & Ammunition from being damag'd by the rain, which were punctualy executed,[.] the Division after Securing their Arms, &c., took to rest,[.]

and about twelve or One Clock, that night, Genl. Wayne came up to me as I was laying under a tree with some of my Officers, and desired we would immidiately get our Men under Arms, that there was an Alarm and that the Enemy were Advancing. I immidiately run to my Men, ordered them under Arms, and I think to the best of my knowledge, in the course of about 10 Minutes from the time I received my orders, from the General, the whole Division was form'd, but unhappily, before a number of fires, which was in front of our Encampment, which gave the Enemy an oppertunity of seeing us, and totaly depriv'd us from seeing them.—

After we were form'd a very heavy fire was given upon our right, by Col. Chambers Regiment [1st Pa.], who were drawn from the Division and lay in a Wood in front of the artilery. Immidiately after this fire Chambers's Regiment gave way, the Enemy Advancing at the same time,[.] Orders was then given for the Division [crossed out: to face to the right, and march by files] to wheel to the left by Sub-plattoons & March by the left, but before we could advance, any distance, the Enemy were upon us, in our rear, and with their charg'd Bayonets, we push'd forward and got into a field adjoining the One in which we were Attackted,[.] we endeavoured to form Our Men, but found it impracticable, the Enemy being then, almost mix'd with us, at the same time calling out, No quarters &c., which in my humble Oppinion caused our Men to make a disparate and indeed obstinate stand,[.] a most severe Bayoneting was the Consequence, and after some time our people retired in the third field, And the Enemy, in the field in which we were first Attacked,[.]

What pass'd further at that time I can't say, as I had unfortunately fell into the Enemys hands,[;] some time after, whilst our people were retiring, I thro' some intrigues &c. got off, and was making for the White-horse, but after passing the third field, in which our troops had been shortly before, I fell in with one of our field pieces, (the carriage of which had lost the hind wheels) and a few Men, amongst which [was] a Captain of Artilery,[.] I found a party of the enemy, Consisting of about 50 men with some light Horse, advancing upon our left but made a halt. I there ralied about 60 Men & form'd a rear Guard, ordered another Horse to be hitched to the piece & drag'd it along[,] which was done, and brought of[f] the piece.

I at this time, whilst we were forming this Guard[,] enquir'd of the Men for Genl. Wayne, some of which inform'd me he was at the Cross roads, ralying the Men.—These roads are nearby ye field in which we were engag'd, however I did not get to see him at that time. I retired with the piece to the White horse, and there halted,[.] I found a number of Troops there, and after inquiry found myself Commanding Officer there. I ralyed the Men and form'd them. after which I went and plac'd several Pickets, about different places. I found it most necessary, but before I could return to the White horse again, I found, thro' Mistakes in Genl. Smallwoods Division, the whole alarm'd, and retiring up the Lancaster road,[.]

I again with the assistance of some officers, routed our Men about half a Mile from the White-horse, Genl. Smallwood then passing, I ask'd what was to be done[.] he desired we would March our Men up the road, about 2 Miles, and then halt. whilst we were on this March, I fell in with Genl. Wayne, which was nearly day break, the Genl. & myself then moov'd down the road towards the White-horse,[.] after being down the road some time the General received intelligence of the Enemies advancing on our left. the General then gave orders, for our troops to March towards the Red Lion, and there remain until further orders.—During the proceedings of the Morning of the 20th. Instant, I had an opportunity of seeing Genl. Wayne, and found him exceedingly Active and Alert, upon all occasions.

Adm. Hubley Jr Lt. Cl. 10th P R

Genl. Wayne to Colo. Hubley

Questn. do you remember how long the troops were Wheeld before they received orders to Mar[c]h?
Ans Immediately.
Question[:] Were you impeded by the left not marching?
Ans Yes sir we were—
Questn. How long were you impeded?
Ans I believe five or six minutes?
Question When you were with the peice of Artillery how near did You understand that Genl. Wayne was to the field of Battle Rallying the men?
Ansr I believe not half a mile.
Question Was the place where Genl. Wayne was ralling the men between the piece and field of battle?
Ans Yes.

(Force Papers, Library of Congress)

Document 15: Testimony of Captain James Wilson, 1st Pennsylvania Regiment
[Paper marked "O"]
Capt. Willsons Evidence
The Evidence of Capt. James Wilson of the 1st Pennsya. Regiment—

That on the Night of the 20th Septr. Genl. Wayne Personally placed me With the Light Infantry, his Orders to me Was, Stand like a Brave Soldier and Give them fire, his Orders I Obeyd as Long as Possible, but the Enimy being too Numerous forsd [forced] me to Give Way to the Middle Fence, Where I Rallied about Thirty men and Gave them the Last Fire.

Ja. Wilson, Capt. 1st Regt.

[Questions on the back of the paper in Lord Stirling's handwriting:]

Quet to the witness. what distance was the light infantry advanced from ye right of ye Division when you received the Enemy?

Anr. 300 Yards.

Quesn. How long was ye placed to oppose the Enemy before they came to you at Firing distance?

answer about 8 minutes, & then not above a rod distance.

(Wayne Papers, Vol. 1, HSP)

Document 16: The Testimony of 2nd Brigade Commander Colonel Richard Humpton
[Paper marked "P"]
Colonel Humptons Evidence

The 20th Sept. between the hours of twelve & one (I believe) in the Morning the Enemy made an Attack upon the Division Commanded by Brgd. Genl. Wayne,[.] the Genl. had received intelligence some hours before the Attack that the Enemy intended it,[.] as Second in Command I think the Genl. ought to have acquainted Me with it, and given orders for the Safety & defence of the Troops,[.]

not more than 15 Minutes before the Enemy Made an Attack upon the Right I was waked by the Noise of a Person calling out, ["]turn out, turn out, the Enemy is Coming, give them (my brave Lads) Your Fire & Charge Bayonets["] or Words to that purpose[.] I jumped up & found it was Genl. Wayne[.] I ask'd what was the Matter[.] He said the Enemy was very near,[.] I desired Him not to ride along in that Manner as possibly it might occasion confusion amongst the Men, to ride back to the Right & that I would get the Men under Arms with all Possible Speed. I immediately ran to the Left of the Brig[a]de & order'd them under Arms and the Brig[a]de was form'd in as short a time as possible[;] at least I saw no Delay, they remain'd form'd a few Minutes waiting for Orders

the Artillery & Waggons was driving very fast along our left flank, being at that time form'd in platoons to the Left, as the Artillery & Waggons greatly incommoded Us either for Action or a retreat I rode to the Left of the Brig[a]de to see if the Fences were down and found a Great Stopage near the Left of the fourth Regt. there I saw Genl. Wayne near the Artillery giving Some Orders to them, & the fourth Regt. I believe. He desired Me to go back towards the Right[.] when I Got near the Centre found the Right in confusion & retreating with the Left Standing fast, which I have Since understood Genl. Wayne orderd'd[.] by the left Standing fast our retreat was greatly delay'd and the Greatest part of the Troops put into the utmost Confusion

after we had retreat'd a few Miles Col. Connor & my self collect'd about 150 Men with a Number of Officers. we halt'd & took post on a Height 'till Day break & then March'd towards the Lancaster Road where I mett Major Ryan who told Me Gen. Wayne Was at the Red Lyon[.] I March'd there & found Him & Genl. Smallwood,[.] The Next Day [Sept. 22] we Marched for Jones Tavern about three Miles from Reading Furnace[.] there I think it was the Genl. read Me a Letter which He proposed sending to His Excellency

We remain'd there two Days and the Morning we March'd [Sept. 25] Lt. Col. Temple of Col. Blands Light Dragoons inform'd Me that Genl. Wayne had notice of the Enemies Intention, which I scarcly could believe as I never before then had heard any thing of the Matter,[.] on My Mentioning this, Major Nicolls of Col. Hartley's [brigade/regiment] Told Me that He had acquaint'd the Genl. that a Picquet was Missing & He was apprehensive the Enemy had carried it off,[.] Notwithstanding all this the Genl. took no Steps (that came to My knowledge) to prepare the Brigade that I commanded either for to annoy the

Enemy or defend themselves, 'till within as near as I can judge 15 Minutes of the Enemies being on Our Right flank with fix'd Bayonets[.] Our Artillery & Store Waggons had very little Notice[;] no Fences laid down or the least preparation Made for a Sudden retreat[;] neither had I any Orders where to assemble the Brigade in case of a defeat[.]

Rich Humpton Col. 11th P. Regt.
Commdng. 2d Brigde. G. Lincolns Division

Questions to Col. Humpton by Genl. Waine

Quest 1st Do you recolect reconnitring any road the afternoon before the attack in Company with myself, Col Hartley & Major Ryan; and what road.[?]

Answr He was on such a Party with Genl Waine and others on that day, on the road to the right of the Division & returned the road near Genl Waines Quarters.

Quesn 2d what was the intention of reconitring that Road.[?]

Answr He Supposes it was in order to change ye Ground of the Division.

Quesn 3 Do you know whether General Smallwood with his Brigade Was to join me that day.[?]

Answer No, he never heard of it, but understood he Was to be at the[White] Horse.

Questn 4 Do you Remember whether the Division Moved one Mile & a half to the left the evening of the 19th; and whether the Fences were down in that Direction.[?]

Answr He does, the evening before the attack, & that the Fences were put down for the wagons & ye rear of the Division, but the Front marchd in the road.

Quesn 5 Whether the division was Wheeled by Sub. Platoons to the left, and how long were they to wheel before they marched.[?]

Answr He thinks his Brigade Was, wheeled to the left, and stood wheeled from 5 to 10 minutes before they Marched.

Quesn 6 For what purpose Was the Division wheeled.[?]

Ansr He thinks to retreat.

Quesn 7 Did you receive orders, to wheel your Brigade.[?]

Answr Does not recollect.

Quesn 8 when the Division was ordered to wheel to the left, did You receive orders to March from the left?

Answr No, he received No orders to March from the left.

Questn 9 Do you know whether the 4th Pena. regt. was formed on the left to favor the retreat[?]

Answr He was told it was.

Quesn 10 Do you know whether the 1st Pena. regt., the light infantry & light drag's were formed to the right to receive ye Enemy & favor the retreat.[?]

Answer He has heard So, by Some of the officers.

Lord Sterling

Quesn Did [you] hear on the evening of the 20th any information of the Enemy's intention to attack[?]

Answer He never did.

General Waine

Quesn 11 Do you know of any Pickets of ours being carried off, that Night[?]

Answr No, he does not know whether it was, or was not, but does not believe it was?

(Force Papers, Library of Congress)

Document 17: Testimony of Major Caleb North, 10th Pennsylvania Regiment
[Paper marked "Q"]
Major North Evidence

The Evidence of Caleb North: Major[,] Relative to the Afair of the Night of the 20th of September 1777—

The first of the Alarm I herd Was by General Wayne who then Came Riding from his Lodgings a Small Distance in the Rear of the Incampment & Desired the Officers to get Up Immediately and Parade their men as he was Inform'd the Enemy were Advancing Towards us; this I had Done as Quick as possible, and the Officers Posted to their Commands as they were Told off in the Evening: Immediately the Picket on the Right fired which was But a Small Distance from the [light] Infantry on the Right who Alsoe fired in Less than Ten Minutes; at which Time I Saw Our Canon Pass in the Rear of the Division and Soon Afterwards the Word was Given ["]to the Left Wheel Retreat in good Order.["] But the Enemy Rushed on So fast which in a Short time threw the Whole in Confusion; in which Order we Retreated Near Quarter of a mile when I fell in with the General at a Cross Road, who was there for[ming]* some men and Desired I would Assist and get Some O[fficer]* to take the Command of them: as he would form the R[ear]* Guard there, to Cover the Canon, &c. this Guard was f[ormed]* and Commanded by Captain Stout when General W[ayne]* Desired me to Ride down the Road Leading towards Chester, and See if the Enemy was Crossing that way which I did and soon Returned Informing him that all was Clear that way. then he Desired I would Ride the Contrary Way Towards the Lancaster Road where I would find General Smallwood: & that I Should Inform him that he had formed the Rear Guard and that he Should Retreat to the White Horse[.] this Messuage I Delivered Agreeable to his Order—

[*torn manuscript]

Caleb North Major
10th P R

[no cross-examination or questions]

(Force Papers, Library of Congress)

County Origins of Continental Regiments and Companies in the Battle of Paoli and the List of Known Casualties

The Battle of Paoli involved more than 2,000 Continental Army troops, most of them in Pennsylvania infantry regiments. Reflecting the newness of the American nation in 1777, many of these soldiers were born overseas, primarily in Ireland, Great Britain, and Germany; others were born in Pennsylvania or other colonies. At least 53 were killed, and more than 200 were wounded or taken as prisoners of war.

Records of the service of these troops in 1777 are incomplete or have been lost over time. The data presented here was compiled from many sources: surviving muster rolls, payrolls, pension applications, period letters, and county histories. To date, the list for Paoli stands at 163 known casualties. The full list—272 casualties were cited by Congressman Samuel Chase of Maryland three days after the battle—may never be identified, unless new material comes to light.

This list organizes Wayne's force by regiment and company. Each company commander's county of origin or place of enlistment is given, based on data provided in Col. John B. B. Trussell's book *The Pennsylvania Line*. The captains were responsible for local recruiting of their companies in 1775 and 1776, but by 1777, the restructuring of the Continental Army by states, along with attrition, caused certain companies and units to be amalgamated. Although some companies retained a local flavor, others became a hodgepodge of men with little or no common origin. Recruitment in 1777 was difficult; an increasingly protracted war and three-year enlistments, not to mention the great hardships of army life, had dampened earlier enthusiasm.

Sources

1. Pennsylvania Archives, ser. 2, vol. X, 1896.
2. Pennsylvania Archives, ser. 5, vol. V, 1906.
3. Dr. Francis Alison, Lancaster Hospital Return, October 11, 1777, HSP.
4. Revolutionary War Muster/Pay Rolls, National Archives.
5. Revolutionary War Pension Papers, National Archives.
6. Compiled Service Records, National Archives.
7. State Pension Papers, State Archives, Harrisburg.
8. Pension Applications, Wagner Collection, State Library, Harrisburg.
9. Heitman.
10. Juliana Wood, *Family Sketches,* 1870.
11. List of Prisoners Wounded and Held Prisoner, 7th Pa., Reed Collection, Valley Forge National Historic Park.
12. Letter of Samuel Hay, 7th Pa., September 29, 1777, HSP.
13. W. W. Davis, *History of Bucks Co.,* 1876.
14. Brodhead's Testimony, October 14, 1777– Library Congerss.
15. Wayne to Wharton, May 2, 1778– Wayne Papers, HSP.
16. British Army Courts-Martial Records, W. O. 71/84, PRO.

Key

KIA	Killed in action
W	Wounded
MIA	Missing in action
POW	Prisoner of war
W/POW	Wounded prisoner of war

COMMANDING OFFICERS

Brig. Gen. Anthony Wayne, Division Commander—Chester County
Col. Richard Humpton, 2nd Brigade Commander—Chester County [b. Yorkshire, England]
Col. Thomas Hartley, 1st Brigade Commander—York County [b. Berks County, Pennsylvania]

1ST PENNSYLVANIA REGIMENT

[Counties: Bedford, Berks, Cumberland, Dauphin, Franklin, Lancaster, Northampton, Northumberland, and Westmoreland
Total Known Casualties: 14 (1 KIA, 10 W, 3 POW)
Estimated Total Personnel: 200 (Army rolls not available for September 1777)
Commander at Paoli: Col. James Chambers, Cumberland and Franklin Counties
    Capt. James Grier's Company, Franklin County
    Capt. David Harris's Company, Northumberland County
        Pvt. Jacob Boyers, POW (5)
        Pvt. Thomas Hawbeard, W (3)
    Capt. James Hamilton's Company, Lancaster County
    Capt. John Holliday's Company, Dauphin County
        Pvt. John McNench, W (3)

Capt. Samuel Craig's Company, Northampton County
Capt. John Matson's Company, Bedford County
 Pvt. James Davis, W (3)
Capt. Michael Simpson's Company, Northumberland County
 Sgt. Atchison Mellen, company clerk, W (1)
Capt. James Wilson's Company, Cumberland County
Capt. James Parr's Company (with Daniel Morgan in New York)
 Drummer John Hutchinson, W (5), "wounded in the thigh"
Unidentified Companies
 Dr. Christian Reinick, surgeon's mate, KIA (1)
 Sgt. William McMurray, W (1)
 Lt. Andrew Johnston, quartermaster, W (1), "in left leg"
 Pvt. John Hutchinson, W (1)
 Pvt. William McCormick, POW (1)
Doyle's Independent Rifle Company, Westmoreland County (?)
 Pvt. William Brown, W (2)
 Pvt. Robert Humphries, W (3)
 Sgt. John Donaldson, POW (6)

2ND PENNSYLVANIA REGIMENT

Counties: Cumberland, Lancaster, Philadelphia, and York
Total Known Casualties: 22 (2 KIA, 6 W, 2 W/POW, 1 POW, 11 MIA)
Total Personnel: 187 (Army rolls available for September 1777)
Commander at Paoli: Maj. William Williams, Philadelphia County
 Capt. Joseph Howell's Company, Philadelphia County
 Pvt. William Dorrington, MIA (4)
 Pvt. William Jackson, MIA (4)
 Pvt. Benjamin Jones, MIA (4)
 Capt. John Patterson's Company, Philadelphia County
 Cpl. Charles Chambers, W (3)
 Pvt. John Stout, W/POW (3,4)
 Pvt. John Nowland, MIA (4)
 Capt. Jacob Ashmead's Company, Philadelphia County
 Sgt. Thomas Parker, MIA (4)
 Capt. John Bankson's Company, Philadelphia County
 Pvt. Balser Barge, W (3)
 Capt. Roger Staynor's Company, Philadelphia County
 Lt. Major Walbron, KIA (1)
 Sgt. John Sullivan, MIA (4)
 Pvt. Edward Dodkins, KIA (4)
 Pvt. Moses Hammer, W (3)
 Capt. George Jenkins's Company, Philadelphia County
 Capt. George Jenkins, W (9)
 Sgt. Patrick Downing, MIA (4)
 Cpl. Thomas Hartnett, MIA (4)
 Pvt. William Dodd, POW (4)

Capt. Christian Staddle's Company, Lancaster and York Counties (?)
Cpl. Thomas Hands, MIA (4)
Pvt. Roger Lane, MIA (4)
Pvt. Samuel Smith, MIA (4)
Capt. Samuel Tolbert's Company, Cumberland County (?)
Unidentified Companies
Lt. John Irwin, adjutant, W (1) "left for dead on the field"
Pvt. John Fagain, W/POW (2) "Wounded in Cheek & leg by bayonet"
Pvt. Peter Jacobs, W (1), "in side"

4TH PENNSYLVANIA REGIMENT

Counties: Bedford, Berks, Northampton, Northumberland, and York
Total Known Casualties: 8 (2 KIA, 6 W)
Estimated Total Personnel: 135 (Army rolls not available for September 1777)
Commander at Paoli: Lt. Col. William Butler, Northumberland County (?)
Capt. Edward Scull's Company, Berks County
Capt. William Gray's Company, Northumberland County
Capt. Benjamin Fishbourne's Company, county unknown
Capt. John McGowan's Company, Northampton County
Lt. Edward Fitz Randolph, W (10), "dangerously wounded, lost an eye"
Pvt. George English, W (3, 7) "desperately wounded in head, shoulder, arm & hand"
Pvt. William McNider, W (3)
Capt. Benjamin Burd's Company, Bedford County
Pvt. Simpson Harris, W (3)
Capt. William Cross's Company, York County
Capt. Robert Connelly's Company, Northumberland County
Capt. John Mears's Company, Berks County
Pvt. Daniel Gillis, W (3)
Pvt. Robert Fasitt, KIA (4)
Unidentified Companies
Maj. Marien Lamar, KIA (1) Philadelphia County
Pvt. William Farrell, W (1), "in head and arm"

5TH PENNSYLVANIA REGIMENT

Counties: Chester and Lancaster Counties
Total Known Casualties: 24 (5 KIA, 5 W, 2 POW, 12 MIA)
Total Personnel: 245 (Army rolls available for september 1777)
Commander at Paoli: Col. Francis Johnson, Chester County
Capt. Benj. Bartholomew's Company, Chester County
Pvt. William Grives, W (3)
Pvt. Galbraith Wilson, W (3)
Pvt. William Graham, POW (4)
Pvt. Gabriel McKnight, MIA (4)
Capt. Thomas Church's Company, Chester County
Pvt. Charles McCahon, KIA (4)
Pvt. Charles Temple, KIA (4)
Pvt. James Reed, W (1, 5)

Pvt. Michael Fennon, MIA (4)
Pvt. Henry Maxwell, MIA (4)
Capt. Alexander Johnson's Company, Bucks County
Pvt. John Noble, POW (4)
Capt. James Moore's Company, Chester County
Lt. Charles McHenry, W (13) "saber blows to head and collarbone"
Pvt. James Donolly, MIA (4)
Pvt. Thomas Fielding, MIA (4)
Pvt. Robert Marshall, MIA (4)
Capt. John Christy's Company, Chester County
Pvt. Dennis McSwine, KIA (1)
Capt. William Oldham's Company, county unknown
Pvt. Thomas Porter, MIA (4)
Capt. Joseph Potts's Company, Chester County
Ens. William Magee, KIA (1)
Pvt. William Campble, KIA (4)
Pvt. Paul Taylor, MIA (4)
Pvt. Philip Trecy, MIA (4)
Capt. James Taylor's Company, Lancaster County
Pvt. Samuel Grunder, MIA (4)
Pvt. George Poke, MIA (4)
Pvt. Charles Quigley, MIA (4)
Capt. Frederick Vernon's Company, Chester County
Unidentified Company
Pvt. Charles Warrington, W (1)

7TH PENNSYLVANIA REGIMENT

Counties: Cumberland and York
Total Known Casualties: 56 (3 KIA, 19 W, 8W/POW, 4 POW, 22 MIA)
Total Personnel: 325 (Army rolls available for September 1777)
Commander at Paoli: Lt. Col. David Grier, York County
Capt. John Alexander's Company, Cumberland County
Pvt. John Bentson, W (2, 3)
Pvt. John Bradley, W/POW (2, 11)
Pvt. Daniel McKessog, MIA (4)
Pvt. Robert Swim, MIA (4)
Capt. William Alexander's Company, York County
Cpl. Henry Gorman, W (2, 3)
Pvt. James Berry, W (2, 3)
Pvt. John McDonald, MIA (2, 4)
Capt. William Bratton's Company, Cumberland County
Pvt. Edward Edgerton, W (2, 3)
Pvt. Michael Wann, W/POW (4, 11)
Pvt. John Connor, MIA (4)
Pvt. Patrick Carter, MIA (2, 4)
Capt. John McDowell's Company, York County
Cpl. Alexander McDonald, W (2, 3)

Cpl. Christopher Morgan, MIA (4)
Pvt. Richard Hamilton, MIA (4)
Pvt. Andrew Kennedy, MIA (2, 4)
Capt. Samuel Montgomery's Company, Cumberland County
Cpl. Patt. Allen, MIA (4)
Cpl. James McClain, W (3)
Pvt. Laurence Keary, W (2, 3)
Pvt. John Henry, POW (4)
Pvt. John Masling, POW (4)
Pvt. Alexander Ross, POW (4)
Pvt. Archibald Basilom, MIA (4)
Capt. Alexander Parker's Company, Cumberland County
Pvt. Neal Hardon, KIA (4)
Pvt. Nathan Hemphill, KIA (4)
Pvt. Robert Elliott, W (2, 3)
Pvt. Jacob Justice, W/POW (2,4,5) "wounded in both legs, head, rear"
Pvt. John Tribble, W/POW (2,4,11)
Pvt. Jacob Carbrough, MIA (4)
Pvt. Cornelius Feril, MIA (4)
Pvt. Benjamin Stevens, MIA (4)
Pvt. Alexander Deney, MIA (2,4)
Pvt. David McClain, MIA (2,4)
Capt. Jeremiah Talbot's Company, Cumberland County
Sgt. John Wilson, W/POW (4, 11), died September 28, 1777
Cpl. John Shoemaker, MIA (2, 4)
Cpl. James Garland, MIA (4)
Pvt. John McKinley, W (2, 3)
Pvt. Samuel Lee, POW (4)
Pvt. John Crowl, MIA (2, 4)
Pvt. John Ferguson, MIA (2, 4)
Pvt. Peter McKinley, MIA (2, 4)
Capt. Robert Wilson's Company, Cumberland County
Capt. Robert Wilson, W (1, 12) "stabbed in the side, cock nail in forehead"
Sgt. John O'Neil, W/POW (2, 3, 11)
Pvt. Joseph Bunner, W (3)
Pvt. John Collins, W (2, 4)
Pvt. John Gibney, W (2, 3)
Pvt. Samuel Gilman, W (3, 7) "wounded in left arm"
Pvt. James Kilpatrick, W (2, 4)
Pvt. Neil McGonigal, W (2, 3)
Pvt. John McSorley, W/POW (2, 3, 11)
Pvt. Joseph Wren, W (1, 2)
Pvt. John Frise, MIA (4)
Pvt. John Smith, MIA (2, 4)
Unidentified Companies
Lt. Col. David Grier, W (1, 12), in the Side slanting towards the backbone
Capt. Andrew Irvine, W (1, 12), "in the thigh"; alleged 17 wounds in all.

Fife Maj. Richard Stack, W/POW (2, 3, 11) "13 wounds"
Pvt. James Lee, W/POW (7)

8TH PENNSYLVANIA REGIMENT

Counties: Bedford and Westmoreland
Total Known Casualties: 9 (9 W)
Estimated Personnel: 225 (Army rolls not available for September 1777)
Commander at Paoli: Col. Daniel Brodhead, Berks County
  Capt. David Killgore's Company, Bedford County
  Capt. Michael Huffnagle's Company, Westmoreland County
  Capt. Matthew Jack's Company, Westmoreland County
    Pvt. John Holton, W (2)
    Pvt. Peter Holton, W (2)
    Pvt. Alexander McKay, W (3)
  Capt. Samuel Miller's Company, Bedford County
    Pvt. James Daugherty, W (3)
  Capt. James Piggott's Company, Westmoreland County
    Pvt. Robert Hunter, W (1)
  Capt. James Montgomery's Company, Westmoreland County
    Pvt. William Gill, W (3)
  Capt. Wendell Oury's Company, Bedford County
    Pvt. Robert Grey, W (3)
    Pvt. Hugh Glen, W (3)
  Unindentified Companies
    Lt. Col. Daniel Brodhead, W (14) "rec'd a small wound"

10TH PENNSYLVANIA REGIMENT

Counties: Lancaster, Philadelphia, Northampton, and York
Total Known Casualties: 8 (8 W)
Estimated Personnel: 170 (Army rolls not available for September 1777)
Commander at Paoli: Lt. Col. Adam Hubley, Philadelphia County
  Capt. James Lang's Company, York County
    Pvt. Abraham Hornick, W (3)
    Pvt. Simeon Digby, W (3)
    Pvt. Andrus Carvin, W (3)
    Pvt. David Stimson, W (3)
  Capt. Henry Shade's Company, Northampton County
    Pvt. Frederick Wilt, W (1), "in right arm and leg"
  Capt. John Stoner's Company, Lancaster County
  Capt. George Calhoun's Company, Northumberland County
  Capt. Robert Sample's Company, Lancaster County
    Pvt. James Reed, W (4), "left for dead w/ numerous bayonet wounds"
  Capt. William Cox's Company, Lancaster County (?)
  Capt. William Wirtz's Company, county unknown
    Pvt. Michael Hatten, W (3)
    Pvt. John Farmer, W (3)
  Capt. Harmon Stout's Company, Philadelphia County (?)

11TH PENNSYLVANIA REGIMENT

Counties: Berks, Chester, Delaware, Lancaster, Philadelphia
Total Known Casualties: 5 (3 W, 1 MIA, 1 W/POW)
Estimated Total Personnel: 202 (Army rolls not available for September 1777)
Commander at Paoli: Maj. Francis Mentges, Chester County (?)
  Capt. Samuel Dawson's Company, Chester County
  Capt. Dr. John Coates's Company, Chester County
  Capt. Adolph Hedrick's Company, county unknown
  Capt. William Scull's Company, Berks County
  Capt. John Douglass's Company, Lancaster County (?)
  Capt. John Harris's Company, Harrisburg
    Capt. John Harris, W (4)
  Capt. Samuel Dean's Company, Chester County (?)
    Pvt. John Brown, MIA (6)
  Capt. George Ross's Company, Philadelphia County
    Pvt. George Beilor, W (2) "in shoulder"
    Pvt. William Leary, W (2) "in hand w/ sword, rt. leg bayonetted, jaw broken"
  Unidentified Companies
    Pvt. John McKie, W/POW (16), British deserter "after he surrendered,
      Sergeant Murphy came up and wounded him with his bayonet."

HARTLEY'S ADDITIONAL CONTINENTAL REGIMENT

Counties and States: Chester, Cumberland, Lancaster, and York Counties, plus states of
  Delaware and Maryland
Total Known Casualties: 14 (11 W, 3 W/POW)
Estimated Total Personnel: 265 (Army rolls not available for September 1777)
Commander at Paoli: Lt. Col. Morgan Connor, Berks County (?)
  Capt. Robert Hope's Company, York County
    Pvt. George Blakely, W/POW (2) 3 Stabs in his body
  Capt. William Nichols's Company, York County
    Pvt. John Casey, W (3)
  Capt. Paul Parker's Company, Cumberland County (?)
    Pvt. Sipera Poring, W (3)
    Pvt. William Meadows, W (3)
    Pvt. John Thomas, W (3)
  Capt. George Bush's Company, Delaware State
    Pvt. John Moriarty, W (3)
  Lt. Andrew Walker's Company, Lancaster County (?)
    Pvt. Edward O'Donald, W (3)
    Pvt. John Steed, W (2, 3)
  Capt. Benjamin Stoddard's Company, Maryland
    Pvt. Felix McGlauglin, W (3)
  Capt. Archibald McAllister's Company, Chester County
  Capt. James Kenny's Company, Chester County
    Pvt. David Hickey, W (3)
    Pvt. Patrick Boyle, W/POW (3, 11)
    Pvt. John Snyder, W (3)

Unidentified Companies
  Drum Maj. Daniel St. Clair, W (5, 8), "wounded several times, lost left eye
    and all fingers on left hand"
  Sgt. James Lee, W/POW (1)

CAPTAIN THOMAS RANDALL'S INDEPENDENT COMPANY OF ARTILLERY, 3RD CONTINENTAL ARTILLERY

States: Massachusetts and New Jersey
Total Known Casualties: 1 (1 W/POW)
Total Personnel: 37
Commander at Paoli: Capt. Thomas Randall, Massachusetts, W/POW (4), "knocked
  down and stabbed in eight places, taken prisoner and paroled"

COUNT PULASKI'S CORPS OF LIGHT DRAGOONS

Total Known Casualties: 1 (1 POW)
  Maj. Julius Count Montfort (10, 15), "taken prisoner at the Paoli"

BLAND'S 1ST CONTINENTAL DRAGOONS

State: Virginia
Total Known Casualties: 1 (1 KIA)
Estimated Total Personnel: 2 troops, estimated 60 horses available, number in camp
  unknown (Army rolls not available for September 1777)
Commander at Paoli: Lt. Col. Benjamin Temple, Virginia
  Capt. Llewellin Jones, 4th Troop, Virginia
  Capt. John Belfield, 6th Troop, Virginia
    Trooper Jones Dean, KIA (4) "killed by the [Maryland] militia"

SHELDON'S 2ND CONTINENTAL DRAGOONS

State: Connecticut
Total Known Casualties: 0
Estimated Total Personnel: 1 troop, 25 horses, number in camp unknown (Army rolls not
  available for September 1777)
Commander at Paoli: Capt. Josiah Stoddard, Connecticut

NOTES

CHAPTER 1

1. Diary of Sarah Logan Fisher [hereafter Fisher], vol. 4, p. 3, Historical Society of Pennsylvania [HSP]; Weather Data, Phineas Pemberton, data for September 26, 1777, American Philosophical Society [APS]; Ernst Kipping and Samuel S. Smith, *At General Howe's Side: The Diary of General William Howe's aide-de-camp Captain Friedrich von Münchhausen* [hereafter Münchhausen] (Monmouth Beach, NJ: Philip Freneau Press, 1974), 36.

2. Don Troiani et al., *Don Troiani's Soldiers in America 1754–1865* (Mechanicsburg, PA: Stackpole Books, 1998), 37. Uniform regulations called for a leather cap with a front plate bearing the queen's cypher and a red horsehair crest, but modified caps were worn on campaign. "The Battle of Paoli," by Xavier Della Gatta (1782), shows the 16th Dragoons wearing a modified cap, complete with visor but no front plate.

3. *The Royal Warrant of 1768 &c.,* Robin May and G. Embleton, *The British Army in North America* (Reading, England: Osprey, Ltd., 1974), 29–31.

4. Ibid.

5. G. D. Scull, "Journal of Captain John Montrésor, July 1, 1777, to July 1, 1778, Chief Engineer of the British Army" [hereafter Montrésor], *Pennsylvania Magazine of History and Biography [PMHB]* 5, (1881): 41.

6. Robert Morton, "Diary of Robert Morton," *PMHB* 1 (1877): 7–8.

7. Letter, Anthony Wayne to Benjamin Franklin, dated "June 13, 1776," *Wayne Papers,* vol. 1, HSP.

8. John B. B. Trussell, *The Pennsylvania Line Regimental Organization and Operations, 1776–1783* (Harrisburg, PA: The Pennsylvania Historical and Museum Commission, 1977), 53.

9. John E. Ferling, *The Loyalist Mind* (University Park, PA: Pennsylvania State University Press, 1977), 7–9. Galloway's wealth, both personal and by marriage, was estimated at £40,000 in 1775; his claim of losses after the war amounted to £45,639.4.3 Sterling, or £75,859.12.0 Pennsylvania Currency. Loyalist Claims, AO 12, vol. 38, 20–80, Public Records Office [PRO], London.

10. Ernest H. Baldwin, "Joseph Galloway, The Loyalist Politician," *PMHB* 26 (1902): 433.

11. Joseph Galloway, *Letters to a Nobleman on the Conduct of the War in the Middle Colonies.* 4th ed. (London: G. Wilkie, 1780), 77. Lord Cornwallis testified that "Mr. Galloway rendered essential Service to the British Governt.—He was in fact the confidential Man in Philadelphia." Galloway stated that he "sent out upwards of 80 different Spies at different times." Loyalist Claims, AO 12, vol. 38, PRO.

12. British regiments of this period often consisted of ten companies of men, one company of which was grenadiers. These were typically the tallest men in the regiment and were

distinguished by their bearskin caps and uniform shoulder wings. On campaign, the grenadier companies were removed from their regiments and battalioned together. Münchhausen states that on the morning of September 26, "General Howe left [Germantown] with these grenadiers, who were all dressed as properly as possible. . . . He accompanied them half way [to Philadelphia]." Münchhausen, 36.

13. John Fanning Watson, *Annals of Philadelphia and Pennsylvania in the Olden Time etc.*, vol. 2 (Philadelphia: J. M. Stoddart, 1877), 282–83.

14. Fisher, vol. 4, 3.

15. "Waste Book 1776," Christopher and Benjamin Marshall, Jr., Apothecary, Marshall Papers, HSP. This book gives detailed inventories of medical equipment and drugs for the Pennsylvania battalions.

16. "Recollections of the Entry of the Army—by a Lady," Watson, vol. 2, 284.

17. Morton, *PMHB* 1, 3–4.

18. May and Embleton, plate C and p. 34; see also Mollo and McGregor, plate 7 and p. 160.

19. Hessian uniforms, as well as those of many other German soldiers of the period, were modeled on Prussian uniforms designed by Frederick the Great. The Prussian drill and system were also largely copied by the German princes. Mustaches were an unofficial requirement for grenadiers; those who could not grow a proper mustache wore false whiskers glued on. See Jay Luvaas, *Frederick the Great on the Art of War* (New York: The Free Press, 1966).

20. Watson, vol. 2, 283.

21. Fisher, vol. 4, 4.

22. Ibid.

23. Münchhausen, 22. Exact numbers are nearly impossible to give, since the daily morning reports are not readily available, if at all. This number is given based on the estimates of the period and the troop lists that survive, along with comments from period sources such as letters and diaries. Variables include the sick, whose numbers fluctuated daily, deserters, and those captured or "on command" or special assignments.

24. Ibid., 36.

CHAPTER 2

1. See Charles M. Lefferts, *Uniforms of the American, British, French and German Armies etc.* (Old Greenwich, CT: WE, Inc., 1917). Also John Mollo and Malcolm McGregor, *Uniforms of the American Revolution* (New York: MacMillan Publishing Co., 1975). Montrésor noted in his journal on September 5: "Three Rebels Light Horse deserted to us—all Irishmen—some with the clothing of our 8th Regt. on [red coats with blue facings]—taken from us by their Privateers and each covered with a rifle shirt." *PMHB* 5 (1881): 414.

2. The Continental Army was a multiethnic force; some regiments were also racially integrated. When the war broke out, many New England units had free black soldiers mixed in the ranks. Congress officially discouraged recruitment of black soldiers, but some New England and Middle States ignored this. In 1778, Congress authorized the raising of two Rhode Island regiments, largely composed of black soldiers. See Benjamin Quarrles, *The Negro in the American Revolution* (New York: W. W. Norton, 1961).

3. John Adams to Abigail Adams, August 24, 1777, Paul H. Smith, *Letters of Delegates to Congress, 1774–1789*, vol. 7 (Washington: Library of Congress, 1981), 538; also Pemberton, *Weather Data*, entry for August 24, 1777. Adams noted, "The Lightning struck in several Places. It struck the Quaker Alms House in Walnut Street, between third and fourth Streets, not far from Captn. Duncan's, where I lodge. They had been wise enough to place an Iron Rod upon the Top of the Steeple, for a Vane to turn on, and had provided no Conductor to the Ground. It also struck in fourth Street, near Mrs. Cheesmans. No Person was hurt."

4. John Fitzpatrick, *The Writings of George Washington,* [hereafter *WW*] vol 9 (Washington: Government Printing Office, 1933), 127–28. "The citizens of Philadelphia were once gratified with the full display of General Washington's whole army. . . . This martial entry passed down the long line of front street. There, thousands of our citizens beheld numerous poor fellows, never to be seen more among the sons of men! They were on their march to meet the enemy, landed at the head of Elk." Watson, vol. 2, 287.

5. Alexander Graydon and John Littell, *Memoirs of His Own Time, etc.* (Philadelphia: Lindsay & Blakiston, 1846), 290.

6. Franklin was in France in August 1777 negotiating the French Alliance. The Quakers, who refused to "take the test" and swear allegiance to Congress, were under suspicion of loyalism. Twenty-one of the leading Philadelphia Quakers were soon placed under arrest without charge and sent into exile in Winchester, Virginia; two of them died in captivity. The Anglican Church in America was destroyed by the Revolution, since many of its clergy remained loyal to the king as head of the Church. Many Methodist clergy also remained loyal to the crown.

7. John Adams to Abigail Adams, August 26, 1777, *Letters of Delegates,* vol. 7, 554. Here Adams refers in general terms to the infantry regiments, which were organized by state in 1777. The dragoons and artillery in Washington's army included soldiers from New England and elsewhere. The Army of the Northern Department was commanded by Horatio Gates, while Israel Putnam had command of the troops in the Hudson Highlands (Peekskill). Congressman Thomas Burke of North Carolina also noted the regional makeup of the army when he wrote on August 26, "General Washington has already marched with a gallant army composed of Southern Troops to oppose them." *Letters of Delegates,* vol. 7, 555.

8. Thomas Tucker, *Mad Anthony Wayne and the New Nation* (Harrisburg, PA: Stackpole Books, 1973), 27.

9. *WW,* vol. 9, 126.

10. Ibid. The road mentioned is now Woodland Avenue in Southwest Philadelphia.

11. John Adams to Abigail Adams, August 24, 1777, *Letters of Delegates,* vol. 7, 538–39.

12. *WW,* vol. 9, 126.

13. Henry Marchant to Nicholas Cooke, August 24, 1777, *Letters of Delegates,* vol. 7, 541.

14. Letter, Anthony Wayne to the Board of War, dated "June 3d, 1777," *Wayne Papers,* vol. 3, 89, HSP.

15. Lefferts, 126–31.

16. Graydon, *Memoirs,* 291.

CHAPTER 3

1. Tavern Petitions, Chester County Archives. Mary Miller was proprietress of the Buck Tavern for five years before the Revolution. Soldiers passed this way during the French and Indian War and the Revolution, but this was the first time that a force of this size, with more than 10,000 men, occupied the area.

   After the war, Delaware County was created out of the eastern portion of Chester County; Montgomery County was created from the northern and western portions of Philadelphia County. Thus, the Buck Tavern (demolished ca. 1965) stood in what is now Delaware County, on the line with Montgomery County; the township names have not changed. The tavern's location is marked by a historical marker on Lancaster Pike (Route 30) between Old Buck Lane and Martin's Lane in Haverford.

2. Weather data, Pemberton manuscript, APS. The outdoor temperature "near Philadelphia" at 7 A.M. was 53 degrees and at 3 P.M. was 67 degrees, very pleasant marching weather. Most of the route of the original Lancaster Road, also called the Conestoga Road, is still used as roadway, though under different names. The army's camp and march are commemorated by two historical markers—one in Merion on Montgomery

Avenue at Meeting House Lane, the other in Garrett Hill opposite the Methodist church. Milestones 8, 9, 10, 12, and 13 have miraculously survived all these years; the 11 and 14 stones have vanished.

3. Letter, Adam Hubley to John Hubley, dated "Camp Lancaster Road Sept. 14th 1777 (Six Clock Eve)," *The Peter Force Collection,* ser. 9, conts. 21–24, MSS 17, 137, reel 104, Library of Congress [hereafter *Force*].

4. Ibid.

5. "That part of the Middle Colonies which has been the scene of the late military operations, cannot, with the least propriety, in the military sense of the words, be called uncommonly strong . . . the hills, when compared with those in this country [England] are by no means high or difficult of access. . . . How then can a country in any military sense be deemed impracticable? . . . A British soldier should blush at finding room for the thought in his heart, and much more at pronouncing it with his tongue. . . . I would, for the sake of my country, erase the words *strong* and *impracticable* from every dictionary, lest it should be renewed to apologize for the military indolence and misconduct of men, who have sacrificed to PARTY and FACTION their own honour, the glory of their Sovereign, and the dignity of the nation." Joseph Galloway, *LETTERS to a NOBLEMAN, on the CONDUCT of the WAR in the MIDDLE COLONIES* (London: G. Wilkie, 1780), 2–6.

6. Journal of Timothy Pickering, Essex Institute [hereafter Pickering's Journal]. Should one presume that Pickering himself set an example by dismounting and walking through the river?

7. Journal, Sgt. John Hawkins of Hazen's Regiment (also known as the 2nd Canadian or Congress' Own Regiment), entry for September 14, 1777, AM 0765, HSP. Washington wrote on September 13 that he intended to march to Swedes Ford. The General Orders for September 14 in Muhlenberg's Orderly Book state, "The Troops are to march to Sweed's Ford." *Part* of the army may have gone there, but other sources mention Swedes Ford and then refer to Merion Meeting and Lancaster Road. Swedes Ford was 8 or 9 miles farther up, and a crossing there, only to return to Merion Meeting, was unlikely. According to Lt. James McMichael: "We crossed the Schuylkill in the centre between Philadelphia and Swedes Ford, 8 miles from each. We reached the great road to Lancaster, at Merion Meeting house, and proceeded up that road, when we encamped in an open field." William P. McMichael, "Diary of Lieutenant James McMichael, of the Pennsylvania Line, 1776–1778" [hereafter McMichael], *PMHB* 16 (1892): 150–51. Capt. Robert Kirkwood wrote, "Forded Schuylkill at Davis's ford, then march'd to the Sign of the Brick [Buck] on the Lancaster Road Chester County & lay in the woods being about 11 miles." Joseph Brown Turner, *The Journal and Order Book of Captain Robert Kirkwood of the Delaware Regiment Etc.* [hereafter *Kirkwood*] (Wilmington, DE: The Historical Society of Delaware, 1910), 173.

8. "Orderly Book of General John Peter Gabriel Muhlenberg, March 26–December 20, 1777" [hereafter Muhlenberg OB], *PMHB* 33–34, (1910): 466.

9. Captain George Smith, *An Universal Military Dictionary, etc.* (London: J Millan, 1779; Ottawa, Ontario: Museum Restoration Service, 1969), 243.

10. *WW,* vol. 9, 220–21.

11. Ibid.

12. Ibid., 225.

13. "Daily Expence Record," *George Washington Papers* [hereafter *GW Papers*], film 36, reel 117, ser. 5, Library of Congress. This tavern, opened by Richard Hughes about 1730 and called the Three Tuns, was bought by Francis Holton in 1760 and renamed the Prince of Wales, but it continued to appear as Richard Hughes's on many eighteenth-century maps. It stood on Montgomery Avenue near Anderson Avenue in Ardmore and was purchased in 1772 by the Irish-born master silversmith Philip Syng, Jr. (1703–89). Thomas Potts wrote to Franklin in 1774, "Good Mr. Philip Syng has

retired into the Country about 10 miles from the city." Charles R. Barker, "Colonial Taverns of Lower Merion," *PMHB* 52 (1928), 211–13.

14. The name of the Plough Tavern was changed just before the Revolution to the Sign of John Wilkes and was kept by Peter Mather in 1774–76. Mather moved to the Admiral Warren Tavern in East Whiteland in 1777. The 1787 tavern petition lists "The Sign of John Wilkes, or the Old Plough." (Tavern Petitions, Chester County Archives.) In local tradition, Peter Mather was a reputed Loyalist. (See chapter 7, note 17; also Futhey and Cope, 85; Burns, *TEHCQ*, 62.) It is odd that a committed Tory would change the name of his tavern from an innocuous name like the Plough to a politically charged name like the Sign of John Wilkes, or even consent to work at such a named establishment. John Wilkes was a radical leader of the Whigs in Parliament, archenemy of the Tories, and hero of the Sons of Liberty. A tavern with this name would not attract a Tory crowd; the name change smacks of a strong political viewpoint.

15. Letter, Anthony Wayne to Thomas Mifflin, dated "Radnor 14th Mile Stone Sepr. 15th 1777," *Wayne Papers*, vol. 4, HSP. Wayne's question was valid: Could the British not move straight on to Philadelphia if the Continental Army moved to the west? The answer is yes; Joseph Galloway emphasized this point in his criticism of General Howe's conduct after Brandywine.

16. "Daily Expence Record," *GW Papers*; also see Tavern Petitions, Chester County Archives. Jacob Waggoner or Wagner took over the running of the Sorrel Horse on the death of his brother-in-law Michael Stadelman in 1777. This was Washington's second known visit to the Sorrel Horse; he dined there on June 3, 1773. See John C. Fitzpatrick, *The Diaries of George Washington,* vol. 2 (Boston: Houghton Mifflin Company, 1925), 114.

17. Letter, Thomas Hartley to William Atlee and Paul Zantzinger, dated "On a Drum Head near the Sorrel Horse Sepr. ye. 15:th 1777," *Force.*

18. Account, dated "Lancaster 12th Sepr 1777—Subscribers to the riders, etc.," *Force.*

19. Letter, Adam Hubley to John Hubley, dated "Camp Lancaster Road Sept. 14th 1777 (Six Clock Eve)"; also Letter, Adam Hubley to William Atlee, Paul Zantzinger, and John Hubley, dated "Camp Lancaster road, near Sorrel Horse Sepr. 15 1777," *Force.*

20. John Adams to Abigail Adams, September 1, 1777, 579; Eliphalet Dyer to Samuel Grey, September 1, 1777, 580; Eliphalet Dyer to Jonathan Trumbull, Sr., September 1, 1777, 581; Henry Laurens to Solomon Legare, August 27, 1777, 563; *Letters of Delegates.*

CHAPTER 4

1. Letter, Anthony Wayne to unknown recipient (probably Abraham Robinson, an in-law), dated "Trap 29th Sepr 1777." Collection of H. Richard Dietrich, Jr., Philadelphia.

2. *WW,* vol. 9, 128–29. It is interesting to note Washington's repeated reference to the fact that these are Congress's orders. The task of organizing militia was not looked upon with enthusiasm by regular officers.

3. Ibid., 147–48.

4. "Journal and Correspondence of the Council of Maryland, 1777" [hereafter JCCM], *The Maryland Archives,* 364–65.

5. Ibid.

6. Ibid., 366–67.

7. Ibid. The "Lower Ferry" crossed the Susquehanna near its mouth, between North East and Havre de Grace, Maryland.

8. *WW,* vol. 9, 198. Washington further instructed Smallwood, "I will not mark out any particular line of conduct for you to pursue, but leave it to you, either to join me or to fall upon the Rear of the Enemy. . . . Your caution upon this occasion cannot be too great, Much is at Stake."

9. JCCM, 369–71.
10. Letter, Samuel Chase to George Washington, dated "Philada. Septr. 15, 1777." *GW Papers*, Library of Congress.
11. Octavius Pickering, *Life of Timothy Pickering*, vol. 1 (Boston: Little, Brown and Company, 1867), 163–64; James Lovell to Robert Treat Paine, September 24, 1777, *Letters of Delegates*, vol. 8, 15.
12. *WW*, vol. 9, 222–23. The postscript stated, "Having spoken to many of my Officers respecting the Line of conduct you should pursue, it is the general Opinion, that you can not render so much Service, as by perpetually hanging on and annoying their Rear. This I wish you to do without you should find it unadvisable from some very particular circumstances."
13. Letter, William Smallwood to George Washington, dated "Oxford Meeting House 7 Miles above Nottingham Septr. 15th 1777" [emphasis added], *GW Papers*. The return was included with the letter.

CHAPTER 5

1. Documentation of troops crossing Swedes Ford is elusive due to the confusion of the ford names in some accounts and in the General Orders. It is possible that some of the army marched to Swedes Ford on September 14; the documents used in chapter 3 confirm that the main part of the army crossed at Levering's Ford. (See chapter 3, note 6.)
2. Tavern Petitions, Chester County Archives. Documents relating to the White Horse Tavern establishment include a bond to James Thomas, Whiteland, 1721; Edward Kinnison's petition "allowed," Whiteland, 1724; John Bromfield, 1728, "about half a mile from Kinnisons," probably the site of the tavern operating in 1777.
3. Swedes Ford was shallow and wide, with a hard, stony bottom that allowed a direct crossing of the river. Many of the other fords were narrow and deep and required a zigzag crossing, using islands or mudflats. Swedes would permit a rapid, safe crossing of an army, whereas other fords could delay an army for hours and present an enemy with an opportunity to strike.
4. *WW*, vol. 9, 229. The most recent British "violent inclination" was the Battle of Brandywine.
5. *WW*, vol. 9, 230. Washington's letter to Hancock on September 16 is headed "Camp between Warren and White Horse Taverns." Lieutenant McMichael wrote, "September 15– At 6 A. M. we marched to the Sorrel Horse, the Spread Eagle and to Paoli, *where we encamped*." McMichael, 151. This would stretch the Continental camp more than 6 miles along the Lancaster Road, from the White Horse to the Paoli.
6. Münchhausen, 32.
7. Orderly Book, "Captain Thomas Armstrong's Company Orderly Book 64th Lt. Infantry," 2nd Battalion of British Light Infantry, *GW Papers*, "Miscellaneous Manuscripts."
8. Journal, "The Journal of Captain-Lieutenant John Peebles of the Grenadier Company of the 42nd, or Royal Highland Regiment," entry for September 15, 1777, Public Records Office, Edinburgh, Scotland. Microfilm of the journal is in the David Library of the American Revolution, Washington's Crossing, Pennsylvania.
9. Montrésor, 35. It is remarkable that the British headquarters knew the correct name of the ford where Washington's army crossed, even though some of the Americans who crossed it did not.
10. "Journal of Sergeant Thomas Sullivan," *PMHB* 34 (1910): 229.
11. Peebles, entry for September 15. Cornwallis's column moved north on modern Route 452 from Aston to Lima, then north on Route 352 to Goshen Meeting House on Paoli Pike in East Goshen. Knyphausen's column (where Howe was) moved northward from Dilworthtown on the Old Wilmington Pike and Route 202 to South High Street

in West Chester, where they marched to the Turk's Head Tavern (High and Market Streets). From there, part of the force under General Mathews continued on the Reading Road (now Route 100) to King Road. The remainder headed northeast on the Road to the Boot, now largely obliterated but roughly paralleling Phoenixville Pike; some headed east over Goshen Road, also mostly obliterated but parallel to modern Paoli Pike to modern Boot Road and Goshen Meeting House, where they rendezvoused with Cornwallis.

12. Münchhausen, 32. Just when the rain began is recorded as early as 8 A.M. and as late as 5 P.M. The heaviest rain seems to have begun about 5 o'clock and remained steady all night.

13. Joseph P. Tustin, *Diary of the American War, A Hessian Journal, Captain Johann Ewald, Field Jäger Corps* [hereafter Ewald] (New Haven: Yale University Press, 1979), 88–89. "General Orders, Head Quarters 17 Septr. 1777. . . . The Commander in Chief thinks him Self Much obligd. to Colo. Donop & Corps of Yeagers for the Spirit & Judgement with which they yesterday Routed & Dispersed the Enemies successfully." Armstrong Orderly Book, *GW Papers.*

14. S. Sydney Bradford, "A British Officer's Revolutionary War Journal, 1776–1778," *Maryland Historical Magazine* 56, no. 2 (June 1961): 171. The Journal of Lt. Henry Stirke, Light Company, 10th Regiment of Foot, 1st Battalion of British Light Infantry [hereafter Stirke].

15. Pickering's Journal, entry for September 16, 1777.

16. J. Smith Futhey and Gilbert Cope, *History of Chester County, Pennsylvania, etc.* (Philadelphia: Louis Everts, 1881; Salem, MA: Higginson Book Company, 1998), 83.

17. Ibid.

18. Ewald, 89.

19. Bernhard A. Uhlendorf and Edna Vosper, *Letters from Major Baurmeister to Colonel von Jungkenn Written during the Philadelphia Campaign 1777–1778* (Philadelphia: The Historical Society of Pennsylvania, 1937), 18–19.

20. Ewald, 89.

21. Münchhausen, 32. Samuel Oliver ran this tavern in 1776; John Bowen ran it in 1778. Tavern Petitions, Chester County Archives.

22. Samuel Shaw to his father, letter dated "Artillery Park, Skippack, about twenty four miles west from Philadelphia, September 30, 1777." Josiah Quincy, *The Journals of Major Samuel Shaw* (Boston: Wm. Crosby & H. Nichols, 1847; Reprint, Documentary Publications, 1970), 37–38.

23. John C. Dann, *The Nagle Journal* (New York: Weidenfeld & Nicolson, 1989), 8. Morgan's Riflemen were not with Washington's army at this time; they were with General Gates. However, many of Morgan's men were Pennsylvanians and many of Wayne's troops, especially the 1st Pennsylvania Regiment, were riflemen. The observation about the difference in sound between the Pennsylvania rifles and the Hessian jäger rifles lends much credibility to this account. The Pennsylvania rifles tended to be long and of small caliber; the jäger rifles were short and of large caliber, giving off a *blam* when fired rather than a crack or snap. The sounds of both weapons were distinctly different from the blast of the smoothbore infantry muskets.

24. Letter, John Laurens to Henry Laurens, dated "November 6, 1777," Laurens Papers, South Carolina Historical Society. Generals' aides were identified by a green sash worn over the left shoulder and under the uniform coat.

CHAPTER 6

1. *WW,* vol. 9, 231–32.

2. Morton, 3. Morton was on his way to Reading to try to visit some of the Philadelphia Quakers, including his stepfather James Pemberton, who were arrested without charge in August.

3. Pickering Journal, entry for September 16, 1777.

4. Letter, Thomas Hartley to William Atlee et al., dated "Camp Septr 17th 1777," *Force.*

5. *WW,* vol. 9, 231–32. "17th march'd and Cross'd French Creek Bridge being 6 miles went 3 miles further there Stayed all night being 9 miles (no tents) Thursday 18th march'd About 3 OClock in the morning, to Reading Furnace being 12 miles." Kirkwood, 175. Local tradition states that Capt. John Ralston guided Washington this way because the only bridge over French Creek was at the Reading Road. See Futhey and Cope, 102.

6. Entry for Wednesday, September 17, 1777. *The Journals of Henry Melchior Muhlenberg,* [hereafter Muhlenberg], vol. 3 (Philadelphia: Muhlenberg Press, 1958), 76.

7. Montrésor, 36–38.

8. The former White Horse Tavern is, as of 2000, a private dwelling at the intersection of Planebrook and Swedesford Roads in Frazer. The section of Swedesford Road west of Route 401 is the original Lancaster Road. Planebrook Road was the "Road to White Horse and Goshen Meeting" in 1777, running south from the tavern all the way up the South Valley Hill (through Immaculata College) to King Road. Just west of the tavern, the small section of Bacton Hill Road south of Swedesford Road is a remnant of the road to the Boot Tavern. Rerouted over the years by railroads and cut off by highways (Routes 202 and 30), most of the original road's path is obliterated in the valley. Phoenixville Pike south from Route 30 to King Road merely approximates the original route. From King Road to Boot Road, however, Phoenixville Pike covers the original road course.

9. These roads include modern Route 352, from Paoli Pike to King Road, then west on King Road to Immaculata College. Troops were spread along King Road farther west, as far as Route 100, the "Road to Pottsgrove." Headquarters was at Boot Tavern, which stood at Phoenixville Pike and Boot Road. Troops camped along Ship Road from Boot Road to beyond King Road, and back along Boot Road and Phoenixville Pike for another mile beyond the Boot Tavern.

10. Münchhausen, 34.

11. Ibid. Discrepancies between times in the accounts are explained by the size of the force, the condition of the roads, and the various duties and functions of the individual writing the account. Some troops halted at the White Horse for only an hour; others had to "hurry up and wait" for several hours.

12. Ibid.

13. *WW,* vol. 9, 235.

14. Ibid., 231–32. Maxwell's Corps of Light Infantry was formed in the summer of 1777, made up of chosen men from the entire army. Its first battle was at Iron Hill ("Cooch's Bridge"), Delaware, on September 3, and it was heavily involved at Brandywine. The General Orders for September 14 state, "Such men Belonging to Genl Maxwells light Corps as have Returned to their Regts are again to Join Genl Maxwell without Delay And the Officers Commanding Regts are to make dilligent Search for those men, & See that they are Sent to Join that Corps Immedietly." (Kirkwood, 174). At Trappe on September 23, Rev. Henry Muhlenberg wrote: "Last night a corps of American light infantrymen, a scouting party, was chased across the Schulkiel toward us by the British. They camped near our house. During the night an old English neighbor came to my house and asked me to get up and speak in his behalf with General Maxwell." (Muhlenberg, vol. 3, 79). The corps seems to have been disbanded sometime in late September, as Maxwell was back with his New Jersey troops before the Battle of Germantown.

15. Letter, Clement Biddle to George Washington, dated "Valley Forge Tuesday Eveng. 9' oClock 16 Septemr 1777," *GW Papers.* Howell's Tavern (now demolished) stood on Swedesford Road between Routes 202 and 252 in "Howellville." The distance from there to "the road to Yellow Springs" is about 1½ miles north (Mill Road to Yellow Springs Road). From there by "this rout[e]" (the roads of that day), the distance to the

Valley Forge (Routes 23 and 252) would be about 4 to 5 miles via Yellow Springs Road, the "Baptist Road" (Valley Forge Road), and the Gulph Road. Bull Tavern, which is greatly modified but still standing, is about 3 miles west of Valley Forge near Pickering Creek.

16. "The light Corps lately under Genl. Maxwell, supposed to amount to 450 Men . . . ." Council of War, September 28, 1777, *WW,* vol. 9, 278. The total number of Pennsylvania militia in the field appears to have numbered about 2,000 or 2,200; Potter's force is estimated at about 1,000.

17. Letter, Thomas Hartley to William Atlee et al., dated "Camp three Miles from the Red Lion Chester County, Sepr. ye 18th 1777 1 oClocke PM.," *Force.* The Red Lion Tavern, no longer a tavern, still stands in Lionville, Uwchlan Township, at the southeast corner of Whitford Road & South Village Avenue. The camp, three miles away, was in the vicinity of Chester Springs.

18. Letter, George Washington to Anthony Wayne, dated "Reading furnace, Septr 18th, 1777," Wayne Papers, vol. 4, HSP.

19. Letter, George Washington to William Smallwood, dated "Camp Sepr. 17:1777," *GW Papers.* The contents of this letter indicate that Washington had not yet left Yellow Springs. It is also possible that Smallwood never received this note; it may have been intercepted.

"Futhay" was probably Samuel Futhey of West Fallowfield Township, who was employed by the Pennsylvania Supreme Executive Council as purchaser of horses for the army. His great-grandson was J. Smith Futhey, coauthor of the 1881 *History of Chester County.* Futhey and Cope, 559.

20. Letter, William Smallwood to George Washington, dated "James Mcclelans Tavern [Parkesburg] September 19, 1777," from Joseph Rubinfine's document catalogue, *The American Revolution in Manuscript* (West Palm Beach, FL: American Historical Autographs, 1994). Smallwood further stated: "I am reduced to the Necessity of sending Officers forward to provide for the Troops which has been the case ever since I set out[.] notwithstanding I have acquainted Mr. Buchanan [of the Commissary Department] with this Defect. I cannot obtain any Remedy." This letter has a number of blanks with coded symbols in place of names and numbers, an indication of the danger of interception.

21. Letter, Hartley to Atlee, September 18, 1777.

CHAPTER 7

1. John Adams to Abigail Adams, May 22, 1777, *Letters of Delegates,* vol. 7, 103.

2. James Lovell to William Whipple, July 7, 1777, *Letters of Delegates,* vol. 7, 315.

3. Washington wrote to Hancock on September 15: "To derange the Army by withdrawing so many General Officers from it, may and must be attended with many disagreeable, if not ruinous, Consequences. . . . The recall of Genl. St. Clair, obliged me to part with Genl. Lincoln, whom I could but illy spare, so that the whole charge of his division is now upon Genl. Wayne, [there being no other brigadier] in it than himself." *WW,* vol. 9, 228. See John Trussell, Jr., *The Pennsylvania Line Regimental Organization and Operations, 1776–1783,* Harrisburg, PA: Pennsylvania Historical and Museum Commission, 1977.

4. Futhey and Cope, 607, 758.

5. As many of the records are incomplete and some of the numbers are based on averages between June and November 1777, a generous margin of error (10 percent or more) should be allowed. The problem of determining exact numbers is partly due to the condition of army affairs in 1777. Dr. Benjamin Rush wrote to John Adams on October 1: "I heard of 2000 who sneaked off with the baggage of the army to Bethlehem. I was told by a captain in our army that they would not be missed in the returns, for as these

were made out *only* by *sergeants* they would be returned on parade, and that from the *proper* officers' neglecting to make out or examine returns General Washington never knew within 3,000 men what his real numbers were." L. H. Butterfield, *Letters of Benjamin Rush*, vol. 1 (Princeton, NJ: Princeton University Press, 1951), 155–56. Washington wrote to Pennsylvania president Thomas Wharton on October 17: "I beg leave to recommend to the Serious Consideration of the Legislature of your State; that is, the falling upon some mode of compleating and keeping up the Quota of your Continental Regiments. *Upon an average, your Battalions have never been above one third full; and now, many of them, are far below even that.*" [emphasis added], *WW*, vol. 9, 386–87.

6. The compiled data of this research—muster and payrolls, letters, General Orders, and Court of Inquiry testimony—has identified the makeup of Lincoln's Division/Wayne's Command in September 1777. Several Pennsylvania militiamen made claims of their presence at Paoli in pension applications; other than these claims, there is no supporting evidence of Pennsylvania militia in the writings of the Continental officers or in the Court of Inquiry testimony. Some militia may have been camped nearby, as they had been at the "Battle of the Clouds," but no other documentation has been found thus far to support the claims.

7. Letter, Hartley, "Camp 3 Miles from the Red Lion, Sept. 18," *Force.*

8. Maj. Samuel Hay of the 7th Pennsylvania wrote on September 29, "You will see by this imperfect scrawl how many sorts of ink I have written with—all borrowed, and the inkstands dry, as I have no baggage, nor have had any these four weeks, more than one shirt and one pair of stockings, besides what is on my back; the other officers are in the same way, and most of the officers belonging to the division have lost their baggage at Colonel Frazer's, taken by the enemy." *PMHB* 1 (1877): 313–15. Col. Persifor Frazer and the division's baggage were captured September 15 near the colonel's home.

9. The memo to Colonel Atlee suggests that this inventory was sent to Lancaster, probably by the established express. The fact that this paper is in the same collection as Hartley's and Hubley's letters to Atlee et al. supports this suggestion. *Force.*

10. Montrésor, 37–38.

11. Pemberton Weather Data, APS.

12. Montrésor, 37.

13. See Harold D. Eberlein and Cortlandt vD. Hubbard, *The Church of Saint Peter in the Great Valley* (Richmond, VA: August Dietz and Son, 1944), 77–82. Pastor Muhlenberg occasionally preached at St. James in Currie's absence.

   Nicholas Cresswell, a young English visitor in Virginia, noted in October 1776: "No service at [the Anglican] Church to-day. Religion is almost forgotten or most basely neglected. In short, the Parsons are not willing to expound the Gospel to people without being paid for it, and there is no provision made for the Episcopal Clergy by this new code of Laws, therefore Religion as well as Commerce is at a stand." Lincoln MacVeagh, *The Journal of Nicholas Cresswell* (New York: The Dial Press, 1924), 165. In short, the "established Church" was disestablished by the Revolution. Currie's reasons for not preaching did not have to do with salary, but with age, health, and stress over his personal crisis, both in family and flock.

14. "Extracts from the Letter-book of Captain Johann Heinrichs . . . ," *PMHB* 22, (1898): 137. The "dissenter" churches tended to support the Revolution; no religious group was more active or militant than the Presbyterian and Congregational churches, whose roots were Calvinist and firmly anti-Anglican. Cresswell makes numerous references to Presbyterian influence on the Revolution: "Sunday, October 20, 1776 . . . The Presbyterian Clergy are particularly active in supporting the measures of Congress from the Rostrum, gaining proselytes, persecuting the unbelievers, preaching up the righteousness of their cause and persuading the unthinking populace to the infallibility of success. Some of these religious rascals assert that the Lord will send his Angels to assist the injured Americans. . . . I am convinced if they establish their Independence that Presbyty will be the established religion on this Continent." Later, when returning to En-

gland, Cresswell wrote, "Saturday, July 19, 1777 . . . The whims, cruelty and caprice of a vile Congress give them Laws, and a set of puritanical Rascals retails the Scriptures. . . . As the Rascally Presbyterian Clergy have all along been the chief instigators and supporters of this unnatural Rebellion, they commonly honour the loyalists with the title of Tory, atheist, Deist, or the most opprobrious name that the most inveterate malice can invent, aided by that cursed enthusiastic, uncharitable, bloody-minded and cruel persecuting spirit which in general constitutes a considerable part of the character of these *fanatic* brawlers, or rather *Bellows* of Sedition and Rebellion." (Cresswell, 165, 261.)

15. Howell's Tavern, now demolished, stood near the modern intersection of Swedesford Road and Bear Hill Road (Route 252) at a crossroads later called Centreville or Howellville. It is interesting to note that the tavern was named the Sign of George III before 1776; the primary references to it in this campaign simply call it Howell's Tavern (see Montrésor; also André's Map), which indicate that the name was changed after independence was declared. Mary Howell applied for the tavern license in 1778 with the following statement: "Your Petioner Lives In the house, which her Late Husband, David Howell Dwelt, which house Hath Been Occupied, as a Tavern, for more then Twenty Years, That your Petioner hath a Large family of Small Children, That the Distresses & great Disasters the British Army Occasioned, as they Passed through the Neiborhood, gives me hopes, to Be Intiled to your Recomendation." (Chester County Tavern Petitions.) Curiously, the tavern bore the name the Sign of George II in the 1780s, a more acceptable name from happier times; economy, no doubt, played its part, as the sign would require one small change rather than full repainting. The house of Samuel Jones is still standing, on Old State Road near Contention Lane.

16. This tavern was opened by George Aston in 1745 and named the Admiral Vernon after a British naval hero, the same hero for whom the Washington estate Mount Vernon was named. Later the name was changed to the Admiral Warren, in honor of Sir Peter Warren, another British naval hero; this was the name during the Revolution. Afterward it was changed to the General Warren in honor of Gen. Dr. Joseph Warren, leader of the Massachusetts Sons of Liberty, who died at Bunker (Breed's) Hill, the first American general killed in the war. (Chester County Tavern Petitions.)

17. Dr. Julius Sachse, *The Wayside Inns of the Lancaster Road,* 2d ed. (Lancaster, PA: Self-published, 1912), 52–53, 55. The tavern was owned in 1777 by John Penn; Mather rented it until after the war. If Mather was a Loyalist, his views were more philosophical than active. Surviving factual evidence raises questions about his allegiance. (See chapter 3, note 14; also, Futhey and Cope, 85; Burns, *Tredffrin-Easttown History Club Quarterly* [hereafter *TEHCQ*], 62.)

18. This term is from a strip map of the Lancaster Turnpike made about 1795.

19. General Paoli lived in exile in England and was a hero of the Whig faction, who saw him as a champion of liberty, as well as an enemy of France. One of Paoli's ardent devotees in the 1770s and '80s was a young Corsican boy, Napoleon Buonaparte. The observation about Anthony Wayne is based on local tradition, which is sometimes plausible but often erroneous. Wayne lived about a mile from the tavern and was noted for his combative nature and "fondness for the bottle." Sachse, 55.

20. "'From Brandywine to Philadelphia,' Extracts from the Journal of Sergeant Thomas Sullivan," *PMHB* 34 (1910): 230.

21. Münchhausen, 34. The "several thousand men . . . behind the Schuylkill" were the forces under Maxwell, Potter, and Armstrong; the "support from Maryland, Virginia, etc." refers to Smallwood and Gist, as well as Virginia troops requested by Washington.

CHAPTER 8

1. *Valley Forge Report,* vol. 3 (Valley Forge, PA: Valley Forge Park Interpretive Association, National Park Service, Valley Forge National Historical Park, 1982), 186.

2. The origin of the names of these "mountains" is shrouded in mystery; tradition holds that they were given by William Penn himself. His daughter, Letitia Penn, was granted thousands of acres on the east side of Valley Creek in the 1680s; this grant was known as Latitia Penn's Manor of Mount Joy. Mount Misery's name is more obscure; evidently it was named long before the encampment.

   The Nutt Road was named after Samuel Nutt, ironmaster of Coventry Forge. This early road was built to convey iron products to Philadelphia from Nutt's Forge and the other ironworks on French Creek.

   Isaac Potts's house served as Washington's Headquarters during the encampment of 1777–78. It is a "Schuylkill Valley mansion" built sometime between 1758 and 1773.

3. From "Memorandum Book of the Committee and Council of Safety; entry for April 22, 1777," *Pennsylvania Archives,* 2d ser., vol. 1, 499; also "August 8, 1777: Estimate of Provisions . . . signed by William Buchanan," *GW Papers,* ser. 4, reel 43.

4. Letter, Col. Clement Biddle to George Washington, dated "Valley Forge Tuesday Evening 9 OClock 16 Septembr 1777," *GW Papers,* ser. 4, reel 43.

5. Ibid.

6. *WW,* vol. 9, 231–32.

7. Henry Lee, *Memoirs of the War in the Southern Department of the United States* (New York: University Publishing Company, 1869), 90–91.

8. Henry Woodman, *History of Valley Forge* (Oaks, PA: John Francis, Dr., 1922), 36–37. It is possible that the Loyalist guide was William Sturge Moore, the grandson of staunch Loyalist judge William Moore of Moore Hall, who "at great personal risque shewed the Ford over the river Schuylkill to the King's Engineers, Captains Montrésor and Moncrieff and *went out of the Lines with a Party of Dragoons to secure Guides and get intelligence.*" [emphasis added] (London: Public Records Office PRO A. O. 12.42, 294–98.) Being from the neighborhood, Sarah Stephens probably would have known William Moore.

9. Münchhausen, 34.

10. Lee, 91.

11. Montrésor, 38.

12. Ibid. Other British and Hessian sources cite the flour at 4,000 barrels; additional items cited in primary sources include iron shot (Seyboldt), nails (André), "but unfortunately no rum" (Münchhausen). The forge manufactured wrought iron from pig iron; it is unknown whether any of the iron goods stored at Valley Forge were actually made there. Specialized iron manufacturing, such as casting houses to make kettles or iron shot, or a smithy to make horseshoes and nails, which also require a slitting mill, do not appear to have been part of the Valley Forge complex. Current evidence would seem to indicate that the finished iron items were made elsewhere and merely stored at Valley Forge.

13. Harold C. Syrett, *The Papers of Alexander Hamilton,* vol. 1 (New York: Columbia University Press, 1961), 326–28.

14. Letter, John Hancock to George Washington, dated "Philada. Septr. 18th. 1777. 10 O'Clock PM," *GW Papers,* ser. 4, reel 44.

15. *Hamilton Papers,* 327, note 2.

16. Morton, *Diary,* 4, note 2.

17. Ibid., 3–4.

18. Fisher, vol. 3, 82–83.

19. Henry Laurens to John Lewis Gervais, dated "18th September 1777," *Letters of Delegates,* vol. 7, 695; Henry Laurens to John Lewis Gervais, dated "York 8th October 1777," *Letters of Delegates,* vol. 8, 80.

20. Elaine Forman Crane, *The Diary of Elizabeth Drinker,* vol. 1 (Boston: Northeastern University Press, 1991), 232.

21. "Military Operations Near Philadelphia in the Campaign of 1777–8, Described in a Letter from Thomas Paine to Dr. Franklin," *PMHB* 2 (1878): 284.

22. Laurens, *Letters of Delegates,* vol. 8, 80.
23. Montrésor, 38.

CHAPTER 9

1. Brodhead's Evidence, paper marked "I"; Hubley's Evidence, paper marked "N"; Letter, Samuel Hay to Col. William Irvine, dated "Camp at the Trap, Sept. 29, 1777," *Irvine Papers,* vol. 1, 94, HSP. Hay stated: "We were ordered by His Excellency to march from the Yellow Springs. . . . We marched early on the 17th [should be the 18th] instant, and got below the Paoli that night." In this case, "below the Paoli" probably meant immediately east of, as Wayne's letters on the 19th are written from Paoli. The distance cited by Brodhead and Hartley from their position on the morning of the 19th to the camp on the heights above the Warren is 1¹/2 miles, which is the distance from the Paoli Tavern to the campsite. (Brodhead's Evidence, paper marked "I"; Hartley's Testimony, paper marked "E.") Yellow Springs is located about 10 miles to the northwest of the tavern, and the Lancaster Road ran east-west at Paoli; thus Wayne's force would have been marching southeastward from Yellow Springs to Paoli. Troops halting anywhere from a few hundred yards to a mile east of Paoli would have been "below the Paoli." A force of 2,200 personnel, wagons, dragoons, and artillery would have stretched in a column for well over a mile.
   Maj. Samuel Hay's regiment, the 7th Pennsylvania, followed the 1st Pennsylvania Regiment, which headed the column. If the Paoli Tavern was halfway between the two brigades, this would place Hay east of, or "below," Paoli, probably on the Darby Road.
   Hay is mistaken in his date; Washington's orders weren't issued until the morning of the 18th. Hartley's letter of the 18th places Wayne near Yellow Springs, "3 miles from the Red Lion," at 1 and 2 P.M. Washington's letter to Wayne telling him to move forward for the third time was written at 6 P.M. on the 18th. If Hay's date were correct, Wayne would have collided with Cornwallis marching to Tredyffrin. Colonels Brodhead and Hubley made the same error in their testimony, stating that they received orders on the evening of the 17th. "About 4 o'Clock in the afternoon, we moved off and about 2 or 3 o'Clock in the Morning arrived within about 1¹/2 Miles from the enemies Encampment." In actuality, the orders arrived on the afternoon of the 18th, and the movements were then set in motion.
2. Letter, George Washington to Anthony Wayne, dated "Readg. Furnace 6 OClock PM [September 18];" John Fitzgerald, aide-de-camp, postscript attached to Washington letter dated "Reading furnace, Septr. 18th 1777." [emphasis added] *Wayne Papers,* vol. 4, HSP.
3. Letter, Anthony Wayne to George Washington, dated "Paoli ¹/2 After 7 OClock AM 19th Sepr 1777," *GW Papers,* ser. 4, reel 44. Two of the prisoners are identified in a "List of British Prisoners of War at Lancaster, Nov. 1, 1777: Artilleryman William McQuelling, taken 19th Sept. at the Paoli; Queens Ranger Thomas Button, taken 18th Sept 1777 near ye White Horse," *Force.*
4. Ewald, 90. With hundreds of fifers, drummers, pipers, trumpeters, and bandsmen in Howe's army, reveille could easily be heard for several miles. Something of a local record was set on May 19, 1778, when Rev. Henry Muhlenberg heard the drums from Valley Forge at his home in Trappe, 14 miles away.
5. Thomas Paine to Benjamin Franklin, dated "Yorktown [Pennsylvania] May 16, 1778," "Military Operations Near Philadelphia in the Campaign of 1777," *PMHB* 2 (1878): 284. Elizabeth Drinker wrote on the night of the 18th, "It has finally cleared up after the Storm, and is now a Serene Butifull night." (Drinker, 232.)
6. Montrésor, 38.
7. Letter, Anthony Wayne to George Washington, dated, "Paoli ³/4 After 10 AM 19th Sepr. 1777," *GW Papers,* ser. 4, reel 44.

8. Montrésor, 38.
9. William Gordon, D.D., *The History of the Rise, Progress, and Establishment of the Independence of the United States of America, Etc.*, vol. 2 (London: Self-published, 1788), 516. Gordon used numerous primary documents in his work. This dispatch appears only in this published source.
10. Brodhead's Evidence, paper marked "I."
11. Hartley's Testimony, paper marked "E."
12. Münchhausen, 34. Lt. Henry Stirke of the 10th Regiment Light Company, 1st Battalion Light Infantry, wrote, "The 1st Battalion of Light Infantry and 1st and 2nd of Grenadiers, march'd at 1 O'Clock to sustain Major Craig, as the Rebels appear'd in large bodys, and made a show of attacking that post." (Stirke, 171.)
13. Peebles, entry for Friday, September 19, 1777. The "fine Prospect from this Hill" at Gulph Road in Valley Forge Park is still one of the most spectacular views in southeastern Pennsylvania.
14. Ewald, 90.
15. Montrésor, 38. The "neighboring height" was the ridge of Mount Joy above Valley Forge east of Valley Creek. Ewald states on September 21 that "the army passed the defile of the Valley Creek, where Lord Cornwallis was situated on the right [east] bank of this creek." (Ewald, 90.) André's map of the British camp at Charlestown shows the 1st Light Infantry, the Guards, and the grenadiers occupying the Mount Joy ridge on September 21.
16. Lt. Col. [John Greaves] Simcoe, *A Journal of the Operations of the Queen's Rangers, &c.* (New York: Bartlett, 1844), 60. On October 15, Simcoe was appointed to command the Queen's Rangers, the most famous Loyalist unit of the Revolution. He was given "the Provincial rank of Major."

CHAPTER 10

1. James Lovell to Robert Paine, dated "Philada. 24th Sepr. A. M.," *Letters of Delegates*, vol. 8, 15.
2. Futhey and Cope, 103, 374. See also *Colonial Records*, vols. 10, 11, 13. These volumes refer to acts of the Supreme Executive Council of Pennsylvania auctioning off property of Loyalists "attainted of High Treason"; Vernon is listed, along with many others.
3. Curtis Lewis, "Memorial of Hannah Lewis . . . Halifax, 5th May 1786," A.O. 12, vol. 40, 78–85; "Memorial of Jacob James," A.O. 12, vol. 38, 355–60; "Memorial of Richard Swanwick," A.O. 12, vol. 42, 29–44; "Memorial of William Sturge Moore of Moore Hall," A.O. 12, vol. 42, 294–98); "Certificate for George Peters," A.O. 13, 71. (Burney Collection, PRO, London.)
4. Wayne's Defense, version 1, inserted at the end.
5. Hartley's Testimony, paper marked "E."
6. Major North's Evidence, paper marked "Q"; see also Humpton's Evidence, paper marked "P." Local twentieth-century tradition erroneously identified the Bowen farmhouse, often called the Griffith house, as Wayne's headquarters, but North and Humpton verify that the Hutchinson house served as headquarters. Futhey and Cope identify Wayne's quarters as "Hutchinson's, later occupied by Jno. King." Determining who lived there at the time is difficult; it appears that the property was owned by Edward Pearce (father of Cromwell Pearce), who died in early 1777, but the house does not appear to have been his residence. Whatever remained of the original building was demolished in 1986.
   Investigation of the deeds for the Bowen properties reveals that both Levi and Ezekiel Bowen bought their farms in 1764 from Jesse Gygar; both farms were sold in March 1777. Levi sold his 96-acre farm to a neighbor, Daniel Cornog; Ezekiel's farm went to Richard Mason, a Philadelphia merchant. Ezekiel resumed ownership of the

farm in April 1778, which suggests that the farm went into receivership. Ezekiel's whereabouts in this period are uncertain. He is listed in the Chester County tax records as having taken the oath of allegiance to the United States in 1778 and is listed in the Willistown Township Company of Chester County Militia in 1780. He died in 1804 and was buried at the Church of St. Peter-in-the-Great Valley; his farm was then sold to the Griffith family. The records disprove the myth that "a Tory named Griffith" refused to permit the soldiers killed in the Battle of Paoli to be buried in a mass grave on his farm. It is not known who occupied the Bowen house during the Paoli Camp; possibly the family was still living there. The house was demolished in the 1950s after a period of abandonment.

7. General Orders, "September 4, 10, 1777," [emphasis added] *WW,* vol. 9, 178–79, 199–200.

8. Brodhead's Testimony, paper marked "I."

9. Ibid. Determining the left, or rear, of camp is a bit confusing. In this case, the men moved out what was to become the left side of camp, which at this time was called the rear, since they had been there only a few hours and were still arranged in a column of march. Viewing the force as a column, the *head* was at the *right* of the camp; thus the *rear* of the column is the *left* flank of camp.

10. Humpton's Testimony, paper marked "P." Humpton may have been referring to the Sugartown Road or to a farm road that led into Sugartown Road. In either case, some openings were made in the fences to enable passage through; the fences mostly remained intact and were not "laid down."

The "front" and "rear" terminology is again confusing. Humpton commanded the 2nd Brigade, which was the *rear* of the *column* on the march. In camp, it became the *left flank.* When evacuating the camp, however, the maneuver went out the *left* of camp, and thus, Humpton's 2nd Brigade now became the *front* of the evacuating column.

11. Wayne's Testimony, versions 1 & 2, *Wayne Papers,* vol. 4, HSP. The original King Road followed the township line exactly and intersected Sugartown Road about 100 yards north of the modern intersection. (Chester County Road Papers.)

12. Münchhausen, 34. From the American accounts, there is no evidence of "great confusion" or of knowledge of a British maneuver. Münchhausen did not observe this himself; his account is based on reports back to headquarters, which may have exaggerated the American evacuation procedure. It is also possible that by comparison with the discipline of the British Army, the American maneuvers appeared confused.

13. Hartley's Testimony, paper marked "E"; Connor's Testimony, paper marked "C."

14. Brodhead's Testimony, paper marked "I."

15. Montrésor, 38.

16. *British Depredations in Chester County in 1777* (unpublished manuscript), CCHS.

17. Ibid.; also Katharine H. Cummin, *Map of Radnor Township . . . Showing Ownership in 1776,* Radnor Historical Society, 1976; *Chester County Deed Books,* "Levi Bowen & ux. to Daniel Cornog (27 March 1777; recorded 31st October 1783)," Chester County Archives; "Daniel Cornog's Will proved 16th March 1802," *Will Book* vol. 16, 313, Chester County Archives. Catherine (d. December 11, 1779, at age 81) and David (d. April 24, 1780) are both buried at Great Valley Baptist Church, as are Daniel and his wife.

18. Muhlenberg, 78.

19. Henry H. Bellas, *Personal Recollections of Captain Enoch Anderson, etc.* (Wilmington, DE: Historical Society of Delaware), 40. The Schuylkill has many bends; depending where Anderson's troops crossed, they may have crossed to the western shore. In this case, he meant the "left bank."

20. Montrésor, 39.

21. Münchhausen, 34. The accuracy of the data provided by von Münchhausen gives much credit to the intelligence gathering of the British Army. Münchhausen's analysis of Washington's maneuver pays a compliment to the American commander in chief.

22. "Extract from a Letter from a Gentleman in the Army dated Septr. 17th. 1777—Camp near Reading Furnace," *Force.*

CHAPTER 11

1. Münchhausen, 34. The term "evening" is somewhat nebulous; it may be used to describe late afternoon, midafternoon, or the entire afternoon, depending on the individual's account. Webster's New World Dictionary gives as one definition, "in parts of England, the period from noon through sunset and twilight." In many accounts, it seems that evening is used to describe any time in the P.M. before dark.
2. James Hunter, *The Journal of General Sir Martin Hunter etc.* (Edinburgh: The Edinburgh Press, 1894), 30. Hunter was a lieutenant in the Light Company of the 52nd Regiment of Foot.
3. Hartley's Testimony, paper marked "E"; Humpton's Testimony, paper marked "P."
4. Hartley's Testimony, paper marked "E"; Wayne's Defense, version 2.
5. Brodhead's Evidence, paper marked "I." Also see Hubley's Evidence, paper marked "N."
6. Hartley's Testimony, paper marked "E."
7. Letter, Hartley to William Atlee, Paul Zantzinger, et al., dated "Camp Sepr. ye 20th 1777, 6 o'Clock PM.," *Force.*
8. Connor's Testimony, paper marked "C"; Hartley's Testimony, paper marked "E."
9. George Wells Bartholomew, Jr., *Record of the Bartholomew Family* (Austin, TX: Self-published, 1885), 445–47. Also see *PMHB* 3 (1879): 100–101. The Bartholomews were actively involved in Chester County government affairs before and after the Revolution. Benjamin was a member of the Provincial Assembly in 1772 and the Chester County Committee of Safety in 1775, serving with Anthony Wayne.
10. Hartley's Testimony, paper marked "E." According to an 1817 newspaper account from Richard Robinson, "old Mr. Jones" was Robert Jones, a neighbor of Wayne's who lived near the Paoli Tavern. (Priscilla L. Cox Richardson, *The Paoli Massacre of 1777*, Paoli Memorial Association, 1996, 11.) Franklin L. Burns states that it was "a patriotic Welsh gentleman, Thomas Jones, a retired farmer of Easttown," but does not specify his source. (Franklin L. Burns, "The Invasion of Tredyffrin," *TEHCQ*, vol. 3, no. 3 (July 1940): 60.
11. Wayne's Testimony, version 1, and insert. Based on Wayne's manuscript map and his description of this reconnaissance, together with Hartley's and Humpton's descriptions and documentation of the roads that then existed, it is possible to locate the modern route of this proposed march to the British right flank. The party would have proceeded south on Channing Avenue on a road (now vanished) parallel with Warren Avenue to Paoli Pike. Turning left onto Paoli Pike, they would have proceeded onto Devon Road to Darby Road. Turning right, they would have taken Darby Road across Route 252 onto Sugartown Road, proceeded a few hundred yards, and then turned left onto Berwyn-Paoli Road. This road would have taken them to the Lancaster Road "near the Blue Ball," which would place them on the British right flank.
12. Hartley's Testimony, paper marked "E"; Humpton's Evidence, paper marked "P."
13. Humpton's Evidence, paper marked "P."
14. Ibid.

CHAPTER 12

1. Hartley's Testimony, paper marked "E."
2. Wayne's map of the Paoli Camp, *Force.* This invaluable map shows the layout of the camp pickets and the roads in the vicinity. From the map and the description of the picket posts, the modern locations can be determined. Picket 1 was located on Route

30 near Cedar Hollow Road (Paoli); Picket 2 was located on Paoli Pike about 50 yards east of Warren Avenue (Malvern); Picket 3 was located on Channing Avenue near First Avenue (Malvern); Picket 4 was located on Old Lincoln Highway at Longford Avenue (Malvern); Picket 5 was located at the Warren Tavern on Old Lancaster Road (Malvern); Picket 6 was located on Sugartown Road 100 yards north of King Road (Malvern). In addition, a horse picket was placed at what is now Swedesford Road and Route 29 (Frazer).

3. Nichols's Testimony, paper marked "D"; Connor's Testimony, paper marked "C"; Butler's "shead" is mentioned in McGowan's Evidence, paper marked "H."
4. Letter, Anthony Wayne to George Washington, dated "Camp near White Mar[s]h 22nd Octr. 1777," *Wayne Papers,* vol. 4, HSP.
5. Ibid.
6. Wayne's Testimony, version 1.
7. Ryan's Evidence, paper marked "F."
8. Wayne's Testimony, version 1; Ryan's Evidence, paper marked "F."
9. C. Willcox, *Major André's Journal* [hereafter André] (Tarrytown, NY: William Abbatt, 1930), 50.
10. WO 12: 1246, PRO; British Commissary Daniel Wier, "Return of the Number of Men Women & Children Victualled the 5th of September 1777 at the Head of Elk," lists the following numbers: Grey's force: 2nd Battalion LI, 661; 42nd Regiment, 1st Battalion, 305, and 2nd Battalion, 336; 44th Regiment, 387 (total 1,689). Musgrave's force: 40th Regiment, 313; 55th Regiment, 287 (total 590). Grand total: 2,279 (*1777 Letterbook of Daniel Wier, Commissary to the Army in America,* Dreer Collection, Case 36, HSP.) Allowances for sickness, Brandywine casualties, desertions, and troops on duty elsewhere would have reduced these numbers significantly. John André cited that "about 1,200" were involved in the Paoli Battle. (Letter, John André to unknown recipient, dated "German Town Sepr. 28:1777," National Army Museum, London.) Most histories of this episode quote the figure of 5,000 British troops involved in the operation. Where this number originated is uncertain; Hartley estimated 4,000 British attackers, but he was on the receiving end of the attack and did not have access to British muster rolls. In the dark, the number of attackers often appears greatly exaggerated. Likewise, British accounts of American casualties were exaggerated. Persistent myth based on a questionable newspaper account describes Hessians involved in the operation; this is absolutely incorrect. The British needed to be swift, silent, and controlled; larger numbers are slower and increase the risk of detection through noise or accidental firing.
11. "Oct. 18, 1776: The Army landed at Pells Point . . . a skirmish took place in the Woods near East Chester when Lt. Colonel Musgrave (with the Light Infantry) was severely wounded." *Ensign Thomas Glyn's Journal on the American Service, etc.* (unpublished manuscript, Princeton University). Also see Hunter, 18. It is unclear who the field commander of the 55th was at this point. The colonel was Gen. James Grant; the lieutenant colonel was William Meadows, who commanded the 1st Grenadier Battalion and was wounded at Brandywine. The major was Cornelius Cuyler, serving as an aide to General Howe. See *A List of the General and Staff Officers, Etc.* (New York: Macdonald & Cameron on Water Street, 1777).
12. The Della Gatta paintings of the Paoli Battle and the Battle of Germantown provide an excellent visual record of British light infantry uniforms on this campaign. Verbal descriptions and clothing returns confirm the nonregulation or unconventional appearance of the light troops on campaign. One light officer noted at the Battle of the Clouds that "the Rebels had not a single Cartridge in their Pouches but what was Wet, *the Light Infy. Accoutrements being mostly Rebel* were in the same Situation." [emphasis added] (*British Journal 1776–1778,* by an unidentified officer of the 1st Light Infantry Battalion, Sol Feinstone Collection, the David Library.) The 2nd Light Infantry Battalion was composed of companies from thirteen regiments: 37th, 40th, 43rd, 45th, 46th,

49th, 52nd, 54th, 55th, 57th, 63rd, 64th, and 71st. (Orderly Book, Capt. Thomas Armstrong, 64th Regiment of Foot, *GW Papers*.)

13. Ibid.; also, André, 50. The journal confirms, "No soldier of either [Musgrave's or Grey's detachment] was suffered to load; those who could not draw their pieces took out the flints."

14. Hunter, 31.

15. PRO, A.O. 13, 57, bundle 2, "L." Testimony of Reuben Haines, sworn in front of Justice Edward Shippen, Philadelphia, 1786, PRO. The following description of the guide survived in local tradition: "Grey's detachment was guided by a local Tory spy who was perfectly familiar with the situation and approaches to the American camp. He has been described as a man who limped badly, who had a wife and seven children eight miles away, and who later with his family departed from Philadelphia with the British army. General Wayne and some of his officers were informed of his identity but his name is not essential here." The description of the large family living 8 miles away fits Curtis Lewis, who was from East Caln Township. Burns, "Invasion," *TEHCQ*, vol. 3, no. 3 (July 1940): 65.

16. Muhlenberg OB, 68–70, referring to the sentence of John Farndon of Hartley's ACR. The quote is from the Journal of Sgt. John Hawkins of Hazen's Regiment, AM 0765, HSP. Farndon is not named by Hazen, but the execution is described, along with the "camp scuttlebutt," which may or may not be accurate. Farndon was tried for "desertion and enlisting with the enemy" on September 25, which would indicate his capture very shortly after Paoli, if not that night. He was found guilty "of desertion but not of enlisting with the enemy" and was hanged October 10, 1777, at Camp Towamencin "on a Gallows erected for that Purpose; he hung there from Noon until Sunset for an Example to deter others from the like or similiar Crimes." (Hazen.)

17. André, 50. Dr. Benjamin Rush described his experience with British Army security after the Battle of Brandywine, when he went under flag of truce to care for American wounded: "I was next struck with their attention to *secrecy* in all their operations. . . . They lock up the houses of every family that is suspected of being in the least unfriendly to them in their marches through the country, and if they are discovered by a countryman whom they suspect, they force him to accompany their army till their route or disposition are so far changed that no mischief can arise from the intelligence he is able to convey." Benjamin Rush to John Adams, October 1, 1777. L. H. Butterfield, *Letters of Benjamin Rush,* vol. 1 (Princeton, NJ: Princeton University Press, 1951), 154.

18. Burns, *TEHCQ,* vol. 3, 61. Mr. Burns and S. Paul Teamer did extensive research in the 1930s and '40s in the region and gathered much local tradition. Unfortunately, Burns cited his source as "MS. Collection of Local Traditions," which makes confirmation of original sources difficult. Combined with the nature of local traditions, use of this material is tricky. In this case, given the documentation of the circumstances of the night and the location of the Bartholomew homestead, the family tradition is plausible; the "rough treatment" is not surprising, given the activities of John and Benjamin Bartholomew. The "aged uncle" was probably their uncle Benjamin, who lived nearby. This Benjamin was born "about 1725" and died in 1784, which would make him fifty-two years old in 1777, though the tradition cited by Burns indicates that he was near eighty and "died shortly afterward." See George W. Bartholomew, Jr., *Record of the Bartholomew Family* (Austin, TX: Published by the compiler, 1885), 440–41.

CHAPTER 13

1. Ferguson's Corps was created in early 1777 as a special corps of riflemen under the command of Capt. Patrick Ferguson. They were equipped with an experimental breechloading rifle invented by Ferguson, which was capable of firing up to six accurate shots per minute. The corps was ambushed at Brandywine and nearly wiped out;

Ferguson himself was severely wounded in the arm. The day before Paoli, the remains of Ferguson's Corps were placed with other British light troops. (Münchhausen.)

The Della Gatta painting of the Battle of Paoli depicts a group of British troops dressed in green in the right center background; independent research and analysis by both Herman Benninghoff II and Stephen R. Gilbert have led each to conclude that they are probably Ferguson's riflemen. Benninghoff's technical analysis of the figures and their weapons, especially the length of the firearm versus the length and position of the bayonet, when compared with the other figures in the painting, draws a fair conclusion that the men are carrying Ferguson rifles. See Herman Benninghoff, "Art and Archaeology and the Study of the American War for Independence," *The American Society of Arms Collectors,* Bulletin 73 (1995): 33–39, and Stephen R. Gilbert, "An Analysis of the Xavier Della Gatta Paintings of the Battles of Paoli and Germantown, 1777: Part 1," *Military Collector and Historian, Journal of the Company of Military Historians* 46, no. 3 (fall 1994): 98–108.

2. Münchhausen, 34.
3. Until the 1950s, Sugartown Road was a continuous road from the Warren Tavern to King Road. The destruction of a bridge over the Pennsylvania Railroad tracks closed this portion of the road, and it has since been abandoned, though the road bed is still partially visible west of the Warren Tavern.
4. "The Crossroads" was on Sugartown Road about 100 yards north of King Road near the railroad. A road opened in 1774 ran on the township line from the "Road from the Warren to Chester" (Sugartown Road) to the "Road from the White Horse to Goshen Meeting House" (Route 352 at King Road, and King Road west to Immaculata). (Road Papers, Chester County Archives.)
5. Hartley's Evidence, paper marked "E." Persistent local tradition holds that the British had learned the American passwords of the night: "Here we are" and "There they go." Hartley clearly states that the vidette reported that he challenged the British three times but received no reply; the British accounts confirm their silence. There is no record of the password in any primary documents found thus far. The tradition came from Dr. R. C. Smedley, who related that the family of Joseph Cox, who lived near Paoli Pike and Sugartown Road, "were aroused by a man outside calling to them. . . . There was borne to them distinctly on that midnight air the sounds of the British as they rushed through the camp in their demon-like madness and murderous intent, crying out with vociferous yell the Americans' watchword of that night, "Here we are and there they go." The Cox residence stands just over half a mile south of the campsite; no doubt some scattered soldiers passed this way in their escape. See Futhey and Cope, 86.
6. Ryan's Evidence, paper marked "F."
7. Hunter, 31.
8. André, 49.
9. Futhey and Cope, 85.
10. Burns, *TEHCQ,* 62. If Mather had any Loyalist inclinations, this episode surely finished them.
11. André, 50.
12. Hunter, 31. A blacksmith shop still stands at the foot of Warren Avenue and Old Lancaster Pike in Malvern, on the southwest corner. It is catercornered east of the Warren Tavern.
13. "Colonel Musgrave marched a different way and took post on the Philadelphia Road at the Paoli. It was thought he would have first fallen in with their outposts. By our attacking them on the flank next to Colonel Musgrave's Post, they retired the opposite way and his Detachment saw nothing of them." (André, 50.)
14. "This May Certifie that George Inglrith a soldier in My Company of the 4th Pennsa. Regiment Served . . . On picquet at the Payola Batle or Sticking Night. . . . [signed] John McGowan Capt." Revolutionary War Pension Files, RG-4, roll 2, State Archives,

Harrisburg. The makeup of this picket is typical; see Nichols's Evidence, paper marked "D," for a description of Picket 1.

15. Hunter, 31; André, 50; Letter, unsigned, "From the Camp on the Field of Battle Near Dilworth on the heights of Brandy Wine September 11th at Night," *Wayne Papers,* vol. 4, HSP. This letter was identified by Stephen Gilbert as having been written by Lt. Richard St. George Mansergh St. George (yes, that is correct) of the 52nd Regiment of Foot Light Company. It was written as an ongoing description of the campaign and was added to on October 2. Most likely it was captured at the Battle of Germantown on October 4 when the 2nd Battalion camp was overrun.

16. Julianna R. Wood, *Family Sketches* (Philadelphia: Self-published, 1870), 22. Dr. David Wood and Edward Fitz Randolph Wood, Jr., provided this rare family anecdote, which was confirmed by the certificate, cited in note 18. The comment "two English soldiers rode by" suggests dragoons; the order not to shoot "to save their ammunition . . . for live rebels" appears at odds with the standing orders not to fire, though the Pearce family anecdote (chapter 19, note 8) supports pistol- or carbine-wielding dragoon activity. Family research by Oris Randolph in 1976, made available to me by Hannah Shipley, noted Lieutenant Randolph's loss of an eye; Randolph died in Philadelphia in 1837.

17. Burns, *TEHCQ,* 64.

18. Certificates signed by John McGowan and Edward Fitz Randolph, Revolutionary War Pension Files, RG-4, roll 2, State Archives, Harrisburg.

19. Mentges's Evidence, paper marked "L." The battle cry "Give them the bayonet through the smoke" seems to have been a favorite rallying cry of Wayne's.

20. Humpton's Evidence, paper marked "P." This exchange may be yet another indication of the strained relationship between Humpton and Wayne. Humpton was obviously somewhere in the camp. That he was awakened by Wayne shouting at the men indicates that Wayne either did not know exactly where in camp Humpton was or Wayne was ignoring Humpton by not sending an officer to inform him of the attack. Humpton's chiding Wayne "not to ride along in that manner" hints again at a strained relationship.

21. Huffnagle's Evidence, paper marked "K." Punctuation added for clarity.

22. Hay's Evidence, paper marked "B."

23. The positions of the 4th, Hartley's, 7th, 1st, and artillery are confirmed in the court testimony. The position of the 8th comes from the pension testimony of Lt. John Findley of the 8th Regiment, who stated that in 1777 "the fourth and eighth Pennsylvania Regiments encamped next each other." (Revolutionary War Pension Files for John Elliot, 4th Regiment, film 27, reel 912.) The relative positions of the 5th and 11th (2nd Brigade) are conjectured, as are those of the 2nd and 10th (1st Brigade).

24. Wayne's Defense, version 2.

25. Wayne's Defense, version 1, inserted at the end.

CHAPTER 14

1. Huffnagle's Evidence, paper marked "K."

2. Wayne's Defense, version 2.

3. Doyle's Independent Company was attached to the 1st Pennsylvania Regiment at this time; at other times it was part of the 6th Pennsylvania. The 1st Pennsylvania had its own light company under Capt. James Wilson. The records for Doyle's Company are sketchy for 1777; an undated return (probably from midyear) and a return from November list twenty-seven NCOs and enlisted men, two musicians, and two officers. In the November return for the 1st Pennsylvania, "Willson's Company" contained two officers, two sergeants, and eighteen privates. Hartley stated that the light infantry at Paoli had thirty to forty men.

4. Wilson's Testimony, paper marked "O." Wilson testified that he was placed 300 yards in advance of the right of the division when he "received the Enemy."

5. Hunter, 31; St. George, Letter, 2.

6. Futhey and Cope, 86.

7. Letter, Anthony Wayne to George Washington, dated "Red Lion 21st Septr. 1777: 12 OClock," *Wayne Papers,* vol. 4, HSP. Emphasis added. British sergeant Sullivan wrote that "their Picquet fired a Volley at the Light Infantry and retreated, but did not hurt a man. Without the least noise our Party by the Bayonet only, forced and killed their out sentries and Picquets." Sullivan, 231.

8. Letter, Thomas Hartley to William Atlee and Paul Zantzinger, "Camp Red Lyon Sepr ye 21st 1777," *Force.*

9. Connor's Evidence, paper marked "C"; Hartley's Evidence, paper marked "E"; Wayne's Defense, version 1, inserted at the end.

10. Capt. George Smith, "Words of command used at the manual exercise," *An Universal Military Dictionary* (London, 1779; Ottawa, Ontario: Museum Restoration Service, 1969), 259.

11. Hartley's Evidence, paper marked "E."

12. Connor's Evidence, paper marked "C."

13. Hunter, 31.

14. Hay's Evidence, paper marked "B." Punctuation added for clarity.

15. St. George, Letter, 3; Hunter, 31.

16. Letter, Hay to Irvine, "Camp at the Trap, Sept. 29, 1777," [emphasis added] *Irvine Papers,* vol. 1, HSP.

CHAPTER 15

1. Hartley, Letter, September 21, 1777.

2. Hartley's Evidence, paper marked "E."

3. "The fences are made of posts fixed in the ground, at ten feet distance, and in general with four or five cross rails, from nine to fifteen inches asunder." (Joseph Galloway, *Letters,* 2.) This is a contemporary general description of fences found in Pennsylvania as explained by Joseph Galloway to the British public. The exact type of fence there at the time is not presently known, but the two most commonly found in the region during this period were the post-and-rail and the snake, or worm, style. The post-and-rail fences usually were four- or five-rail, rather than the three-rail versions often seen today; the posts stood about 5 feet high and were firmly planted in post holes. The bottom rails of the snake, or worm, fence were held off the ground by staggered stones laid at the rail ends. Other rails were then laid in a perpendicular fashion to connect the sections, giving the fence a zigzag appearance, like a snake or worm. Four or five rails would thus be piled alternately on top of each other, supported at the joints by crisscrossing stakes and a rider rail laid in the notch created by the stakes.

4. St. George, Letter, 4.

5. Capt. William Nichols enlisted Daniel St. Clair as drum major in Hartley's Additional Continental Regiment in early 1777 for "three years, or during the war." Years later, the only battle his widow could remember that he had participated in was Paoli. Federal pension papers indicate that he served as drum and fife major of the Invalid Corps for two years and was discharged in 1780. The records indicate that his service to the Invalid Corps began sometime in 1778. The nature of his injuries and the circumstantial evidence suggest that Paoli made a major impression on him and that if his convalescence was six to nine months, he would have returned to service sometime in the spring of 1778. He was placed on the State Invalid Pension Rolls in the 1790s. His wounds and service are described in his pension applications of the 1830s and his widow's application of 1850. (Wagner Collection, vol. 2.) Daniel must have presented quite a sight as drum major of the Invalid Corps, with an eye patch, head scars, no fingers on the left hand, drum major's mace in his right hand, proudly if painfully carrying on his duty.

6. Montrésor, 39.
7. Hartley's Evidence, paper marked "E."
8. Pennsylvania Archives 2, vol. 10, 1896, 407; *Delaware County American,* Media, June 24, 1857.
9. Wayne's Testimony, version I.
10. Humpton's Evidence, paper marked "P."
11. Maj. Caleb North (10th Pennsylvania) confirmed the artillery's route of escape: "I Saw Our Canon Pass in the Rear of the Division and Soon Afterwards the Word was Given 'to the Left Wheel Retreat in good Order.'" North's Evidence, paper marked "Q." See also Humpton's Evidence, paper marked "P."
12. Hubley's Evidence, paper marked "N."
13. Letter, Anthony Wayne to George Washington, dated "Camp near White Mash [*sic*] 22nd Octr. 1777," *Wayne Papers,* vol. 4, HSP. Wayne's court-martial testimony, given less than a week after this letter was written, does not mention the disabled gun impeding the column.

CHAPTER 16

1. Letter, Adam Hubley to William Atlee, et al., dated "Red Lion September 21, 1777," *Force.* British casualties were actually very light, not considerably more.
2. Hubley's Evidence, paper marked "N." Hubley's statement about the British shouting, "No quarters," is at present the only documented primary source of this battle cry from the British. A British grenadier officer who was not at Paoli, Capt. William Hale, wrote in October 1777, "As our Light Infantry gave no quarter, very few prisoners were taken." (See chapter 18, Note 5.)
3. Futhey and Cope, 86.
4. According to *Webster's New World Dictionary* (2nd college ed., 1980), a banshee, in Irish and Scottish folklore, was "a female spirit believed to wail outside a house as a warning that a death will occur soon in a family."
5. May and Embleton, 40. The Kilmarnock bonnet or Highland cap of the 1770s consisted of a wide headband ornamented with three checkered rows, the top and bottom rows red and white, and the middle row red and green. On top was a blue wool tam surmounted by a red touri, or pompom. Completing the headgear was a single black ostrich plume fixed to a black ribbon, or cockade, and a button on the left side of the headband, the plume overhanging the top of the cap. Highland dress was in transition during the war; it is likely that most troops were in "trews" (trousers) or overalls by 1777, rather than belted plaids or kilts. The belted plaid in 1777 was a piece of tartan wool cloth about 12 feet long, partially pleated; it was wrapped around the hips and thighs (the kilt part) and held with a waistbelt. The remainder was then looped up the back and fastened to the shoulder like a cape.
6. The map "British Camp at Trudruffrin," published in London in 1778, shows the 42nd Regiment as two distinct battalions labeled "H." Under "References" is stated, "The 42d. Regiment *in* Reserve, *following without breaking their Ranks.*" André's map titled "Surprize of a Rebel Corps in the Great Valley" also shows the 42nd as two battalions in a solid line.

There is presently no documentation that bagpipes sounded in this battle. There were pipers with the regiment on the campaign, and it is very possible that some came along with the regiment at Paoli. Given the nature of this battle, the spine-chilling "skirl o' the pipes" certainly would have added yet another dimension of "romantic terror" to an already terrifying scene.

7. Sullivan, 231. The 49th Regiment was not present at Paoli; this is "secondhand primary" information. Sullivan's account is quite accurate in its details of the battle, including what at first glance appears to be a minor error about "gaining the Enemy's

left." Several secondhand British accounts repeat the same statement, including Howe's letter to Lord Germain. The sometimes ethereal descriptions of left, right, rear, and so forth are based on perceptions of an enemy's position at a given moment. Viewing Wayne's force as a column with the head facing the left of the camp, as it was when the British entered the camp, the British were, in fact, attacking the *rear* and the *left* of the column.

8. Hunter, 31. This account may appear to contradict Sullivan's statement as to when the camp was set on fire and by whom. Chances are that both accounts share a large measure of truth.
9. Humpton's Evidence, paper marked "P."
10. Ryan's Evidence, paper marked "F."
11. *Pennsylvania Archives,* ser. 2, vol. 10 (1896): 548; Pension Narrative of Benjamin Burd, 1818, Revolutionary War Pension Rolls, film 27, reel 409.
12. Ryan's Evidence, paper marked "F."
13. North's Evidence, paper marked "Q."

CHAPTER 17

1. Letter, William Smallwood to Gov. Thomas Johnson, dated "Bucks [Berks] County Jones Tavern Sept. 23, 1777," MSS. 1875, Maryland Historical Society.
2. Letter, Anthony Wayne to George Washington, dated "Camp near White Mar[s]h 22nd Octr. 1777", *Wayne Papers,* vol. 4, HSP.
3. Letter, Mordecai Gist to John Smith, Esq., Baltimore, dated "Camp at Jones' Tavern Near Reading [Furnace] 23d. Sept. 1777," MSS. 6610, Emmet Collection, New York Public Library; also Smallwood. The distance was actually about four or five miles.
4. Smallwood. Colonel Chambers's refusal to take the force any farther was a proper decision, especially since this force was militia, most of them poorly trained. The proof of this wisdom lay in their performance that night.

   Wayne wrote to Washington the next day, "Gen'l Smallwood was on his march but not within supporting distance[;] he Order'd his people to file off toward this place [Red Lion Tavern, Lionville] where his Division and my own now lay." (Letter, Wayne to Washington, dated "Red Lion 21st Sepr. 1777: 12 OClock," *Wayne Papers,* vol. 4, HSP.) Wayne's statement was not accurate on two counts: First, Smallwood *was* within supporting distance and actually attempted to cover the withdrawal, and second, by hasty omission, Wayne minimalized Smallwood's presence and performance, implying that Smallwood acted on his own and ordered a withdrawal to the Red Lion. In defense of Wayne, he obviously was not acquainted with the full truth of Smallwood's situation at the time he wrote the letter. Later, in his defense testimony, Wayne partially rectified the omission by stating, "at which time he [Gen' Smallwood] was Advancing and *by my Orders* Retreated to the White Horse." [emphasis added] (Wayne Testimony, version 1.)
5. Smallwood; Gist.
6. Smallwood. This description indicates the appearance of the line of march. Heading toward the camp was Smallwood's infantry, followed by commissary wagons, ammunition wagons, and the artillery. A few hundred yards behind this was Gist's column. Smallwood was able to stop, have the wagons and guns turn around, and order the infantry "to the right about, face" to proceed back down the road.
7. Gist says, "We were within a mile and a half of the place, *but not being made acquainted with Circumstances, continued our Rout[e]* until we were fired upon by the Enemy." [emphasis added] The evidence indicates that this was not another case of "friendly fire," but in fact a case of "independent fire" on the part of enthusiastic British light infantry. There was also "friendly fire" in this area, which resulted in casualties and near death for Smallwood himself.

8. Letter, Richard St. George, HSP, emphasis added to quoted material. The poor grammar and dismal lack of punctuation in this letter make interpretation cloudy. Taken by itself, the "scattering shots" could be describing either side. Put together with Smallwood's and Gist's statements, it seems likely that St. George is describing British "scattering shots."

9. Gist; Smallwood.

10. Gist.

11. Smallwood. Pinpointing exactly where this occurred is difficult based on the descriptions, but the most likely area is south of King Road and north of Forest Lane, in the general area between Hickory Lane (then called the Road to Ashbridge's Mill) and Chester Road (Route 352, then also called the Road to Goshen Meeting). The main reason for the British not pursuing further is that they had already gone far from their main force and were scattered; regrouping and control were essential in military discipline.

12. North's Evidence, paper marked "Q."

13. Gist; Smallwood. These militia casualties have yet to be identified.

14. Smallwood. This episode took place somewhere on "the road to the White Horse," probably in the vicinity of Immaculata College.

15. Speech, written for Caleb North's campaign for sheriff of Philadelphia County, "To the Freemen of the City and County of Philadelphia," by "An American," "Published in the *Daily Aurora* . . ." October 8, 1819, Society Collection, "North, Caleb, 1819," HSP.

16. Muster and Payroll Returns, National Archives, emphasis added to quoted material.

17. Smallwood. This likely occurred between the South Valley Hill (site of today's Immaculata College) and the White Horse Tavern. The Red Lion Tavern is 5 miles from the White Horse; Smallwood says he ordered "the Retreat to be made to the Red Lyon abt. 5 Miles higher up the Country."

18. Hubley's Evidence, paper marked "N."

19. Smallwood.

20. "Papers Related to the Paoli Massacre," *PMHB* vol. 1 (1877): 315. Limekilns were prevalent in southeastern Pennsylvania in the eighteenth century, especially in the Great Valley.

21. Gist.

22. Smallwood.

CHAPTER 18

1. Hay to Irvine, September 29, 1777, *Irvine Papers,* vol. 1, HSP.

2. James Murray, *An Impartial History of the War in America Etc.,* vol. 2 (Newcastle upon Tyne, England: T. Robeson, 1783), 271–72. This book was written while the war was still in progress.

3. Letter, Adam Hubley to William Atlee, dated, "Camp at Jones's Tavern Septr. 23, 1777," *Force.*

4. André, 50. John Robert Shaw, a British soldier in the 33rd Regiment, noted at the massacre of Baylor Dragoons in 1778, "a most inhuman massacre took place near Tappan in New-Jersey . . . [of] a small regiment of light horse, (raised a short time before in Virginia, and known as Lady Washington's regiment) . . . general Gray undertook the barbarous task . . . The 33d regiment, to which I belonged, was about three miles off when the cruel carnage began; but as we approached, the shreiks and screams of the hapless victims whom our savage fellow soldiers were butchering, were sufficient to have melted into compassion the heart of a Turk or a Tartar.—Tongue cannot tell nor pen unfold the horrors of that dismal night . . . *To preserve, however, some appearance of clemency, 43 were admitted prisoners of war* . . . [emphasis added] Let Britain boast no more of her honour, her science and civilization; but with shame hide her head in the dust; her fame is gone; Tappan will witness against her.—Having performed this igno-

ble exploit, the few prisoners that were spared being conducted to New-York by a guard of British soldiers, and the wounded sent off in waggons, we returnded to Long-Island to be ready for another scene of British barbarity." John Robert Shaw, *A Narrative of the Life and Travels of John Robert Shaw, the Well-Digger, Now Resident in Lexington, Kentucky.* (Lexington, KY: Printed by Daniel Bradford, 1807), 20–21.

5. Hunter, 29; Capt. William Hale, "Letters Written During the American War of Independence," *Regimental Annual,* Sherwood Foresters Regiment, 1913. Dr. Benjamin Rush observed the same attitude after Brandywine regarding the care of the American wounded: "British officers called every morning upon our officers to know whether their surgeons did their duty. You must not attribute this to their humanity. They hate us in every shape we appear to them. Their care of our wounded was entirely the effect of the perfection of their medical establishment, which mechanically forced happiness and satisfaction upon our countrymen perhaps without a single wish in the officers of the hospital to make their situation comfortable." Rush to John Adams, October 1, 1777. *Letters of Benjamin Rush,* 155.

6. Murray, 273–74.

7. Hubley to Atlee, September 21, 1777, *Force.*

8. Deserter description, *Maryland Journal,* October 28, 1777, in Lefferts, *Uniforms, etc.,* 130. [emphasis added to quoted material]

9. Hubley to Atlee, September 21, 1777, *Force.* Fortunately, Hubley's letters were preserved as well as his Court of Inquiry testimony, for the testimony merely states, "What passed further at that time I can't say, as I had unfortunately fell into the Enemy's hands,[;] some time after, whilst our people were retiring, I thro' some intrigues &c got off," a bland passing reference to an intriguing episode.

10. Hubley's Evidence, paper marked "N." Hartley wrote later that morning that "Colonel Hubley and some of his officers behaved very galantly in Saving a Piece of artillery." (Hartley to Atlee, September 21, 1777, *Force.*)

11. Letter from Maj. Samuel Shaw to his father, dated "Artillery Park, Skippack, about twenty four miles west from Philadelphia, September 30, 1777," Josiah Quincy, *Journals of Major Samuel Shaw* (Boston: Wm. Crosby & H. Nichols, 1847), 37–38.

12. "George Inman's Narrative of the American Revolution," *PMHB* 7 (1883): 241. Inman was with the 1st Light Infantry Battalion, stationed at Valley Forge the night of the Paoli Battle. Timothy Pickering wrote on October 13, 1777, "Captain Randall, of the artillery, now a prisoner of war on parole, told me he was going home to Boston." *Life of Pickering,* vol. 1, 172.

13. Hutchinson, Stack, St. Clair, Revolutionary War Pension Rolls, film 127, National Archives. (See chapter 15, note 5.)

14. Justice, Leary, Stead, Revolutionary War Pension Rolls, film 127, National Archives.

15. British Army Court Martial Records, W. O. 71/84, 333–34. PRO, London. McKie was court-martialed on October 2, 1777 and found guilty of desertion. He was sentenced to death but "in consideration of some circumstances favourable to the prisoner . . . the Court beg leave to recommend him mercy."

16. John Dann, *The Revolution Remembered* (Chicago: University of Chicago Press, 1980), 149–50.

17. Payroll for September 1777, 13th Virginia Regiment, Muster and Payroll Returns, National Archives.

CHAPTER 19

1. Unidentified Officer in the 1st Light Infantry Battalion, "British Journal 1776–1778," 39–40, Sol Feinstone Collection, David Library; also Payroll Returns for the period June 24–December 25, 1777, 49th Regiment of Foot, Capt. Nicholas Wade's (Light) Company, WO 12: 6032; 16th Light Dragoons, Maj. Francis Edward Gwyn's Troop,

WO 12: 1246, PRO. The return for Capt. Thomas Armstrong's Company, 64th Regiment, lists "Drummer William White Dead 20th Sept. 1777" (WO 12: 7313); whether he was killed at Paoli or died in camp is unclear. A careful search of all the returns for the troops involved at Paoli failed to disclose the identity of the sergeant stated as killed. Also Montrésor, 39.

2. Hunter, 31–32.
3. Montrésor, 39.
4. André, Journal, 50; also Letter in André's handwriting, unsigned, dated "German Town Sepr. 28: 1777," National Army Museum, London.
5. André, 50; also Letter, Anthony Wayne to Thomas Wharton, dated "Mount Joy 2nd May 1778," "Julius Count Montfort—taken Prisoner at the Paoli in the Action of the night of the 20th Sepr . . . Major in Count Pulaski's Corps [Continental Dragoons]," Wayne Papers, vol. 5, HSP; also Montrésor, 39: "prisoners, amongst which was a Major and a French officer." Adam Hubley wrote the next morning, "[I] sent my Major with 4 of our Horsemen on the field who counted our Dead bodys, the enemy's were taken off, they were inform'd in large numbers." (Hubley to Atlee, September 21, 1777, Force). Timothy Pickering wrote, "Next day Wayne buried fifty-six of his men, and the inhabitants said the enemy buried twenty-three of theirs, and carried off four or five wagon-loads." (Life of Pickering, 162) A possible explanation for the discrepancy is that many American wounded were carried off in the dark. It may also be that some of the Americans were in red uniforms.
6. Return of Prisoners, dated "Philadelphia April 5th 1778," lists among others: "Delivered over by Sir William Howe to the American Surgeons at Trydefferin . . . 22 Privates. [signed] Joshua Loring, Commissy. Genl. Prisrs." 2690, Emmet Collection, New York Public Library.
7. Harold Donaldson Eberlein and Cortlandt Van Dyke Hubbard, The Church of St. Peter in the Great Valley, 1700–1940 (Richmond, VA: August Dietz and Son, 1944), 83. The prominence of this church on the Faden map is remarkable, especially since other conspicuous landmarks are absent, the most glaring omission being the Warren Tavern. It is also curious that the map refers to the attack as "near White Horse Tavern." After thoughtful consideration, I have reached the following conclusion: The officer who drew the map was probably a 40th Regiment officer, a "brother officer" of Capt. William Wolfe, who was killed. The 40th Light Company was attached to the 2nd Battalion of Light Infantry. The 40th Regiment battalion companies, commanded by Col. Thomas Musgrave, were near the Paoli Tavern, together with the 55th; this force did not engage. The officer may have visited the Paoli battle site a few hours after the fight, as did several British officers. If he took the Lancaster Road route, he would not have passed the Warren Tavern, which might explain its omission. He drew his map based on his own observations and firsthand descriptions from those in the battle. This is how most battle maps are drawn, since it is nearly impossible to observe all places and events at once, especially at night.

The actual road to St. Peter's goes off Swedesford Road about 2 miles west of Howell's Tavern, yet the Faden map shows the road leading directly from the 2nd Battalion of Light Infantry camp to the church. If the officer went to the church for Wolfe's burial, he drew the route as he observed it and perhaps relied on his memory from the march on the 18th from White Horse Tavern to mark the route of the attack. This would explain the attack labeled as "near White Horse Tavern"; the absence of the Warren Tavern; and the skewed representation of the road to St. Peter's with the actual roads.

The road from the light infantry camp to the upper right leads to a road parallel to Swedesford Road. I believe that these roads are modern Mill Road and Yellow Springs Road, respectively. Rev. Currie's Parsonage (not indicated on the map) is on Yellow Springs Road just 1 mile east of this intersection. It is presently part of Valley Forge

Park and is known as Stirling's Quarters, used during the Valley Forge encampment as headquarters for Gen. William Alexander, Lord Stirling.

Even today, St. Peter's is in an obscure, isolated location, yet it features as the largest structure in the center of the map. This fact, together with the orientation of the map's compass and the alignment of the 40th and 55th Regiments at the Paoli Tavern, both of which help guide the eye to the church, suggest that the church was significant to the cartographer and those for whom he drew the map. Captain Wolfe's grave is unknown; given the circumstances of the Paoli Battle, it has warranted little or no attention, and its anonymity has protected it from desecration. Based on the evidence presented, I believe that Wolfe and the other British dead from Paoli, together with some American dead (as many as eight pickets from Randolph's Post 4, according to tradition) are buried at St. Peter's, and that British officers who acquired copies of the Faden map would know why St. Peter's was so prominently featured.

8. Stewart Pearce, *The Pearce Family* (Privately printed, 1909), 10. Mrs. Catharine Simmons, a descendant of Cromwell Pearce, provided the family history.
9. Letter, Abraham Robinson to Anthony Wayne, dated "East Town Septr: 22nd. 1777," *Wayne Papers,* vol. 4, HSP.
10. Letter, Sir William Howe to General Washington, dated "Head Quarters 21st September 1777," *GW Papers.*
11. Münchhausen, 34–35. Emphasis added to quoted material.
12. Kirkwood, 176. Here is another indication of "growing pains" among Continental forces.
13. Peebles, Diary entry for Sunday, September 21, 1777. [Emphasis added]
14. "Short Description of the Journey of the Hon. Hessian Troops, etc., Lieutenant-General von Heister," *The Hessian Documents,* Letter F. Z., microfiche 45, 112–18, Morristown NHP.
15. *Archibald Robertson, Lieutenant General of Royal Engineers, His Diaries and Sketches in America* (New York: New York Public Library and Arno Press, 1971), 148.
16. Loyalist Claims, Certificate for George Peters, signed "W. Howe," PRO, AO, 13, 71.
17. *WW,* vol. 9, 245. For a detailed history and map, see "The Thompson Family and the Jeffersonville Inn," *Historical Sketches of Montgomery County* 1, (1895): 348–61.
18. Letter, George Washington to Lt. Genl. Howe, dated "Head Qrs. 21st September 1777," *GW Papers.*
19. Typescript of Letter, Sir George Osborn to his Brother John in Saxony, dated "Camp near Schuylkill, September 30th. [1777]," 2. Courtesy of Mrs. Sarah Saunders-Davies, England.
20. Typescript of Letter, Loftus Cliffe to Jack [?], dated "Camp near Philadelphia 24 October 1777," 2. William L. Clements Library, Ann Arbor, Michigan.
21. Hunter, 32.

CHAPTER 20

1. Letter, Anthony Wayne to General Washington, dated "Red Lion 21st Septr 1777: 12 OClock," *Wayne Papers,* vol. 4, HSP.
2. Testimony, Wayne's Defense, version 2, dated "Camp at White Marsh 1st Nor. 1777," *Wayne Papers,* vol. 4, HSP. The "contrary way" was west and southwest across Sugartown Road into the fields, as opposed to the "proper route" north to King Road and west-northwest toward White Horse Tavern. The remark about "those who went a contrary way" has generally been interpreted by the better historians of this battle to mean that Humpton countermarched his men eastward toward the right flank of the camp instead of toward the left as ordered, which would have had them heading into the British attack instead of away from it, all the while moving in front of their campfires. This was a fair interpretation, given that it was based almost entirely on Wayne's

description. The Court of Inquiry documents are invaluable in clearing up this misin-
terpretation. They also clarify Wayne's statements about "staying on the ground above
an hour" and "the Enemy not pursuing," which conflict with British accounts. The
documents also help pinpoint just who was where at what point in the sequence of
battle. Wayne's account suggests that the British did not pursue because of his formidable appearance; this type of statement is consistent with Wayne's bravado. Smallwood
suggested the same based merely on the presence of his large militia force rather than
its fighting capacity. Both were mistaken. The reason the British did not pursue was
that they had achieved their aim: They had effectively neutralized Wayne's force as a
threat to their line of march. Further pursuit in the dark would accomplish little, from
the British perspective, although seizing the American artillery would have been a
juicy bonus.

3. Humpton's Testimony, paper marked "P." Punctuation added for clarity.

4. Wayne's Defense, version 1.

5. Richard Willson's Evidence, paper marked "G." This data alone dispels the persistent
   myth that Wayne escaped from the scene by turning his coat or cloak inside out to
   show a red lining. Anthony was intrepid, sometimes to the point of foolhardiness.

6. Hubley's Evidence, paper marked "N." This activity took place on modern Swedesford
   Road (the original Lancaster Road) in East and West Whiteland Townships, between
   Planebrook Road and Ship Road. The place where Smallwood called for a halt would
   be in the vicinity of Swedesford Road and Ship Road.

7. The Uwchlan Monthly Meeting record for October 9, 1777, states: "Our preparative
   meeting Informs this that meetings are kept up as Usual Except one first day meeting
   which was uncommonly small at Uwchlan Occationed by Thronging of the American
   Army. Love & unity subsists in a good degree & when disorders appear care is taken."
   Abstracts of Uwchlan Monthly Meeting, Records 1763–1829, Ch20F, Genealogical Society
   of Pennsylvania, HSP.

8. At Uwchlan Meeting, "traces of blood therein are still visible from the wounds of the
   Revolutionary soldiers who for months were lodged in it, many being of the wounded
   at Paoli." (Futhey and Cope, 100) The route of this march was over modern Swedesford Road west to Ship Road, then northwest on Ship Road to Pottstown Pike
   (Route 100) north to South Village Avenue in Lionville. The Red Lion Tavern still
   stands on the southeast corner of South Village Avenue and Whitford Road. Uwchlan
   Meeting House stands on the north side of Route 113, a stone's throw from the tavern.
   Tradition holds that soldiers are buried in the meetinghouse yard. This meetinghouse
   was used as a hospital during the Valley Forge encampment; the soldiers may have been
   from that time or the Paoli Battle or both but this is not known for certain.

9. Humpton's Testimony, paper marked "P."

10. Wayne's Defense, version 1.

11. Wayne to Washington, September 21, 1777. *Wayne Papers*, vol. 4, HSP, emphasis added
    to quoted material. One letter was copied and endorsed by Robert H. Harrison, an
    aide of Washington; the other copy is in an unidentified hand. Curiously, someone
    attempted to scratch out Humpton's name on the Harrison copy.

    A number of statements in this note are striking. It is imperative to make allowances
    for errors or misperceptions, as this letter is primarily based on Wayne's own observa-
    tions. There are, however, some obvious distortions created by gross minimization of
    negative facts and overexaggeration of positive facts. For example, Wayne did not send
    "two or three Regiments" to support the light infantry; he sent one only, which he
    personally placed. Two or three regiments in battle formation might have changed the
    outcome of the night. Stating that "part of the Division were a little scattered" is a
    gross understatement, quickly followed by an optimistic "but are collecting fast."
    Wayne admitted to losing one or two wagons; British accounts indicate the capture of
    eight to ten, a significant discrepancy.

The blithe statement praising all of the officers is nothing short of blandishment. This might be understandable, were it not so inconsistent with later acerbic statements made by Wayne about some of the same officers, especially Colonel Humpton, who were critical of his judgment that night.

12. Letter, Samuel Chase to Gov. Thomas Johnson, dated "Lancaster Septr. 25. 1777." *Letters of Delegates,* vol. 8, 18.

13. *Life of Pickering,* vol. 1, 162. The statement that "the inhabitants said the enemy buried twenty three of theirs" raises some questions, as British sources consistently state the numbers of their dead as three. Is it possible that the number was originally "two or three" and became distorted into "twenty-three" by the time it reached Pickering?

14. Hubley to Atlee, September 21, 1777; Letter, Adam Hubley to William Atlee, Paul Zantzinger, et. al., dated "Camp at Jones's Tavern Septr 23, 1777," *Force.*

15. Futhey and Cope, 86. This account says that fifty-three were buried originally and that the soldier found two weeks later in the woods was buried where he was found. The monument placed in 1817 states that fifty-three soldiers are buried in the mass grave.

   Family tradition states that Conrad Acker of Uwchlan "was a firm patriot, and assisted in burying the victims of the Paoli massacre." (Futhey and Cope, 461) In the papers of the Acker family at the Chester County Historical Society Library, an undated late-nineteenth-century to early-twentieth-century published account from a collection of biographical sketches of Delaware and Chester Counties states, "He was one of a party who helped to bury the bodies after the Paoli Massacre." Whether these were the dead found at the battlefield or some who were taken to Uwchlan Meeting/Red Lion Tavern and later died is unclear.

16. "About 1000 of G. Washington's army are without Shoes & Stockings. About 500 of Genl. Waynes Division lost theirs & their Blankets in the late shameful Surprise." Chase to Johnson, *Letters of Delegates,* vol. 8, 18.

17. Futhey and Cope, 86.

CHAPTER 21

1. Münchhausen, 35.

2. McMichael, 152.

3. Ewald, 90.

4. Robertson, 149. The five fords along the British camp, from west to east, were noted by Captain Montrésor, along with the distances between each: "Gordon's Ford, Mouth of French Creek, (1 mile to) Longford—Moorehall, (1 mile to) Richardson's, (1 mile to) Paulins, (2 miles to) Fatland. Can ford it with Horse by people who know it and in low tides." The next ford downstream was Swedes Ford, 5 miles below. Montrésor, *Collections of the New York Historical Society,* 1882, 419.

5. Montrésor, 39.

6. Letterbook, Deputy Commissary of Purchases Ephraim Blaine to Commissary William Buchanan, dated "Camp New Hanover 24th Septr 1777," *Force,* series 8D, item 12, 4–7, reel 75. The letter continues: "Pray have an Eye to the Army 'till I return, that nothing may be wanted; daily complaints are making to the General, tho' never was Troops better Served with Flour, Beef and Rum. Several of the Issuing Commissarys, by no means, answers their appointments, the neglect making applications for proper supplys, and indeed issues great waste in the Issuing."

7. Wayne might have quartered at the farm of Daniel and Ester Evans. "They built a house in 1766. . . . The house is said to have been for a time the headquarters of Gen. Wayne, while his forces were encamped on the farm." (Futhey and Cope, 542.) This house is located 3 miles northeast of the Red Lion.

8. Letter, Anthony Wayne to Mary "Polly" Wayne, dated "Red Lion 22nd Sepr. 1777," *Wayne Papers,* vol. 4, HSP.

9. Humpton's Testimony, paper marked "P."
10. Estelle Cremers, *Reading Furnace 1736,* Elverson, PA: Reading Furnace Press, 1986, 144; also Trussel, *The Pennsylvania Line,* 42. Jonathan Jones's home still stands on the south side of Route 23, about 1 mile east of Morgantown and a few hundred yards east of the Pennsylvania Turnpike. Jones's Tavern is believed to be a private farmhouse located on the north side of Route 23 just west of Route 401, between Elverson and Morgantown. The building has been significantly altered, and only the basement reveals its eighteenth-century character. It is also possible that one of two other nearby early buildings on the same tract was the tavern. Thanks to Pam Shenk and Estelle Cremers, I was able to locate these obscure places and actually see the interior of the structure believed to be Jones's Tavern.
11. Hay to Irvine, September 29, 1777, *Irvine Papers,* HSP.
12. Dann, 149–50; Muster and Payroll Returns, Nat. Archives.
13. Revolutionary War Pension Papers, reel 2015, National Archives. In early 1777, the 4th Pennsylvania Battalion became the 5th Pennsylvania Regiment of the Continental Line. Wayne was promoted from colonel to brigadier general in February, 1777.
14. John W. Jordan, "Continental Army Hospital Returns 1777–1780," *PMHB* 23 (1899): 35. Given its location on the Lancaster Road west of Downingtown, and Dr. Alison's orders, it is possible that the Ship Tavern served as a rendezvous point for wounded being transported to Lancaster from both Howell's Tavern and the Red Lion, along with the men picked up by local farmers. A possible explanation for Corporal Martin's sojourn all the way to McClellan's Tavern may be that the wounded at the Ship Tavern were transported to Lancaster before the morning of September 23. Hypothetically, the Quaker farmer who found Corporal Martin on the "second morning after the Paoli Massacre" may have taken him first to the Ship Tavern, only to find the wounded and surgeons already gone, and then moved on to the next place where he could find American soldiers, namely McClellan's Tavern.
15. The original Ship Tavern still stands as a private house at the edge of Downingtown borough, on the east side of Lloyd Avenue just south of Route 30 and the railroad.
16. Revolutionary War Pension Papers, reel 2015, National Archives.

CHAPTER 22

1. "Weather fine, rather cold wind, frost at North West." Montrésor, 40.
2. Orderly Book, Capt. Thomas Armstrong, entry for September 22, 1777, *GW Papers.*
3. *WW,* vol. 9, 258–59.
4. Montrésor, 35.
5. *WW,* vol. 9, 245.
6. Ewald, 90–91. A captured British memorandum book found in the George Washington Papers contains the following entry: "The 22 the 2 Light Infentory on a Recnghting part found a Pouder Mill A Magazien and Some Armers Shops and Store houses Which they Burnt and Distroid all that Came to hand & With Stores of Provishons and Furage." ["the 22nd, the 2nd Light Infantry on a reconnoitering party found a powder mill, a magazine, and some armorers' shops and storehouses, which they burnt, and destroyed all that came to hand, along with stores of provisions and forage."] "A Memmorandum List for 1777," *GW Papers,* reel 118. Ewald specified that it was his Jägers and Hessian grenadiers involved here; no doubt this was all part of General Erskine's patrol up the Pottsgrove/Reading Road.
7. "General von Knyphausen to His Serene Highness the Landgrave, 17 October, 1777," *Correspondence of General von Knyphausen, 1776–1779,* letter G., microfiche 56, 79. Hessian Documents, Lidgerwood Collection, Morristown National Historical Park. The site of the Powder Works is found on Rapp's Dam Road at Pickering Creek, next to a National Guard armory. The ruins of a nineteenth-century linseed oil mill stand on the site.

8. See John B. Linn and William H. Egle, "Minutes of the Board of War," *Pennsylvania Archives*, 2nd ser., vol. 1, 1874, 17–68.

9. Futhey and Cope, 67.

10. *Pennsylvania Archives*, 2nd ser., vol. 1, 499.

11. Futhey and Cope, 70.

12. *Short Description of the Journey of the Hon. Hessian Troops, etc., Lieutenant-General von Heister*, letter F. Z., microfiche 45, 112–18, entry for September 22. Hessian Documents, Morristown NHP.

13. Ibid.

14. Münchhausen, 35.

15. "Memorial of Richard Swanwick," AO 12, vol. 42, 29–44, PRO; Osborn Letter September 30, 1777.

16. Peebles, entry for September 22 and 23.

17. Armstrong's Orderly Book, 64th Regiment; also Peebles, entry for September 22.

18. Peebles, entry for September 22.

19. Henry Woodman, *The History of Valley Forge* (Oaks, PA: John U. Francis, 1922), 38. Woodman stated that Caleb North "informed me thirty-nine years after the event, that he saw the conflagration from the top of Mount Joy, near the place." In his letter to Washington on September 21, Wayne wrote that North had just notified him of the British march to the Schuylkill, which confirms that North was on reconnaissance duty. Hubley sent North to the Paoli battlefield that same day; Hubley's letter from Jones's Tavern on the 23rd begins "I'm just informed" about the British crossing of the Schuylkill, probably by North, who was from Coventryville and knew the area very well.

North's services were noted in an 1819 campaign speech when he successfully ran for sheriff of Philadelphia: "The next morning North was detached, with a few horse, by General Wayne to watch the movements of the enemy, and give him intelligence. This critical and dangerous service he performed entirely to the satisfaction of the General; he never lost sight of their flank and rear until they had crossed the Schuylkill." Speech, "To the Freemen of the City and County of Philadelphia," October 8, 1819, Society Collection, HSP.

Woodman could not remember the exact date of the burning of the forge but believed that it happened prior to the Paoli Massacre. On September 23, Montrésor states, "On leaving the ground of our last Encampment we set fire to the Valley Forge and destroyed it," and Peebles says, "The Stores at Valley forge that could not be brot. away were set on fire &ca."

CHAPTER 23

1. Letter, Adam Hubley to William Atlee and Paul Zantzinger, dated "Camp Jones's Tavern Sep. 23, 1777," *Force*.

2. Letter, William Smallwood to Gov. Thomas Johnson, dated "Bucks [should be Berks] County Jones Tavern near Reading [Furnace], Sept. 23, 1777," MSS 1875, Maryland HS. "Infatuation" in this sense means "lacking sound judgment; foolish."

3. Letter, Thomas Hartley to William Atlee and Paul Zantzinger, dated "Camp Johnses Tavern Little Cannestogoe, Tuesday Eveng. Sepr. ye. 23d. 1777," *Force*.

4. Letter, Anthony Wayne to Abraham Robinson [?], dated "Trap[pe] 29th Sepr 1777," Collection of H. Richard Dietrich, Jr., Philadelphia.

5. Letter, Adam Hubley to William Atlee and Paul Zantzinger, dated "Camp, at Trap, Septr. 26th 1777," *Force*; Quincy, *Journals of Samuel Shaw*, 39.

6. "John Adams' Diary, 1777 Septr. 21. Sunday," *Letters of Delegates*, vol. 8, 7–8.

7. "James Lovell to William Whipple [?] Philadelphia 20 Sept. 1777," *Letters of Delegates*, vol. 8, 6–7.

8. "John Adams' Diary, 1777 Septr. 21. Sunday," *Letters of Delegates*, vol. 8, 16.

9. "Henry Laurens to John Lewis Gervais, York 8th October, 1777," *Letters of Delegates*, vol. 8, 80; "Henry Laurens to John Lewis Gervais, York 6th Octobr. 1777," 69–70.
10. Humpton's Evidence, paper marked "P."
11. Letter, Anthony Wayne to George Washington, dated "Trap, 27th Sepr 1777," *Wayne Papers*, vol. 4, HSP.
12. Letter, Tench Tilghman to Anthony Wayne, dated "Head Quarters 27:th Sepr. 1777," *Wayne Papers*, vol. 4, HSP.
13. Hay to Irvine, September 29, 1777, *Irvine Papers*, vol. 1, HSP.
14. St. George Letter, 4.

CHAPTER 24

1. Münchhausen, 38. Münchhausen was ordered to arrest "a man named Reichell," who was working for the Continental Army Assistant Quartermaster General Lutterloh.
2. Hunter, 33–34.
3. Ibid, 22, 34. On page 22, Hunter mistakenly stated that St. George "got a shocking wound in the head at the Battle of Princeton," but he later corrected this in his description of Germantown on 34. The Battle of Germantown painting by Della Gatta (1782) depicts a British light infantry officer with a head wound being carried off the field in the lower left foreground. The Payroll of the 52nd Light Company identifes the "man of the Company named Peacock" as Corp. George Peacock (WO 12/6240, PRO).
4. Hunter, 34.
5. Letter, Anthony Wayne to Mary "Polly" Wayne, dated "Camp near Pawling Mill 6th Oct. 1777," *Wayne Papers*, vol. 4, HSP.
6. Cliffe, 2.
7. Hunter, 34–35. Della Gatta's painting also depicts a mounted general officer with his back to the viewer. The general's horse is rearing up, and two cannonballs are near the horse's feet, no doubt an artistic interpretation of this episode.
8. Münchhausen, 38.
9. Ibid.
10. For a fully documented, detailed description of this phase of the Battle of Germantown, see Thomas J. McGuire, *The Surprise of Germantown* (Gettysburg: Thomas Publications, 1994).
11. *London Chronicle*, January 3–6, 1778.
12. McGuire, *Surprise of Germantown*, 82–84.
13. Anthony Wayne to Polly Wayne, October 6, 1777, *Wayne Papers*, vol. 4, HSP.
14. McMichael, 153. Describing Germantown in his own inimitable style, McMichael wrote:

> I then said, I had seen another battle o'er
> And it exceeded all I ever saw before,
> Yet thro' the danger I escap'd without receiving harm
> And providentially got safe through firing that was warm,
> But to my grief tho' I fought sore, yet we had to retreat
> Because the cowardice of those on our left was great.

15. *WW*, vol. 9, 312.
16. Letter, Adam Hubley to William Atlee, et al., dated "Towamencing Township, Octor. 9th 1777," *Force*.
17. A. Wayne to P. Wayne, October 6, 1777, *Wayne Papers*, vol. 4, HSP.

CHAPTER 25

1. Muhlenberg OB, 68–70; also Hawkins, entry for October 10, 1777, HSP. See chapter 12, note 16.

2. Letter, Anthony Wayne to George Washington, dated "Octr 11th 1777," *Wayne Papers,* vol. 4, HSP.
3. "Papers Related to the Paoli Massacre," *PMHB* 1 (1877): 315.
4. Court of Inquiry Document, List of Evidences, dated "At a Court of enquiry held at the House of Houfer in Camp the 13th of Octor 1777," *Wayne Papers,* vol. 4, HSP. The "Camp Towamencin" region was largely inhabited by people of Dutch, Swiss, and German extraction in 1777. At first glance, the script word Houfer appears as Houser, the *f* resembling a long *s*. Close examination of the handwriting, however, reveals it as an *f;* the name may be a variation of the Dutch-German name Huver or Hoover. Spelled with an *s,* the name would be Houser, a variation of Heiser. Investigation of the Skippack area residents in the period reveals a Hiser family farm near Skippack Creek west of Skippack Road (today's Evansburg State Park). A manuscript map in the HSP showing Camp Towamencin depicts a house on the North Wales Road labeled "Heister's." Definitive identification of where this court was held remains elusive.
5. Ibid. The testimony was given in the following order: *October 13:* Lt. Col. William Butler (4th Pennsylvania), paper A; Maj. Samuel Hay (7th Pennsylvania), paper B; Lt. Col. Morgan Connor (Hartley's ACR), paper C; Maj. William Nichols (1st Brigade Major), paper D; Col. Thomas Hartley, (Commander, 1st Brigade), paper E; Maj. Michael Ryan (Acting Division Adjutant), paper F; Capt. Richard Wilson (Hartley's ACR), paper G. *October 14:* Capt. John McGowan (2nd Brigade Major), paper H; Col. Daniel Brodhead (8th Pennsylvania), paper I–J; Capt. Michael Huffnagle (8th Pennsylvania), paper K; Maj. Francis Mentges (11th Pennsylvania), paper L; Capt. George Ross (11th Pennsylvania), paper M; Lt. Col. Adam Hubley (10th Pennsylvania), paper N; Capt. James Wilson (1st Pennsylvania), paper O; Col. Richard Humpton (Commander, 2nd Brigade), paper P; Maj. Caleb North (10th Pennsylvania), paper Q.

  Each officer signed his testimony; Colonel Humpton signed his paper "Rich Humpton, Col. 11th Pa. Regt. Comdg 2nd Brig. G[enl]. Lincoln's Division," a proper professional description of his position and also a backhanded needle at Wayne.
6. The disparity of distances may be explained several ways. The first is that the officers were simply mistaken. The exact distance from Wayne's main camp to Howe's main camp was about 4 miles by foot, depending which route one took. However, if the camps were measured from Wayne's outposts to Howe's, then the distances cited are more accurate. Wayne took issue with these numbers to discount the validity of the testimony. See Wayne's letter to Washington cited in note 10.
7. Nichols's Testimony, paper marked "D." By court time, Nichols was aware that the picket had not been taken away, although for several days after the battle, he had believed it was captured. Had Wayne told Nichols of his mistake in a reasonable manner (see chapter 12, notes 3 and 4), much of the discord among the officers would have dissipated.
8. Ibid., List of Evidences. This paper is not among Pickering's extensive papers.
9. Letter, Anthony Wayne to General Washington, dated "Skippack 17th Octr. 1777," *Wayne Papers,* vol. 4, HSP.
10. Letter, Anthony Wayne to General Washington, dated "Camp near White Mash 22nd Octr. 1777," *Wayne Papers,* vol. 4, HSP.
11. St. Clair was recalled for evacuating Fort Ticonderoga without a fight; Lincoln was with the Northern Army in New York; Smallwood was "on tour" with the Maryland militia; DeBorre was cashiered after Brandywine; and Nash died after Germantown. Two more Frenchmen may be added with qualification: Lafayette was a new general without troops and was wounded at Brandywine; du Courdray was a controversial French "volunteer" who drowned in the Schuylkill River on September 15.
12. "September 15 . . . Tho' I would willingly pay every attention to the Resolutions of Congress, yet in the late instance respecting the recall of Genl Sullivan, I must [beg leave to] defer giving any order about It. . . . I am obliged to observe, in justice to my

own Charactr. that I cannot be answerable for the consequences which may arise from a want of Officers to assist me." *WW,* vol. 9, 227–29.

Adam Stephen was recalled and cashiered in November 1777 for numerous occasions of "public drunkenness" and "unofficer-like behavior" (he was seen "taking snuff from the boxes of strumpets!"). John Sullivan faced two inquiries: one for his Staten Island expedition and the other for Brandywine.

13. "Whitepain October 24: A Genl. Court Martial Whereof Genl. Sullivan is appointed President, is to sit tomorrow morning at 9 O'Clock at the President's Quarters for the Trial of Brigr. Genl. Wayne. . . . Genls. [Peter] Muhlenberg, [Joseph] Weedon, [Thomas] Conway & [Jedidiah] Huntingdon; Cols. [Edward] Stephens, [Elias] Dayton, [Alexander] McClenachan; [Walter] Stewart, [Philip Burr] Bradley, [Lt. Cols.] [William] Davis, [William] Dehart, [James] Thackson, are appointed members of this Court." (*Muhlenberg's Orderly Book,* 157.)

The choice of Sullivan as president of this court-martial and the closing remark of Wayne's defense, "I rest my Honor & Character . . . in the Hands of Gentlemen—who when Deciding on my Honor will not forget their own," raise some interesting issues. Sullivan's writings in October–November 1777 are consumed with his asking numerous officers to testify on his behalf regarding Brandywine. Nowhere in his published papers from this period is Wayne's court-martial mentioned or even alluded to. Given Sullivan's own impending hearings and Wayne's raging fury, such circumstances raise questions about how impartial the court-martial truly was.

14. Court-Martial Document, Anthony Wayne to the Printers, dated "2nd Novr. 1777 Determination of a Genl Court Martial," *Wayne Papers,* vol. 4, HSP; Montrésor, 53–54. Long-held tradition asserts that Wayne's court-martial was held in the parlor of Dawesfield, the house used by Washington at Camp Whitpain October 19–November 2, 1777. This house is located on Lewis Lane between Skippack Pike and Morris Road, Ambler, Montgomery County. The General Orders state that it was to be held "at the President's Quarters," which would be Sullivan's Quarters, location unidentified.

15. One clue as to the whereabouts of the court-martial documents surfaced in a postscript note to a letter written by Anthony Wayne to Sharp Delany on May 21, 1778: "I have received a hint from a friend that some gentlemen of the Committee of Congress, who were in camp [Valley Forge], were not acquainted with the circumstances of the court-martial held on me and that some caitiffs had attempted to place it in a very unfavorable point of view. The whole of the proceedings are in the hands of Richard Peters, Esq. [Secretary of the Board of War] You will do me a particular favor to show it to some of these gentlemen—for from what I can learn it has not been transmitted to Congress—although all others are regularly sent up." Letter, Anthony Wayne to Sharp Delaney, dated "Mount Joy May 21, 1778," *Wayne Papers,* vol. 4, HSP. The documents have not been found in the Peters Papers. Possible explanations for this include fire, time, dispersal for sale, or descent into obscurity. Deliberate destruction is unlikely, for Wayne's personal papers preserve much material relevant to the case, including rough-draft letters that are not exactly flattering to him. Besides, he was exonerated by the court-martial, and the records would be a personal vindication for him. It is possible that because of the army's critical paper shortage, the inquiry evidences were used at the court-martial. On the other hand, the courts-martial of Generals Arthur St. Clair and Charles Lee fill volumes of pages in published form. It is also possible that Wayne's court-martial papers are in an unidentified collection or archive. Wayne's Court of Inquiry documents lie in the Force Collection at the Library of Congress all but unknown and, to my knowledge, are used here for the first time in publication. The trial's lack of mention in other papers, though, is not so easily explained. Timothy Pickering, the adjutant general of the Army, blithely remarked in his extensive journal, "Nothing material in camp" in the latter part of October, but wrote detailed commentary about the activities at the Delaware River forts.

16. Ibid., Court-Martial Document.
17. Letter, September 29, 1777, Collection of H. Richard Dietrich, Jr., Philadelphia.
18. Letter, Daniel Brodhead to Benjamin Lincoln, dated "Camp White Mash Novr. 7th 1777," Western Reserve Historical Society, Cleveland.

CHAPTER 26

1. *Baurmeister,* 20.
2. Letter, Samuel Chase to Gov. Thomas Johnson, dated "Lancaster Septr. 25. 1777," *Letters of Delegates,* vol. 8, 18.
3. Document, Gen. John Armstrong to Capt. David Denny, dated "Camp near the Fox Chase [Haverford Township] 3d. Novembr. 1777," Pension Claim of the Widow of David Denny, Revolutionary War Pension Claims, RG 15, M804, roll 797, W9834, State Archives, Harrisburg.
4. Burns, "Invasion," *TEHCQ* 3, no. 3 (July 1940): 64. Burns unfortunately does not cite his sources, but the information given is plausible local tradition. Taken with the usual caveats, he states: "Two excavations for foundations to monuments, 1817 and 1877, in which the remains of seven or eight bodies were removed to one side, revealed an equal number of bayonets and proved [*sic*] that these men had been slain before the removal of their bayonets from the scabbards. In 1877 there were little left beyond a few of the larger bones (the thigh bones of one man appeared those of almost a giant), besides small pieces of cloth, cloth-covered pewter buttons, bayonets and a knife blade or two."
5. Futhey and Cope, 86.
6. "Proceedings on the Occasion of the Erection of the Monument in 1817, Monument Committee Report," *One Hundredth Anniversary of the Paoli Massacre* (West Chester, PA: F. S. Hickman, 1877), 74–75.
7. Glenn Tucker, *Mad Anthony Wayne and the New Nation* (Harrisburg, PA: Stackpole Books, 1973), 257.
8. Futhey and Cope, 475 (Barnard); 676–77 (Pearce).
9. In 1809, the Society of the Cincinnati erected a monument to Anthony Wayne at St. David's Church in Radnor, Pennsylvania. Isaac Wayne, the general's son, traveled to Erie with the intention of bringing his father's remains home. When the remains were exhumed, the body was still intact, so the surgeon at the fort, Dr. J. G. Wallace, had the corpse boiled and dissected. The bones were cleaned and returned to St. David's, while the flesh and viscera were reinterred at Erie. Thus Anthony Wayne is one of a very few people who are actually buried in two places. See Tucker, *Mad Anthony Wayne,* 257.
10. Letter, Richard North to Mr. Barnard, dated "Philadelphia Augt 16th 1817," Author's Collection. The monument resembles an obelisk at a distance because it is incomplete due to nineteenth-century vandalism. The capstone and base, which were square, flat stones, are missing. The pyramid, whose tip is broken off, has been attached directly to the "die," or dado ("the sollid part"), without a capstone. The 1809 monument on Anthony Wayne's grave at St. David's Church and Benjamin Bartholomew's 1813 monument at Great Valley Baptist Church are intact examples of this type of monument, whereas a true obelisk is defined as "a tall, four-sided stone pillar tapering towards its pyramidal top" [Webster's New World Dictionary]." The 1877 granite Paoli Monument is a pedestal surmounted by a true obelisk.
11. *Chester and Delaware Federalist,* West Chester, September 24, 1817, CCHS.
12. Ibid., "Proceedings . . . Monument Committee Report," 74. The report continues on page 75 with a description of how the committee removed "specimens" of the articles found with the corpses and "have accordingly reserved a few of these specimens, which are subject to their orders." What became of these objects is unknown.

13. Ibid., 75. Work to complete the wall was done on September 10, 1817, by the artillerists. Isaac Barnard Papers, CCHS.

14. The Napoleonic Era and the decades immediately after were the heyday of elaborate military fashion. Militia regiments especially vied with each other to create the most outlandish examples of military garb. Shakoes were tall, cylindrical hats made of leather or felt, often heavily ornamented with cords, tassels, embossed metal badges, and plumes.

   The regiments marched in the following order: Union Troop of Chester and Delaware, Republican Artillerists of Chester County, Captain Cooper's Junior Artillerists, Chester County Volunteer Light Infantry, the Montgomery Blues, the Delaware Fencibles, Captain Holstein's Montgomery County Troop, Captain Smith's Delaware County Troop.

15. *Federalist,* September 24, 1817.

16. This was Jones's last public appearance; he died in 1820. (Futhey and Cope, 617.)

17. Speech, untitled, Address Delivered by Major Isaac Barnard at the Dedication of the Paoli Monument, September 20, 1817, *Isaac Barnard Papers,* CCHS.

18. *Federalist,* September 24, 1817; also Futhey and Cope, 617.

19. "Proceedings, etc.," 76.

EPILOGUE

1. Marian Klamkin, *The Return of Lafayette 1824–25* (New York: Charles Scribner's Sons, 1975), 46.

2. John C. Dann, *The Revolution Remembered* (Chicago: University of Chicago Press, 1980), xv.

3. Benson Lossing, *Pictorial Field Book of the Revolution,* 2nd ed., vol. 2 (New York, 1860), 164.

4. Harry Emerson Wildes, *Anthony Wayne: Trouble Shooter of the American Revolution* (New York: Harcourt, Brace and Co., 1968), 132.

5. John Hyde Preston, *A Gentleman Rebel: The Exploits of Anthony Wayne* (New York: Farrar & Rinehart, 1930), 118. Preston's account has the dubious distinction of being the most distorted, ludicrous farrago of myth, legend, fabrication, poor interpretation, and outright silly-minded nonsense I have found describing Paoli.

6. Ibid., 119. Preston states, "The criticisms of Mad Anthony's conduct at Paoli were mostly the criticisms of drill masters and people who did not understand the circumstances." A list of such people would have to be headed by Preston himself.

7. Revolutionary War Pension Papers, reel 2479, National Archives.

8. In 1996, I contacted a direct descendant of Colonel North in the hope of locating North's papers. The descendant regretfully informed me that North's house had been sold shortly after his death and that his papers had been taken into the yard and burned during the "housecleaning."

9. Letter, Wayne to Robinson, dated "Trap 29th Sepr 1777," Dietrich Collection.

BIBLIOGRAPHY

MANUSCRIPT SOURCES

American Philosophical Society
  Phineas Pemberton [?], "Weather data kept near Philadelphia March 1777–May 1778"
Chester County Archives
  Deed books, road papers, tavern petitions, tax records, will books
Chester County Historical Society
  British Depredations Book
  Letter, Isaac Barnard to William Brooke, September 10, 1817
  Speech, Isaac Barnard, delivered at Paoli Monument, September 20, 1817
William L. Clements Library
  Letter, typescript, Loftus Cliffe to Jack [?], "Camp near Philadelphia 24 October 1777."
David Library of the American Revolution
  "British Officer's Journal 1776–1778," Officer of the 1st Battalion Light Infantry
Dietrich Collection
  Anthony Wayne to unknown recipient [Abraham Robinson?], "Trap 29th Sepr. 1777,"
    Collection of H. Richard Dietrich, Jr., Philadelphia, Pa.
Essex Institute
  Journal, "Journal of Timothy Pickering, Adjutant General of the Continental Army."
Historical Society of Pennsylvania
  Journal, "Journal of Sergeant John Hawkins, Hazen's Regiment, 1777."
  Letterbook, Christopher Marshall, 1777, Marshall Papers
  Letterbook, Daniel Wier, Commissary to the [British] Army in America, Dreer Collection
  Speech, signed, "An American," Caleb North's Campaign for Sheriff, Society Collection
  Waste Book, 1776, Christopher Marshall Jr.'s Apothecary Store, Marshall Papers
Wayne Papers, HSP (vol. IV unless otherwise noted)
  Letter, Anthony Wayne to Benjamin Franklin, "June 13, 1776," vol. I.
  Letter, Anthony Wayne to Thomas Mifflin, "Radnor 14th Mile stone Sepr. 15th 1777."
  Letter, George Washington to Anthony Wayne, "Reading furnace, Septr 18th, 1777."
  Letter, George Washington to Anthony Wayne, "Readg. Furnace 6 OClock PM [Sep-
    tember 18, 1777]."
  Addendum, John Fitzgerald to Anthony Wayne, "Reading furnace, Septr 18th 1777."
  Letter, Anthony Wayne to George Washington, "Red Lion 21st Septr. 1777: 12 OClock."
  Letter, Anthony Wayne to Polly Wayne, "Red Lion 22nd Sepr. 1777."
  Letter, Abraham Robinson to Anthony Wayne, "East Town Septr: 22nd. 1777."
  Letter, Anthony Wayne to George Washington, "Trap, 27th Sepr 1777."
  Letter, Tench Tilghman to Anthony Wayne, "Head Quarters 27:th Sepr. 1777."

Letter, Richard St. George [?] to fiancee, "From the Camp near Beggars Town 2d Octr. 1777."

Letter, Anthony Wayne to Polly Wayne, "Camp near Pawling Mill 6th Oct. 1777."

Letter, Anthony Wayne to George Washington, "Octr. 11th 1777."

Evidences, "At a Court of enquiry held at the House of Houfer in Camp the 13th of Octor 1777."

James Wilson's Evidence, Paper marked "O" [October 13–14, 1777; see Force Papers]

Letter, Anthony Wayne to George Washington, "Skippack 17th Octr. 1777."

Letter, Anthony Wayne to George Washington, "Camp near White Mash 22nd Octr. 1777."

Defense of Wayne, dated "2nd Novr, 1777 Determination of a Genl Court Martial," Version I.

Court Martial Defense of Wayne, Version II.

Court Martial Defense of Wayne, Version III [fragment].

Library of Congress

   The Peter Force Papers, L of C

      Account Record, "Lancaster 12th Sepr 1777—Subscribers to the riders, etc."

      Letter, Adam Hubley to John Hubley, "Camp Lancaster Road Sept. 14th 1777 (Six Clock Eve)."

      Letter, Thomas Hartley to William Atlee, et al., "On a Drum Head near the Sorrel Horse Sepr. ye. 15th 1777."

      Letter, Adam Hubley to William Atlee, et al., "Camp Lancaster road, near Sorrel Horse Sepr. 15 1777."

      Letter, "Extract from a Letter from a Gentleman in the Army Septr. 17th 1777— Camp near Reading Furnace."

      Letter, Thomas Hartley to William Atlee, et al., "Camp Septr 17th 1777."

      Letter, Thomas Hartley to William Atlee, et al., "Camp three Miles from the Red Lion Chester County, Sepr. ye 18th 1777 1 oClocke PM."

      Letter, Thomas Hartley to William Atlee, et al., "Camp Sepr ye 20th 1777, 6 o'Clock PM."

      Letter, Thomas Hartley to William Atlee, et al., "Camp Red Lyon Sepr ye 21st 1777."

      Letter, Adam Hubley to William Atlee, et al., "Red Lion Septembr 21, 1777."

      Letter, Adam Hubley to William Atlee, et al., "Camp at Jones's Tavern Septr. 23, 1777."

      Letter, Adam Hubley to William Atlee, "Camp Jones's Tavern Sep. 23, 1777"

      Letter, Thomas Hartley to William Atlee, et al., "Camp Johnses Tavern Little Cannestogoe, Tuesday Eveng. Sepr ye. 23d. 1777."

      Letterbook, Ephrain Blaine to William Buchanan, "Camp New Hanover 24th Septr 1777."

      Letter, Adam Hubley to William Atlee, et al., "Camp, at Trap, Septr. 26th 1777."

      Letter, Adam Hubley to William Atlee, et al., "Towamencing Township, Octor. 9th 1777."

      Manuscript Map of Paoli Camp and Camp Pickets, Anthony Wayne, October 13–14, 1777.

   Testimony of Officers at Wayne's Court of Inquiry, October 13–14, 1777

      [William Butler, paper marked "A"]

      Samuel Hay's Evidence, paper marked "B"

      Morgan Connor's Evidence, paper marked "C"

      William Nichols's Evidence, paper marked "D"

      Thomas Hartley's Evidence, paper marked "E"

      Michael Ryan's Evidence, paper marked "F"

      Richard Willson's Evidence, paper marked "G"

      John McGowan's Evidence, paper marked "H"

      Daniel Brodhead's Evidence, paper marked "I–J"

Michael Huffnagle's Evidence, paper marked "K"
Francis Mentges's Evidence, paper marked "L"
George Ross's Evidence, paper marked "M"
Adam Hubley's Evidence, paper marked "N"
James Wilson's Evidence, paper marked "O" [see Wayne Papers]
Richard Humpton's Evidence, paper marked "P"
Caleb North's Evidence, paper marked "Q"

Prisoner List, "List of British Prisoners of War at Lancaster, Nov. 1, 1777."
The George Washington Papers
"Estimate of Provisions, etc., signed by William Buchanan, August 8, 1777."
"Daily Expence Record, September, 1777"
Letter, Samuel Chase to George Washington, "Philada. Septr. 15, 1777."
Letter, William Smallwood to George Washington, "Oxford Meeting House 7 Miles above Nottingham Septr. 15th 1777." Troop Return enclosed.
Letter, Clement Biddle to George Washington, "Valley Forge Tuesday Eveng. 9'oClock 16 Septemr 1777," Col. Dewees's Inventory of Public Stores enclosed.
Letter, George Washington to William Smallwood, "Camp Sepr. 17: 1777."
Letter, John Hancock to George Washington, "Philada. Septr. 18th 1777. 10 O'Clock PM."
Letter, Anthony Wayne to George Washington, "Paoli 1/2 after 7 OClock AM 19th Sepr 1777."
Letter, Anthony Wayne to George Washington, "Paoli, 3/4 after 10 AM 19th Sepr. 1777."
Letter, William Howe to George Washington, "Head Quarters 21st September 1777."
Letter, George Washington to William Howe, "Head Qrs. 21st September 1777."
British Memorandum Book, "A Memmorandum List for 1777."
British Orderly Book, "Captain Thomas Armstrong's Company Orderly Book 64th Lt. Infantry."

Maryland Historical Society
Letter, William Smallwood to Thomas Johnson, "Berks County Jones Tavern Sept. 23, 1777."

McGuire, Thomas J.
Richard North Letter, to Isaac Barnard, "Philadelphia Augt 16th 1817."

Morristown National Historical Park, The Hessian Documents, Lidgerwood Collection
Letter, "Short Description of the Journey of the Hon. Hessian Troops, etc., Lieutenant-General von Heister."
Letter, Wilhelm von Knyphausen to the Landgrave, "17 October 1777."

National Archives
Revolutionary Muster Rolls/Payrolls
Revolutionary War Pension Papers

National Army Museum, London
Letter, John Andre to unknown recipient, "German Town Sepr. 28: 1777."

New York Public Library, Emmet Collection
Letter, Mordecai Gist to John Smith, "Camp at Jones' Tavern Near Reading 23d. Sept. 1777."
Return of Prisoners, signed by Joshua Loring, "Philadelphia April 5 1778 . . .[includes number of prisoners] Delivered over by Sir William Howe to the American Surgeons at Trydefferin."

Pennsylvania State Archives
Revolutionary War Pension Files

Pennsylvania State Library
Wagner Collection, Typescript Copies of 500 Revolutionary War Pension Files.

Princeton University
    Ensign Thomas Glyn's Journal on the American Service, etc.
Public Records Office, London, Loyalist Claims
    Reuben Haines, "Testimony of Reuben Haines"
    Jacob James, "Memorial of Jacob James"
    Curtis Lewis, "Memorial of Hannah Lewis"
    William Sturge Moore, "Memorial of William Sturge Moore of Moore Hall"
    George Peters, "Certificate for George Peters"
    Richard Swanwick, "Memorial of Richard Swanwick"
Public Records Office, Edinburgh, Scotland
    "The Journal of Lieutenant John Peebles of the 42nd, or Royal Highland Regiment."
Rubinfine, Joseph, Document Catalogue
    William Smallwood to George Washington, "James Mcclelans Tavern September 19,
        1777," *The American Revolution in Manuscript* West Palm Beach, FL: American His-
        torical Autographs, 1994.
Saunders-Davies, Sarah [Osborn]
    Letter, George Osborn to John Osborn, "Camp near ? [probably Schuylkill], September
        30, 1777," Family Papers, England.
Western Reserve Historical Society
    Letter, Daniel Brodhead to Benjamin Lincoln, "Camp White Mash Novr. 7th 1777."

PUBLISHED SOURCES

Bartholomew, George. *Record of the Bartholomew Family.* Austin, TX: Self-published, 1885.
Bellas, Henry Hobart. *Personal Recollections of Captain Enoch Anderson, etc.* Wilmington, DE:
    Historical Society of Delaware, 1896.
Benninghoff, Herman. "Art and Archaeology and the Study of the American War for
    Independence." *The American Society of Arms Collectors Bulletin* 73 (1995).
Bradford, S. Sydney. "A British Officer's [Lieutenant Henry Stirke] Revolutionary War
    Journal, 1776–1778." *Maryland Historical Magazine* 56 (June 1961): 150–73.
Burns, Franklin. "The Invasion of Tredyffrin." *Tredyffrin Easttown History Club Quarterly* 3,
    no. 3 (July 1940).
Butterfield, L. H. *Letters of Benjamin Rush.* Vol. 1. Princeton, NJ: Princeton University
    Press, 1951.
Crane, Elaine F. *The Diary of Elizabeth Drinker.* Vol. 1. Boston: Northeastern University
    Press, 1991.
Cremers, Estelle. *Reading Furnace 1736.* Elverson, PA: Reading Furnace Press, 1986.
Dann, John C. *The Nagle Journal.* New York: Weidenfeld & Nicholson, 1989.
———. *The Revolution Remembered.* Chicago: The University of Chicago Press, 1980.
Eberlein, Harold D., and Cortlandt van Dyke Hubbard. *The Church of Saint Peter in the
    Great Valley.* Richmond, VA: August Dietz and Son, 1944.
Egle, William H. *Pennsylvania Archives.* 2nd ser. Harrisburg, PA: E. K. Meyers, 1888, 1896.
Ferling, John E. *The Loyalist Mind.* University Park, PA: Pennsylvania State University
    Press, 1977.
Fitzpatrick, John C. *The Diaries of George Washington.* Vol. 2. Boston and New York:
    Houghton Mifflin Company, 1925.
———. *The Writings of George Washington.* Vol. 9. Washington, DC: Government Printing
    Office, 1933.
Futhey, J. Smith, and Gilbert Cope. *History of Chester County, Pennsylvania, etc.* Philadelphia:
    Louis Everts, 1881. Reprint. Salem, MA: Higginson Book Company, 1998.
Galloway, Joseph. *Letters to a Nobleman on the Conduct of the War in the Middle Colonies.* 4th
    ed., London: G. Wilkie, 1780.

Gilbert, Stephen R. "An Analysis of the Xavier Della Gatta Paintings of the Battles of Paoli and Germantown, 1777." *Journal of the Company of Military Historians* 46, no. 3 (1994).

Gordon, William. *The History of the Rise, Progress, and Establishment of the Independence of the United States of America, Etc.* Vol. 2. London: Self-published, 1788.

Hunter, James. *The Journal of Gen. Sir Martin Hunter, etc.* Edinburgh, Scotland: The Edinburgh Press, 1894.

Ketchum, Richard. *The American Heritage Book of the American Revolution.* New York: American Heritage Publishing Co., 1958.

Kipping, Ernst, and Samuel Stelle Smith. *At General Howe's Side: The Diary of Captain Friedrich von Munchhausen.* Monmouth Beach, NJ: Philip Freneau Press, 1974.

Lee, Henry. *Memoirs of the War in the Southern Department of the United States.* New York: University Publishing Company, 1869.

Lefferts, Charles M. *Uniforms of the American, British, French and German Armies etc.* Old Greenwich, CT: WE Inc., 1917.

"Letters Written during the American War of Independence by Captain William Hale." *Regimental Annual for 1913.* Sherwood Foresters Regiment, Nottinghamshire, England.

Lossing, Benson J. *Pictorial Field Book of the Revolution.* 2nd ed. New York: Harper & Bros, 1860.

Luvaas, Jay. *Frederick the Great on the Art of War.* New York: The Free Press, 1966.

MacVeagh, Lincoln. *The Journal of Nicholas Cresswell.* New York: The Dial Press, 1924.

Maryland Archives. *Journal and Correspondence of the Council of Maryland, 1777.*

May, Robin, and G. Embleton. *The British Army in North America.* Reading, England: Osprey, Ltd., 1974.

Mollo, John, and Malcolm McGregor. *Uniforms of the American Revolution.* New York: MacMillan, 1975.

Monument Committee Report, "Proceedings on the Occasion of the Erection of the Monument in 1817," *One Hundredth Anniversary of the Paoli Massacre.* West Chester, PA: F. S. Hickman, 1877.

Muhlenberg, Henry M. *The Journals of Henry Melchior Muhlenberg.* Vol. 3. Philadelphia: Muhlenberg Press, 1958.

Murray, James. *An Impartial History of the War in America Etc.* Vol. II. Newcastle upon Tyne, England: T. Robson, 1783.

Pearce, Stewart. *The Pearce Family.* Compiled 1866–1909 and published by the family.

The Pennsylvania Magazine of History and Biography

Baldwin, Ernest H. "Joseph Galloway, The Loyalist Politician." Vol. 26 (1902).

Barker, Charles R. "Colonial Taverns of Lower Merion." Vol. 52 (1928).

Futhey, J. Smith. "Papers Relating to the Paoli Massacre." Vol. 1 (1877).

Heinrichs, Johann. "Extracts from the Letter-book of Captain Johann Heinrichs, etc." Vol. 22 (1898).

Inman, George. "George Inman's Narrative of the American Revolution." Vol. 7 (1883).

Jordan, John W. "Continental Army Hospital Returns 1777–1780." Vol. 23 (1899).

McMichael, William P. "Diary of Lieutenant James McMichael of the Pennsylvania Line 1776–1778." Vol. 16 (1892).

Morton, Robert. "The Diary of Robert Morton." Vol. 1 (1877).

Muhlenberg, John Peter Gabriel. "Orderly Book of General John Peter Gabriel Muhlenberg, March 26, December 20, 1777." Vol. 34 (1910).

Paine, Thomas. "Military Operations Near Philadelphia in the Campaign of 1777–8, Described in a Letter from Thomas Paine to Dr. Franklin." Vol. 2 (1878).

Scull, G. D. "Journal of Captain John Montresor, July 1, 1777, to July 1, 1778, Chief Engineer of the British Army." Vols. 5 & 6 (1881, 1882).

Sullivan, Thomas. "Journal of Sergeant Thomas Sullivan." Vol. 34 (1910).

Wayne, Anthony. "Letter of Anthony Wayne to Sharp Delany." Vol. 9 (1885).

Peterson, Harold. *The Book of the Continental Soldier.* Harrisburg, PA: Stackpole Co., 1968.

Pickering, Octavius. *The Life of Timothy Pickering.* Vol. 1. Boston: Little, Brown and Company, 1867.

Preston, John Hyde. *A Gentleman Rebel: The Exploits of Anthony Wayne.* New York: Farrar & Rinehart, 1930.

Quarrles, Benjamin. *The Negro in the American Revolution.* New York: W. W. Norton, 1961.

Quincy, Josiah. *The Journals of Major Samuel Shaw.* Boston: William Crosby & H. P. Nichols, 1847. Reprint. Documentary Publications, 1970.

Richardson, Priscilla L. Cox. *The Paoli Massacre of 1777.* Malvern, PA: Paoli Memorial Association, 1996.

Robertson, Archibald. *Archibald Robertson, Lieutenant General of Royal Engineers, His Diaries and Sketches in America.* New York: New York Public Library and Arno Press, Reprint. 1971.

Sachse, Julius. *The Wayside Inns of the Lancaster Road.* 2d Ed. Lancaster, PA: Self-published, 1912.

Simcoe, John G. *A Journal of the Operations of the Queen's Rangers, &c.* New York: Bartlett, 1844.

Smith, George. *An Universal Military Dictionary, etc.* London: J. Millan, 1779. Reprint. Ottawa, Ontario: Museum Restoration Service, 1969.

Smith, Paul H. *Letters of Delegates to Congress.* Vols. 7 & 8. Washington, DC: Library of Congress, 1981.

Stille, Charles. *Major General Anthony Wayne and the Pennsylvania Line.* Philadelphia: The Historical Society of Pennsylvania, 1893.

Syrett, Harold. *The Papers of Alexander Hamilton.* Vol. 1. New York: Columbia University Press, 1961.

Thibaut, Jacqueline, et al. *Valley Forge Report.* Vol. 3. Valley Forge, PA: Valley Forge Park Interpretive Association, National Park Service, 1982.

Troiani, Don, et al. *Don Troiani's Soldiers in America 1754–1865.* Mechanicsburg, PA: Stackpole Books, 1998.

Trussell, John B. B. *The Pennsylvania Line Regimental Organization and Operations, 1776–1783.* Harrisburg, PA: The Pennsylvania Historical and Museum Commission, 1977.

Tucker, Thomas. *Mad Anthony Wayne and the New Nation.* Harrisburg, PA: Stackpole Books, 1973.

Turner, Joseph Brown. *The Journal and Order Book of Captain Robert Kirkwood of the Delaware Regiment,* part II. Wilmington, DE: The Historical Society of Delaware, 1910.

Tustin, Joseph P. *Diary of the American War, A Hessian Journal, Captain Johann Ewald, Field Jager Corps.* New Haven: Yale University Press, 1979.

Uhlendorf, Bernhard A., and Edna Vosper. *Letters from Major Baurmeister to Colonel von Jungkenn, etc.* Philadelphia: Historical Society of Pennsylvania, 1937.

Watson, John Fanning. *Annals of Philadelphia and Pennsylvania in the Olden Time, etc.* 3 vols. Philadelphia: J. M. Stoddart, 1877.

Wildes, Harry Emerson. *Anthony Wayne: Trouble Shooter of the American Revolution.* New York: Harcourt, Brace & Co., 1968.

Willcox, C. DeW. *Major Andre's Journal.* Tarrytown, NY: William Abbatt, 1930.

Wood, Julianna R. *Family Sketches.* Philadelphia: Privately printed, 1870.

Woodman, Henry. *History of Valley Forge.* Oaks, PA: John Francis, 1922.

Wright, Esmond. *The Fire of Liberty.* New York: St. Martin's Press, 1983.

INDEX